On Behalf of the Mystical Fool

C000156525

Jung's understanding of the religious tendency of the psyche addresses many sides of the contemporary debate on religion and the role that it has in individual and social life. This book discusses the emergence of a new mythic consciousness and details ways in which this consciousness supersedes traditional concepts of religion to provide a spirituality of more universal inclusion.

On Behalf of the Mystical Fool examines Jung's critique of traditional Western religion, demonstrating the negative consequences of religious and political collective unconsciousness, and their consequent social irresponsibility in today's culture. The book concludes by suggesting that a new religiosity and spirituality is currently emerging in the West based on the individual's access to the sense of ultimacy residual in the psyche, and seeking expression in a myth of a much wider compass.

This book will be of interest to scholars and students at all levels who are engaged in the expanding field of Jungian studies. It will also be key reading for anyone interested in the theoretical and therapeutic connections between the psyche and religious experience.

John P. Dourley is Professor Emeritus, Department of Religion, at Carleton University, Ottawa, Canada. He graduated as a Jungian analyst from the Zurich/Kusnacht Institute in 1980 and has published widely on Jung and religion. His most recent books include *Paul Tillich, Carl Jung, and the Recovery of Religion* (Routledge, 2008).

On Behalf of the Mystical Fool

Jung on the Religious Situation

John P. Dourley

Routledge
Taylor & Francis Group

LONDON AND NEW YORK

First published 2010 by Routledge
27 Church Road, Hove, East Sussex, BN3 2FA

Simultaneously published in the USA and Canada
by Routledge
270 Madison Avenue, New York, NY 10016

Routledge is an imprint of the Taylor & Francis Group, an Informa business

Typeset in Times by Garfield Morgan, Swansea, West Glamorgan
Printed and bound in Great Britain by TJ International Ltd, Padstow,
Cornwall
Paperback cover design by Andy Ward

This publication has been produced with paper manufactured to strict
environmental standards and with pulp derived from sustainable forests.

British Library Cataloguing in Publication Data
A catalogue record for this book is available from the British Library

Library of Congress Cataloging-in-Publication Data
Dourley, John P.
  On behalf of the mystical fool : Jung on the religious situation / John P.
Dourley.
       p. cm.
  Includes bibliographical references and index.
  ISBN 978-0-415-55222-6 (hardback) – ISBN 978-0-415-55223-3 (pbk.)
  1. Psychology, Religious. 2. Jungian psychology–Religious aspects. I. Title.
  BL53.D65 2010
  200.1'9–dc22
                                                              2009017281

ISBN: 978-0-415-55222-6 (hbk)
ISBN: 978-0-415-55223-3 (pbk)

Contents

Preface

In 1936–1937 Carl Jung conjured up a prophet who, thirty years earlier, would have foreseen the face of then current Europe with its "medieval persecutions of the Jews", with its collective submission to militant fascism and restored Roman salute, and with its homage to the swastika as the *representation collectif* replacing the Christian cross but imbuing its followers with the same fidelity onto death. Jung rightly suspects that such a visionary thirty years before his time would have been "hooted at" by his contemporaries as a "mystical fool" (Jung 1968l: 48).

And what similar horrors might the mystical fool see in today's world? The three variants of monotheism, each proclaiming an objective God of universal and privileged truth and claim, provoke the same hostility and loss of life among their competing communities that has characterized their interface from almost the outset. Under stress from each other and from social forces such as a morally superior secularity, they turn to their founding scriptures as literal and historical accounts of their being the chosen. In doing so they lose the sense of the religiously poetic, the symbolic and the mythic, for a literal sense of the transcendent who so favors them in history. The resultant and now spreading fundamentalism coarsens the human spirit by reducing it to the more superficial levels of human consciousness. It removes humanity from its own depths to external accounts of past divine exploits in history rather than leading the human into the profundities from which both humanity, its history and the deities derive. Such fundamentalism, even in its more sophisticated theological exponents, lies at the insuperable tension between individuals and communities bonded by their one and only Gods or even by families of Gods in the world's polytheistic persuasions. The situation now drives scholars more insistently to identify the links between religion and violence in the past and present. More than fifty years later, no in-depth psychological or theological analysis of the holocaust has surfaced adequate to its religious enormity. The mind seems incapable of grasping intellectually and facing historically the "absolute evil" that Jung identified as resident to the human psyche (Jung 1968n: 10). Indeed the enormity continues with the atrocities of 9/11, and the response to it. "Ethnic cleansing" has become a new phrase describing the lethal interaction of religiously and ethnically based communities. The grim irony of the Balkans rests in the fact that the dissolution of a "secular/political" religion served as the occasion of the ensuing slaughter among religiously based ethnic communities.

In continuity with these observations, geopoliticians have come to locate the religious foundations of the world's civilizations in their supporting religions now themselves perceived as the root of the tensions between civilizational groupings. In the current and future "clash of civilizations" all wars become religious wars. Politically the most powerful democracy in the world has been reduced to a theocracy by a leader inspired by God in the justification of two current wars whose real motivation is now widely perceived to be questionably divine in origin. By and large the religious leaders of the civilizations engaged in them have not condemned the waging of these wars. Where there has been criticism it is *sotto voce*, though ringing condemnations of other moral violations – sexual indiscretion and social injustice being widely favored – continue to bellow forth from such sources frequently unable or unwilling to remove such iniquity from their own communities.

In the ecological sphere a mind severed from its own depths and so from its continuity with nature, often through religious conceptions of a dubious "transcendence", continues to ravage the natural world that, through evolution, brought the mind into existence and seeks to sustain it in existence now through a human community reflecting the process of organic complexity evident in the making of the human brain. Should the human project somehow avoid elimination through faith based conflict, political and/or religious, the rape of nature threatens her generosity and with it the long term survival of the species.

And so the mystical fool would have much to ponder in today's world. As the creator of the mystical fool and as one himself, the senior Jung was of the opinion that the species would have to seek its joint salvation in a "symbolic death" if it was to avoid a literal one in a "universal genocide" (Jung 1976d: 735). By a symbolic death Jung would point to the emergence of a new symbolic sense, a new religious sense, which would enable the species to survive the congealed paralysis of its current religious, political and civilizational differentiations. Jung's understanding of the psyche is thus of an evolving living reality now seeking a wider sense of compassion or universal embrace than the current state of religious development, East or West, can easily provide.

The psyche's current movement toward a more encompassing consciousness is the object of this work. It seeks to identify this spirit underlying Jung's psychology and to show its social significance in the context of variants of the religious imagination with which he saw it incompatible. These incompatibilities serve to illustrate the wider and negative consequences of failure to attain a religious perspective at once deeper and more inclusive than the current religions can readily sponsor. To delineate the full compass of Jung's understanding of the religious propensities of the psyche the inquiry dwells on wider metaphysical and cosmological themes that make Jung's psychology unique. It details some of the far ranging consequences of his understanding of divinity and humanity as agencies wholly contained within the psyche engaged in an eternal and ongoing reciprocity of mutual redemption. Finally it appeals to Jung's sense of radical interiority as the key to revisioning the divine/human commerce through the portals of the depths native and natural to humanity. The work concludes by turning to the mystics to whom Jung turned throughout his work, mystics who experienced these depths most intensely, some to the point of momentary dissolution in them. Their sense of the natural universality of the divine in whom they momentarily dissolved in an identity beyond distinction could today restore a living sense of God as the common universal ground of individual and of nature beyond the individual. The sense of the human and the natural as joint manifestations of an immanent divinity could serve as the basis of a sacred communality beyond discrete and transcendent Gods and their disparate communities. In the end the turn inward may evoke an ever widening universal embrace of the external. Such interiority could give rise to a symbolic birth on the other side of the current need for a symbolic death, a birth marking the survival and enrichment of consciousness in a restored resonance with its ground as the guarantor of the survival of the earth and the planet themselves.

Introduction

Carl Jung's understanding of the religious propensity of the psyche, when understood and engaged, continues to address, to enrage and to confirm many sides of the contemporary discourse on religion and its role in individual and social life. Obviously the most important of these is the nature and state of religion itself, both in the predominantly Western monotheisms and throughout the world. On the one hand the very credibility of religion continues to diminish in the light of Western liberal secularity whose values inform a now emerging social myth of deeper religious sentiment and moral concern. The profundity and universalism of religious secularity threatens to supersede the more traditional orthodoxies unable to meet the religious needs of a developing humanity increasingly aware of its inner resources and their external deployment in the service of humanity. Democracies in varying hues tend to replace the theism and theocracy with which religion is more comfortable. Human rights base themselves on other than religious grounds such as the natural law purified of a religious referent. The ongoing contest for the separation of church and state and the increasing reluctance of most Western governments and leaders, with the notable exception of the United States, to use language derivative of any identifiable religion are examples of the emergence of an ethical and religious sense that surpasses a commitment to specific religions. In all of this a broader, deeper and more inclusive perspective obviates a narrower one.

Recent outbreaks of militant atheism attack as a dangerous infantilism the beliefs and practices of any of the various forms of theism understood as a biblically based relationship to a personal and wholly transcendent God. They rightly ask why religious tolerance should be extended to such unlikely viewpoints and certitudes when their connection with violence, not only among themselves but often toward surrounding cultures of greater tolerance, becomes increasingly apparent (Dawkins 2006: 301–308; Dennett 2006: 278–307; Harris 2006). Such atheism has no problem documenting the hatred addressed to those who question religious faith and the reality of God on which it is based. This questioning is most acute when religious faith supports political commitment and military aggression. The twenty-first century lives under the shadow of the holocaust with still sparse attention paid to aspects of the Christian revelation and history which provided, at least to some degree, the conditions of its possibility. Geopoliticians like Huntington now document the religious bases of conflicting civilizations. They more than imply that these religiously based cultures insure that present and future wars are and will be religious, whether fought under explicitly religious banners or disguised as deeper human, even secular, values such as human rights understood to be held by one combatant and not the other. War has been and continues to be a consistent historical reality in the interface of monotheistic communities, especially where One or Other of the One and Only Gods has vested a particular community with a claim to land, most tragically in cases where two or more communities have divinely based claims on the same piece of geography.

On other fronts religion engages in its own self-discrediting in its ambiguous relationship to the gay community, to the concerns of feminism and to causes inspired by a higher concern for life and dignity such as the opposition to war, to capital punishment, and to state, or any, use of torture. Women are excluded from admission to the Roman Catholic hierarchy. Priests are forbidden marriage. Homosexuality is described as an "objective disorder" when a significant proportion of the male Roman clergy are homosexual themselves. Possible connections between institutional excesses such as universally imposed celibacy and the widespread practice of pedophilia are consistently denied by ecclesial leadership without being examined in any depth. In the face of the undeniable shadow hanging over contemporary institutionalization of religion, West and East, the civilized mind now moves to the search for salvation from religion rather than through it. The situation raises the question of whether religion can be saved from the religions through a more immediate experience of the authentic power of religion at the personal level with the social consequences such experience may foster. Among such consequences would be a more inclusive universalism based on the now surfacing sense that religion in its wondrous variety derives from the depths of a commonly held humanity in the interest of enhancing the humanity from whose womb it springs.

And yet, even in its present condition, religion flourishes. Fundamentalism thrives. Religious institutions continue to split between left and right. In most the right continues to prevail. In the face of a narrow but overwhelmingly conservative majority, liberal individuals and forces withdraw leaving the institutions bastions of a defensive but powerful regression frequently resting on an inherited revelation, the only true one, still to be imposed on others. In Roman Catholicism it took less than fifteen years to destroy the liberating spirit of Vatican II (1962–1965). More statements of rejection, caution or outright condemnation have proceeded from the Vatican since the ecumenical council than at any time since the condemnations of Catholic theological thought in the early twentieth century under the name of "Modernism".

Some of the experts at the Council itself, like Edward Schillebeeckx of the University of Nijmegen, Netherlands and Karl Rahner of Germany and Hans Küng of Switzerland, were subjected to scrutiny either by Rome or their more conservative colleagues. Marxist theologians in South America were wholly rejected. Politicians who were priests were forced to give up elected seats in democratic governments in Canada and the United States. Nor is the split between left and right confined to Catholicism though it is most obvious there. The Anglican tradition is split, as are many ecclesial bodies, on the issue of homosexuality in both the priestly caste and in the laity. In the United States, identifiable groups in conservative reformed communities known demographically as "Jesus land" voted the second Bush administration into power. This administration turned into a theocracy doing God's will in Iraq under the direction of a president in immediate touch with divinity. Needless to add that potential and actual violence in the Balkans and the Middle East owes its energies to religious division.

In the face of such startling evidence that the civilized mind sees so clearly the shadow side of religion and seeks to surpass its religious past, especially in the wake of the Western Enlightenment, only to be confronted with an intransigent and violent tribal religious barbarism, Jung's contention that the human psyche and so humanity itself are ineradicably religious is worth sustained examination. In his conviction of the permanence of religion, Jung joins such modern thinkers as Paul Tillich in the conviction that religion is endemic to human self-consciousness itself. The major option is then not to accept or reject religion but to determine how it can serve rather than destroy its constituencies and, by extension, the species itself (Dourley 2008). If this line of analysis proves valuable, Jung's psychology could identify the factors in the human psyche which ground humanity's religious instinct. Further it could identify the teleology of this instinct in individual and society. In this manner Jung's understanding of religion could both diagnose religious pathology and foster religion's legitimate contribution to human well being. More his understanding of religion would be able to identify religion when it is present and operative in ways that are not explicitly and obviously religious and frequently unseen by more superficial observers. Religion in such disguise would appear in the various forms of allegedly secular commitment in the form of political mass movements, past and present, movements themselves archetypally grounded and so driven by the same energies that drive religion.

The ineradicable nature of religion would thus serve as the presupposition for a reflection on religion's profound ambiguity. Its shadow would appear as among the greatest of current threats to human survival; its common root in the human psyche as one of humanity's potentially greatest resources. This line of reflection would respect the archetypal suasion that religion works on human consciousness, a suasion that so easily devolves into a threat to humanity when it claims a privileged and exhaustive possession of the truth. Such exclusivism would most obviously be the case with any group taking on the designation of "chosen" or its equivalent on the basis of a specific revelation from a sole wholly transcendent God. This side of Jung's thought would be profoundly iconoclastic in its reduction of such a claim to the status of a dangerous collective inflation and currently an anti-social and so immoral form of consciousness. Monotheistic faith in all religious and political variants would be increasingly perceived as immoral and socially irresponsible. Yet because Jung would understand the religions as expressions of the deepest, commonly possessed, and universal stratum of the human psyche, each monotheistic variant could be seen as treasured resources to human self-understanding when shorn of their lethal tendency to take themselves as final truths exhaustive of the human revelatory potential. In this sense the very fecundity of their archetypal and so sacred origins would be at the same time the basis of their relativity and their enduring truth and worth.

Though the foregoing reflection may be of some use in corroding the anti-social nature of the collective religions' understanding of "faith", it does not fully address a significant side of the contemporary religious problem. This problem is directly connected to Jung's understanding of the psychic origin of the manifest religions. In efforts to preserve the meaning of their symbols, religions (and especially Western religions) have deprived their symbols and their initially protective dogmatic formulations of a living meaning. In Jung's view the meaninglessness of symbolic discourse and its dogmatic elaboration is true not only for contemporary educated minds but also for the mind natively attuned to religion. The main culprits in the emasculation of symbolic discourse and meaning have been literalism, historicism and externalism. Each of the foregoing understand the referent of symbolic discourse to be as literal as everyday discourse. They reduce the referent of symbolic statement to objective events in the past and so external and foreign to the individual seeking meaning in the symbols. Jung felt strongly that modern spokespersons for religion had failed to put forth a compelling apology for the enduring fact of symbolic expression itself with its unusual propensities for the non-literal, and irrational vested with a profundity defiant of a more mundane and superficial rationalism (Jung 1966a: 226, 227). With loss of the symbolic sense the credibility and humanizing power of religion also vanished. What Jung is suggesting in these passages is that religion in its more modern form severed its adherents from the human depths from which its symbols and myths rose to consciousness, took itself literally and historically and, in so doing, committed spiritual suicide. Jung's sustained efforts to show that religious and mythic expression owe whatever power they have to their archetypal origins fell on deaf or rejecting ears. The admission that the woeful "sacrosanct unintelligibility" of current religious symbol and dogma reflected an ignorance of the archetypal origin of religious experience and its native symbolic expression remained impossible to the mind of faith (Jung 1969e: 109). Such admission would ground the referent of the religious myth and symbol as well as their dogmatic elaboration in the foundational movements and energies of the psyche itself and not on a foreign and wholly other God as the source of an interventionist revelation then to be given assent in a demeaning and mind destroying obedience of faith in unlikely past events.

Jung's effort to demonstrate the archetypal basis of revealed truth consumed much of his energies in the construction of an apology that came, as he aged, to extend beyond Christianity. Jung's apology became an apology for religion as such. Jung was convinced that the credibility of religion itself would have to precede the recovery of the credibility of any particular religion. In this matter Jung's strategy is closely aligned with that of Paul Tillich who also thought that the apology for religion was of greater import and had to be the prelude to any apology for Christianity (Dourley 2008). In spite of his sustained efforts as an apologist of religion, it is questionable if Jung's efforts in this regard were wholly successful. If they were, it is less likely that the widespread search for a life-giving spirituality no longer to be found for many in specifically ecclesial environments would be so extensive. Nevertheless Jung's efforts to identify the archetypal basis of all religious experience, including the Christian, remain relevant in the contemporary search for a viable spirituality because one of the earmarks of such a sought for spirituality is the immediacy of spiritual experience it seeks. The Christian community and other orthodoxies proved in the end unable to revitalize their symbols by living them in the unique variant of the individual's life immediately under the unmediated and experiential impact of their psychic origin. Rather the symbols remained a body of distant revealed information simply accepted by a mind able to function quite well in its own right without them, though their reception would add important facts to their holder's intellectual repertoire, facts gained only through revelation. The symbols divested of their ability to recreate or reactivate in the individual psyche the power of their psychic origin killed them as a source of anything but intellectual meaning, a supplement to what reason could know about God. As a result the search for a spirituality of such immediacy continues to inform today's spiritual quest.

Commentators on the contemporary spiritual quest can identify many of its component characteristics. Whether the newer spirituality is practiced by one within or beyond an identifiable religious institution, it has as its core an emphasis on an interiority based on the practitioner's experience of ultimacy. In other words, regardless of its religious dynamic the new spirituality must be accessed as a psychological reality. As such it is less related or wholly unrelated to entities transcendent to the individual, a transcendence usually lodged in an existent thought of as divine and wholly other than the individual engaged in such spirituality. Many theologians fear the radical immanence present in one form or another in an emerging spirituality lest the sense of their particular version of the wholly other God be badly compromised or even undone. Rather in the spirituality emerging in contemporary culture transcendence becomes a function or consequence of a sense of an immanent power native to humanity. Spirituality becomes the process in which this power becomes conscious in the consciousness of the practitioner throughout a lifetime. Transcendence becomes a function of immanence in so much as the power native to the human always transcends its realization at any given moment in an individual's development. There is always more to be assimilated. One can never say, "It is over." One can only say, "It is alive and goes on." In this side of itself modern spirituality shares a discernible affinity with Jung's understanding that the self can be only approximated never exhaustively realized. The self is a power wholly natural and so immanent to the individual psyche and yet it always outstrips its conscious realization in the life of an individual at any time in the course of that life. On the basis of this similarity it is not surprising that both the new spirituality and Jung's understanding of psychic maturity relate the ongoing integration of the individual to a deepening sense of the interconnectedness of what is because Jung would also ground the individual self in the universality of the unconscious. Through its role in uniting the ego with its origin in the unconscious, the self is at once the author of one's intensified sense of personal uniqueness and of one's ever extending embrace of the totality. In this respect individual growth, the integration of the complexes contributing to one's uniqueness as the basis of personal wisdom, unites rather than contradicts an extended sense of participation in the totality as the basis of an ever extending compassion. The process is wholly internal to the psyche as productive of personal unification and universal relatedness. It is one that never ends.

At this point it would appear that Jungian psychology, a now widely surfacing spirituality, and what has been called the New Age share some common ground. No less an authority than the Vatican itself would support this hypothesis. In a document entitled, *Jesus Christ, the Bearer of the Water of Life*, issued under the joint sponsorship of the Pontifical Council for Culture and the Pontifical Council for Interreligious Dialogue on 21 February 2003, Jung is explicitly identified and rejected as not only a member but a founding member, "an Aquarian conspirator" of the New Age movement (2.3.2). Elements of the movement compatible with Jungian psychology are understood as "incompatible" with Christianity (6.1). Logically such incompatibility would have to be extended to Jung's psychology itself because the points of incompatibility are foundational to it. In its broader sweep the document attacks all forms of traditional and contemporary gnosticism and neo-gnosticism (7.2) which it rightly associates with the internalization of religion and the sacralization of the psyche so that conversation with the psyche becomes functionally conversation with divinity. In this error Jung is associated with William James (2.3.2).

Perhaps most importantly the New Age rejects a wholly transcendent and personal divinity and so defies an acceptable Christian theism (7.2). Here Jung is cited and rejected for his views on the essential divinity of the individual (2.3.2). It further condemns all forms of pantheism (2.3.1) and panentheism (7.2) closely linked to a monism supportive of a universal sensitivity in an all encompassing totality allowing and needing no divine intrusion from beyond (6.1; 7.2). In such a vision and the experience informing it, every individual and existent would participate in the being of such an organic and contained universe. The conscious development of such participation would then become the foundation of a newer spirituality and human maturation. Jung would have to plead guilty as charged to all counts of the above indictment. More, he would have to thank the authors of this document for giving a synthetic presentation of varying but essential threads in his thought which he, by and large, failed to systematize in his own copious writings. Once again the Inquisitor had done the heretic a favor in a systematization that evaded the heretic.

The document becomes yet more interesting when it turns to a critique of Jung and his psychology by name. In a questionnaire sent to 210 people asking them who had influenced them most as "Aquarian Conspirators" Jung ranked second only to Pierre Teilhard de Chardin (endnote 15). Both thinkers treasured the experience of the divine as immanent to the human and driving toward greater configurations of personal integration and universal relatedness. Due to ecclesial opposition Teilhard died with the burden of his work unpublished. Yet his fuller work shared much with Jung who had some of his work available prior to his own death (personal information). Jung's understanding of the God within would mean effectively that the relationship with God was really with the self or energies endemic to the nature of the psyche. Such a conception of an intrapsychic relation to the divine would be significant failure to relate to the wholly transcendent God of theistic Christianity. Further Jung is accused of making causality relative to correspondence, a reference no doubt to Jung's thought on synchronicity which does indeed undermine the type of causality imagined in the relationship of a wholly transcendent God creating the world and humanity as does a potter a pot (endnote 24). Jung's sense of interiority extends the divine/human relation well beyond the boundaries of divine efficient causality. Further in the Vatican document Jung's inner God is related to Abraxas (6.1) in connection with the problem of evil and Jung's contention that what unquestionably exists in existence must unquestionably emanate from its source (7.2). It may be indicative that this thorny problem is not addressed at any great length in the document other than to reaffirm the absence of evil in an acceptable Christian God. Again in the index at the end of the document Jung is mentioned in relation to depth psychology where certain features of his psychology are listed without comment. Perhaps the foregoing was enough. In excluding Jung and Jungian psychology from the realm of Christian orthodoxy the imagination at work in the document is that of a wholly transcendent objective and self-sufficient God who has revealed himself definitively, and exhaustively in the historical personage of Jesus never to be confused with one among many religious notables. By implication this revelation is final and universally valid in its extension to global humanity itself. As such it has to be universally inclusive meaning exclusive of other religions and spiritualities and, relevant to this discussion, rejective of an immediate and experiential relation to the divine as the ground of the individual's personal being and so as the basis of the individual's relation to the totality.

None of this is to say that Jungian psychology can be reduced to or identified with the New Age movement if there is such a unified movement. This would be to mistakenly identify the specific reality of Jung's psychology and its understanding of the psyche with a grouping of disparate spiritualities which no doubt have much in common but lack the organic unity in Jung's thought on the psyche when the latter is taken in its totality. Nevertheless the document is of great value in delineating some of the major features of Jung's understanding of the psyche and its relation to religion and to Christianity. The document is obviously based on a sense of divine transcendence which Jung forcefully rejected in his heated exchanges with Martin Buber and in his more sustained conversation with Victor White. Both conversations revealed that the Jewish and Catholic Christian conceptions of divine transcendence were not compatible with Jung's understanding of the psychogenesis of religion, of religious maturation and the direction in which the psyche was currently leading the evolution of religious consciousness, at least, in the West.

Finally, the document hostile to the New Age is highly critical of a mysticism which would culminate in a fusion between the divine and the human so that the distinction between them would be wholly defeated (7.2). In fact the Christian mystics to whom Jung turns in his corpus undergo such a loss of distinction in a nothingness in which their personal identity is fused with the divine in an abyss beyond all separation. This mystical experience is described as apophatic in the Christian tradition and is currently undergoing something of a revival at least in academic circles. Jung would understand all mystical experience as archetypal in origin but did have a greater appreciation for the mystics of the apophatic. But the nothingness they undergo carries with it a certain passivity or resignation that moderate the drive of the archetypes to become conscious in human consciousness the unconscious creates for that purpose. Penetration into an area of psyche beyond archetypal urgency, though best described in religious and mystical terms, could be a valuable asset in ushering the archetypes into consciousness, individual and collective, in such a way as to preserve and enhance consciousness in the process and offset the enmity between archetypally constellated communities now threatening the species.

No doubt profound archetypal differences would still mark discrete cultures and their supportive religions but the recognition of their common origin in a psyche preceding their differences whose further reach is in the stillness of the nothing prior to all form and drive to form could well lend them less lethal in their conscious interface.

Reflection then on what Jung has to offer to the search for a modern and vital spirituality unites many apparently disparate dimensions in contemporary religious culture. It would point to a religious vision grounding a spirituality which would appreciate even as it transcended the concretions of collective and often conflicted religions currently threatening humanity itself. The search for such a spirituality would touch, perhaps deeply, the contemporary political and societal reality in enabling cultures to move beyond their current joint petrifaction and resultant clashes. It could point to depths in the human soul, spirit or psyche as the common origin of all significant human expression but especially of extant religions. The exposition of these depths could lead to their wider cultivation in a growing collective sense of a common humanity appreciative of the shared origins of its deepest differences as the basis of an embrace not beyond but through these differences. What follows is simply a more extensive presentation of what Jung has to offer in these many areas of a now growing human concern.

Chapter 1

Jungian psychology and spirituality

Carl Jung's psychology, taken in its totality, contains a radical critique of current Western societal religiosity and the spirituality attaching to it. When his psychology is read as itself an expression of and contributor to a widespread emerging religious consciousness, it is found to promote a new societal myth which both appreciates and undermines all three mainstream monotheistic variants on which the Western religious tradition rests. The myth embedded in Jung's psychology would radically revision the relation of the divine to the human and in so doing sponsor a new individual and societal religiosity with far-reaching repercussions on Western culture and its religious foundations. For these reasons a closer examination of the spirituality endemic to Jung's myth is of some interest and value in offering a critical understanding and discerning appreciation of the shifts in current religious sensitivities within what is loosely called current Western culture.

What is spirituality and why now?

The latter section of this question should be answered first. The term "spirituality" has gained its current widespread currency in the wake of the failure of institutional agencies to provide their constituencies with the resources needed to nourish and sustain the human spirit. The paradox at the heart of this situation is that spirituality is now a growing personal and social concern because its traditional sponsors and mediators have lost their ability to fulfill this role. The current usage of the term with its peculiar meaning may be new but as a noun the term dates from the fifth century (Wulff 1997: 5). It is also a term with a wide range of meanings. In its narrowest and more historical sense, it usually described the spiritual discipline and practice of a given specific religious tradition exercised in the interests of imbuing the practitioner with the spirit of divinity at the heart of that tradition. One can speak of a Hindu or a Buddhist or a Christian spirituality and distinguish many variant spiritualities in each of these larger categories. Thus within Christianity one might speak of a spirituality based on the exercises of Ignatius of Loyola, or John of the Cross or the

Rhineland mystics or Luther or Calvin. However in contemporary usage spirituality has taken on another and wider meaning. It has come to describe a religious consciousness and discipline entirely free of a conscious and committed relation to any religious institution (Wulff 1997: 5–7). Analysts of contemporary religiosity now identify a significant segment of the religiously concerned who describe themselves as spiritual but not religious. They mean their spirituality has for them no relation to an institutional religion. People in this stance usually do not form counter or alternative institutions. On the contrary, frequently they are explicitly seeking a religious life free of significant institutionalization. The experience of people in this situation has convinced them that institutional religion is irrelevant to and even repressive of their personal spiritual needs. They tend to go it alone in the face of a frowning sociology which cannot understand their concern and so brands and rejects their efforts as "privatization", i.e., not easily fitting into existing sociological categories and consciousness.

For these privateers, whose numbers can no longer be denied, spirituality is relatively dogma free though adherents of such spirituality are capable of clearly expressing their own rudimentary convictions usually grounded on their immediate experience. They are able to live with doubt as an inescapable component of an ongoing development toward a life-giving truth never wholly to be possessed, a truth beyond certitude whose wealth remains inexhaustible and so beyond full capture and confinement in creed and defining proposition. They remain hostile to any creed, ritual and morality allowing of little if any ambiguity or flexibility unless these realities contribute to rather than repress their personal religious maturation. They have affinities with a mystical immediacy though usually are not dependent on a specific religious tradition as were many mystics. Theologically they would be understood to be vested with a profound sense of an immanent often impersonal divinity though this sense can move into a sense of loss or emptiness or the absence of God. At the same time spirituality thus understood is frequently fostered by a personal discipline. Psychologically they would be understood as sensitive to the depths of the human spirit and open to what Jung describes as a sense of the numinous and its demands. There is a very real sense in which a Jungian spirituality can encompass both of these populations, those of institutional and non-institutional spirituality, because Jung traces the origins of both institutional spiritualities, resting on their scriptures, dogmas, morality and rituals, as well as the more recently emerging spirituality of the single seeker to their common origin in the archetypal unconscious (Jung 1968a: 9).

Spirituality in a Jungian context is thus all embracing. As such, a Jungian perspective could be used to formulate a generic and universal description of spirituality. Such an understanding of spirituality would encompass every avenue of conscious access to the energies of the Gods and spirits whether through an institution, on an individual basis, or in combinations of both. In this sense spirituality would extend to every practice that enabled the practitioner to appropriate the energies that create conscious life and make it ever fuller, namely those of the archetypal unconscious. This understanding of spirituality would obviously include Jungian analysis within itself since, at least in its classic form, it engages consciousness with the energies that give rise to all religious experience and so to the religions and their divinities themselves (Jung 1968a: 9). And what are the energies or spirits which a Jungian spirituality would usher into consciousness? Writes Jung on the topic, "The world of gods and spirits is truly 'nothing but' the collective unconscious inside me" (Jung 1969a: 525).

Jung could hardly be more succinct. In this citation the qualifier "nothing but" is not reductive or dismissive. If anything it is ironic and refers to those who cannot take the psychic origin of the divine and spiritual seriously. The phrase "nothing but" is referenced more than twenty times in the index to Jung's *Collected Works*, evidence of his concern for a consciousness unable to accept the human origin of the sense of the divine in the creation of divinity (Jung 1979: 484). The remark is based on what to Jung was a fact, namely, that the Gods and spirits owe their existence to humanity's experience of the archetypal unconscious. Such experience then serves as the basis of their externalization or projection beyond the individual into the questionable objectivity of a transcendent other. What is specific to a Jungian understanding of the contemporary development of spirituality is that the Gods created through such externalization are now to be consciously returned to their place of origin and addressed in the containment of the inner forum (Jung 1969b: 85). Thus Jung's understanding of the Gods, spirits and spirituality carries with it a much wider world view, a view inclusive of a metaphysic, a cosmology and a religious perspective supportive of the contemporary emergence of a new mythic consciousness centered on unmediated dialogue with the powers of human interiority. Like all myths of cosmic proportion, the myth inherent in Jung's psychology addresses and embraces the totality in its vision. Thus it is worthwhile unpacking the full implications behind Jung's suggestion that spirituality of every kind ultimately implicates, consciously or unconsciously, an immediate commerce with the spirits and Gods within. The priority of the inner dialectic between ego and archetype on an intrapsychic basis sounds a foundational note in the evolution of contemporary spirituality.

Jung's naturalism and psychic containment

Jung understood the collective unconscious to be nature itself but a nature in need of its greatest creation, the ego and its consciousness, as the only agency capable of humanely ushering the infinitely fecund unconscious into consciousness (Jung 1940: 283; 1960g: 540; 1966a: 62). It is often overlooked that in equating nature with the creative unconscious and understanding consciousness as its needed offspring, Jung is effectively containing within a vastly extended psyche both the totality of what is or can be as well as the human cognitive capacity to experience what is or can be. If metaphysics is understood in its classical sense to be made up of the disciplines of ontology, the study of what is, and epistemology, the study of how what is is known, then Jung is engaged in a sophisticated metaphysics of being and knowing when he grounds both in an all containing psyche. Needless to say this containment would extend to humanity's experience of the divine. All of this is made explicit when Jung writes, "Not only does the psyche exist, it is existence itself" (Jung 1969b: 12). He denies in this same passage that the psyche has an Archimedean point transcendent to itself which enables it to know itself from a position or through agencies wholly outside itself. No God who first creates the psyche looks upon the psyche from beyond it. The energy of the unconscious "of indefinite extent with no assignable limits" infinitely transcends the ego from within the psyche, but nothing transcends the psyche itself (Jung 1969c: 258). Jung, citing Archimedes, who discovered the laws of buoyancy, would strongly suggest God and humanity are in the same bath tub. A move by either effects the other. This reciprocity works within the containment of the psyche where it takes on the form of the relation of the unconscious to consciousness and so of the divine to the human as the two move to unity as the meaning of human history.

Jung is thus quite consistent with his own ontology and epistemology in describing the origin of all deity beyond the psyche as projections funded by the archetypal energies of the psyche. Externalization of the deities was perhaps a needed moment in the development of human religiosity. Having the major energies of the psyche depicted as divinities other than the psyche intersecting with humanity from without was valuable in an earlier stage of religious development. Such projection at least contributed to humanity's awareness of the greater movements in its own profundity. However, Jung's psychology reverses the psyche's creation of divinities beyond itself with his recognition that the object of all divine revelation are not the divinities but the foundational movements within the psyche itself. As humanity comes to realize that rather than being created by God or Gods, it creates the Gods out of the commerce of consciousness with the archetypal unconscious, a new moral and psychological imperative calls for a return of all the Spirits to their origin in the psyche as the basis of a new understanding of and dialogue with them there (Jung 1969b: 85). Such positions give rise to the obvious question of whether a God or Gods exist as objective entities beyond the psyche.

Lionel Corbett has identified the only alternatives to this question responsible to Jung's understanding of the psyche (Corbett 1996: 6–9). In this Corbett has done Jung and Jungians a great favor. Corbett starts from

Jung's seminal position that the divine manifests most directly and power-fully through numinous experience generated by the archetypal or collective unconscious as the basis of all religious experience and so of the religions. From this foundational position only two options about God's existence remain open. Either the unconscious creates the spirits and Gods as pro-jections of its major psychic energies, or God creates the unconscious as the medium through which God, in a second movement, makes itself known to humanity. Corbett suggests that a decision between these options is beyond human competence and that Jung, by implication, left them open. No doubt Corbett is here referring to Jung's prolonged waffling on the issue often in the face of theological criticisms aware of the threat his psychology posed to the objective existence of their presiding God.

For Jung would frequently take the position that as a scientist he could only show the empirical evidence of humanity's experience of itself as an image of God and refrain from making statements about the reality or nature of a God which this experience imaged. It is important to state here that Jung's understanding of humanity as an image of God is never of two distinct entities imaging each other in and through their distinction as the moose on a Canadian quarter would image a moose in a Canadian bush. The rare texts where this may be suggested after lengthy and somewhat tortured grammatical analysis are exceptional. Rather Jung's understanding of humanity as an image of God is always experiential, based on approxi-mations of the experience of the total expression the self as mediator of the unconscious seeks in consciousness. Such expression is the power operative in images and art capable of triggering that experience (Jung 1969c: 261). The experience itself could not be used to establish the reality of an objective divinity beyond and distinct from the experience. With an appeal to Kant Jung would frequently fortify his position that only the experience of humanity as an image of divinity and not divinity itself fell within the range of his inquiry (Jung 1969c: 245, 246). Humanity's experience of God fell within the field of empirical phenomena, the legitimate field of psychology and of Jung's phenomenological approach. This experience and the images it left in its wake were simply empirical facts. Beyond the phenomenal thus understood and into the realm of the noumenon, Jung, in his cautious Kantian moments, would fear to tread.

Nevertheless at times the waffling broke down, especially as he grew older. In fact the caution vanished entirely in his late bald and repeated statements about the end of monotheism in the face of humanity's evolving religious consciousness. About the dubious existence of a God wholly independent of the psyche and unqualifiedly good, Jung could hardly be more explicit than when he writes, "The naive assumption that the creator of the world is a conscious being must be regarded as a disastrous prejudice which later gave rise to the most incredible dislocations of logic" (Jung 1969d: 383, fn. 13). One such dislocation was the conviction that God was perfect and the corresponding negative inflation that humanity was the source of all evil. And again in reference to the evolution of religious consciousness evident in the book of Job he repeats, "An unusual scandal was blowing up in the realm of metaphysics, with supposedly devastating consequences, and nobody was ready with a saving formula which would rescue the monotheistic conception of God from disaster" (Jung 1969d: 385). Indeed Jung describes as "peculiar people . . . those who think that one can make anything but a conceptual distinction between the individual experience of God and God himself" (Jung 1933: 321). Two such peculiarities will be dealt with at length in ensuing chapters.

And what precisely was this monotheistic conception of God that the evolution of humanity's religious consciousness left defenseless and abandoned in its wake? As will be seen in subsequent chapters, Jung's lengthy discussions with both Martin Buber, a Jewish thinker, and Victor White, a Dominican Roman Catholic theologian, the monotheistic God would be an objective entity creating humanity from beyond humanity and in no need of humanity and its developing consciousness for its own well being let alone developing self-consciousness. Nor would humanity be possessed of an immediate awareness of such a divinity. Such experiential divestiture would then serve as the precondition for the need of revelation and the supremacy of the religion that received it. Jung's prolonged discussions with both Buber and White were really one discussion with exponents of two major variants of the monotheistic family of Gods (Dourley 1994). These discussions clearly reveal that such a divine being and its relation to humanity is simply not compatible with Jung's understanding of the human psyche and the commerce with divinity the psyche sponsors. The failure of both dialogues forces the conclusion that, from Jung's perspective, all interchange with divinity, once removed from the skies, is now to become a wholly intrapsychic process around the interior dialectic of the ego with the unconscious under the orchestration of the self. When Jung's total work is weighed and considered, the first of Corbett's options prevails. The unconscious creates the Gods and spirits wholly out of is own archetypal resources and the evolution of human religious consciousness and its attendant spirituality is presently coming to realize this fact. The option that a divinity external to the psyche creates it to reveal itself through the psyche adds an unneeded element to the encounter between the divine and the human and, in Jung's hands, falls under Occam's razor.

Are we then to conclude that Jung having dissolved the illusion of humanity's relation to a variety of one and only Gods abandoned humanity to a Godless life? Such abandonment would convict Jung of the same charge he brings against Albert Schweitzer. For Jung, the latter's relativizing picture of the biblical Jesus as the bearer of an apocalyptic message soon to meet historical disappointment shattered the culture's previous faith in a literal historical Jesus leaving a spiritual vacuum throughout

Christendom in its wake (Jung 1953d: 140–142; 1953e: 144–145). Jung's admiration of Schweitzer's religious genius and the continued need for it in the Europe of his time lies behind his caustic critique of Schweitzer's flight to a life of heroic sanctity in Africa leaving the consequent spiritual desolation in his home culture to be addressed by psychologists like Jung then forced to play the role of spiritual directors (Jung 1952d: 39, 40; 1952e: 85; 1953c: 125). Jung hardly followed suit. Rather he took up the spiritual plight of Europe in the wake of the loss of a too simple faith induced in part by the very valid biblical and theological scholarship such as Schweitzer's and others'. In addressing the spiritual sterility in his culture Jung effectively contributed to the rise of a new myth which would revalidate the reality of religion but, in doing so, question the capacity of extant religions, and especially the monotheisms, to meet its religious perspective and demands. Paul Tillich has much to support his contention that only a symbol replaces a symbol and only a myth a myth (Tillich 1957: 43). Tillich's formulation means that symbol and myth are not the sole product of reason nor can reason replace or manipulate them out of its own resources. Rather the emergence of symbol and myth is from a depth of reason which precedes reason itself and manifests most intensely through reason in the form of myth and symbol. Tillich's depth of reason has much in common with Jung's archetypal unconscious. Both are the source of symbol and myth created in response to the conscious situation of individual and society.

Read from this perspective what Jung left the West was a substantial contribution to a new myth and its spirituality expressive of the unconscious urgencies compensating collective consciousness toward a greatly expanded and inclusive compassion and so completeness. Archetypal in origin and power, such compensation would bear nothing less than the force of a developing new religious and societal revelation. In its fostering of this dawning consciousness Jung's myth revisioned humanity's relation to the divine as the ground movement of the psyche itself in which both the divine and the human are inescapably implicated from the outset in the conferral of mutual redemption on each other. The dissolution of the distant and powerful Gods foreshadowed in the book of Job evolved into the growing contemporary realization that God, natural reality and humanity at some point coincide and that authentic religion enables the experience of this coincidence. The point of coincidence lies in the psyche as the source of what is. Jung puts it this way, "It was only quite late that we realized (or rather, are beginning to realize) that God is Reality itself and therefore last but not least man. This realization is a millennial process" (Jung 1969d: 402).

Since the substance of Jung's psychology is devoted to the furthering of this millennial process and to the formulation of the myth and spirituality that would now foster it, the cardinal features of that myth are worth spelling out.

The now emerging myth

The myth embedded in Jung's psychology would cap the unconscious in its creation of the Gods understood to be other than and totally transcendent to humanity. This capping would end all variants of supernaturalism understood to point to divinities wholly other than the human, addressing the human from beyond the human and immune to the outcome of such address. In doing this Jung wholly dissolves the three transcendental gentlemen populating the monotheistic heavens: Yaweh, God the Father with Trinitarian associates, and Allah. All are understood as variants of the same archetypal constellation now seeking its own supersession at the insistence of the same unconscious energies that produced all three individuals. In their stead he understands transcendence as the intrapsychic transcendence of the archetypal unconscious to its ongoing incarnation in human consciousness of which the three aforementioned Gods are indeed outstanding manifestations. In thus revisioning the process of incarnation as the progressive penetration of consciousness by the archetypal unconscious, it is important to note that the only legitimate sense of the word "transcendence" in Jungian parlance rests on the fecundity of the archetypal which will always transcend its valuable but ever partial incarnations in historical consciousness. In the sense of William James there will always be a "more" yet to become incarnate (James 1979: 486–488). This is the only legitimate understanding of transcendent divinity in a Jungian universe and its referent is to the commerce between the conscious and unconscious moments of the psychic life in which the latter will always transcends the former.

This understanding of incarnation denies to any religion or archetypal equivalent the status of unqualified ultimacy or an exhaustive finality. It is to this archetypal agency of the psyche creating the sense of God and attendant symbols and myths that Jung refers when he boasts of "my demonstration of the psychic origin of religious phenomena" (Jung 1968a: 9). Elsewhere in this work he repeats that his researches have laid bare, "the empirical foundations of all religious experiences" (Jung 1968a: 14). It is not only the two unnamed theologians Jung refers to in the first above cited passage who have missed his demonstration of the psychic origins of religion and its import for reflection on the nature of religion itself and so of the religions. So too have many Jungian scholars and analysts addressing Jung on matters religious. The implications of Jung's demonstration of the wholly intrapsychic origin of religious experience and so of the religions remain largely unacknowledged and unexplored by both Jungians and non-Jungian scholars. Some of the more important and immediate implications would be the fact that Jung grounds each of the religions, past and extant, on archetypal experience and expression, and in so doing, makes each of them relative and (let us hope), in the present world context, safer for a humanity increasingly aware of the origin of religion in itself.

Jung's demonstration of the psychic origin of all religious experience and so of all the religions is the foundation of everything he has to say about religion. With it he can give a succinct and credible statement about the total historical development of humanity's religious consciousness. The many Gods dwelling on mountain tops became one God. The one God became human and humanity recognized its natural divinity. Even in the face of the very real danger of inflation, the "common man" is now to become conscious of his native divinity as the completion of his humanity and as the capstone of the evolution of divinity in relation to the human, individually and collectively (Jung 1969b: 84). The spreading sense of humanity's native divinity is why divinity no longer presides at the centre of the modern mandala and the wholeness of the human does (Jung 1969b: 82). More importantly, once the unconscious is identified as the creator of the Gods, Jung can go beyond a general history of the evolution of religious consciousness to identify where the ongoing drama of the evolving sense of the divine is currently acting out.

For Jung, humanity's present religious maturation lies in the conscious recall of the Gods to their origin in the unconscious and to the subsequent unmediated dialogue with them there. Jung writes:

> But since the development of consciousness requires the withdrawal of all projections we can lay our hands on, it is not possible to maintain any non-psychological doctrine about the gods. If the historical process of world despiritualization continues as hitherto, then everything of a divine or daemonic character outside us must return to the psyche, to the inside of the unknown man, whence it apparently originated.
>
> (Jung 1969b: 85)

What does "apparently" mean in this citation? It would probably best be understood as "evidently" because it implies no doubt in Jung's mind. Rather it means that the origin of the Gods from the "inside of the unknown man" had become all too apparent to Jung, to the evolution of religious consciousness itself and to ever widening circles in the current discussion on spirituality.

The ongoing return of the Gods to their psychic origins would have great societal and personal value. On the social level it would mean that each community bonded by a totally transcendent divinity would have to realize that its allegedly unique and exclusive God was a valued variant of the family of one and only Gods created by the psyche as humanity now moves through and (let us hope) beyond its once much needed monotheistic moment. Such a realization would produce a moderating and humanizing relativity in the claims for universal and exhaustive religious validity made by each of the contending one and only Gods and free their constituencies from the need to convert or kill each other ultimately in the name of these claims. The link between what even a Paul Tillich could call a "final revelation" in Christianity and the final solution would become much clearer and so avoidable (Tillich 1951: 135–137). In the end the tracing of the monotheistic Gods to their psychic origin would question not only the maturity but also the morality and social responsibility of an unqualified faith in any variant of monotheistic divinity given the shadow side of their historical and societal performance especially in relation to each other. Such relativizing of the major divine contenders and their conflicting communities combined with the heightened moral sensitivity such relativity would engender could serve as the major resource in helping humanity through its monotheistic phase if it is indeed to survive it. Needless to say the identification of the archetypal basis of political and ethnic monotheistic faiths would have much the same result. It would force those bonded by any political faith to recognize its relativity and force the political believer to face the common human problem of societal archetypal bonding which lowers the consciousness and so moral responsibility of the individual in favor of a cohesive but unconscious group, nation or tribe (Dourley 2003). Chapter 6 will address this issue at greater length.

At the personal level the recall of the Gods to their common psychic matrix would have equally radical effects. It would destroy what Jung calls the "systematic blindness" and "prejudice that God is *outside* man" (Jung 1969b: 58, italics Jung's). Rather the restoration of divinity to its natural containment in the psyche would point to a dialectical "identity of God and man" (Jung 1969b: 61). The revisioning of humanity as naturally divine, and driven by divinity itself to an ever fuller conscious recovery of its native divinity, would be for Jung a universal truth of human nature. And yet it would have a devastating effect on orthodox religious conceptions of figures of the self on which these religions are built. Facing the problem in its Christian variant, Jung concedes that the participation of every human in a natural divinity borders on heresy (Jung 1969b: 60). Official guardians of religious truth, at least in the monotheisms, would think it was well over the border and deeply into the heartland of heresy. Undaunted Jung goes on to extend the *homoousia*, the unity of divine and human natures in Christ, to everyone and to claim that nature works to unite in all, the human and the divine, a union Christianity reserves to the single person of the Christ figure. Jung could hardly be more explicit, "it would be considered blasphemy or madness to stress Christ's dogmatic humanity to such a degree that man could identify himself with Christ and his *homoousia*." The extension of divinity to humanity universal and the implied extension of the sacred to all that is remains unacceptable to the Church. Continuing the above passage Jung goes on, "She [the Church] may even have to condemn any approach to these experiences, since she cannot admit that nature unites what she herself has divided" (Jung 1969b: 61). In this citation "nature" means the archetypal unconscious, divinity, working through the self toward an ever greater ingression in consciousness, the human. As this union occurs humanity attains its divinity and incarnation becomes an equally universal reality. What the Church has divided is the divine from the human both in human nature and throughout nature itself and in so doing has removed humanity from a sense of the sacred nature of itself and of nature beyond the human.

When Jung reunites the divine and the human universally, he is not using the substantial categories of the Christological councils who identify two substantial natures united in the uniqueness of the person of Christ. Rather he would see divinity as the experience of a universal human latency driving to become ever more conscious in human consciousness as the base dynamic in a human spirituality now equated with human maturation. Collectively this drive becomes the *telos* or movement of history itself. Jung's understanding of alchemical transformation is the best example of this process at the individual level. What he means by the human recovering a native divinity as the meaning of psychological maturation is explicitly spelled out when he writes:

> It looks as if the idea had dawned on the alchemists that the Son who, according to classical (and Christian) tradition, dwells eternally in the Father and reveals himself as God's gift to mankind, was something that man could produce out of his own nature – with God's help of course (*Deo concedente*). The heresy of the idea is obvious.
>
> (Jung 1968b: 112)

In this passage Jung clearly identifies the alchemical effort as one which made conscious to the individual adept the divinity native to the adept's humanity. Since alchemy compensated what Christianity had removed from the realm of the sacred, the divinity that alchemy made conscious in humanity was a divinity capable of embracing and resacralizing the totality of creation which Christian theology and spirituality could not do. In this sense the entire alchemical effort constitutes an effort to compensate the one-sidedness of Christianity by fostering a more inclusive and, ultimately, an all inclusive sense of the sacredness of what is.

The birth of the divine Son in consciousness through the alchemist's role of midwife is effectively the birth of the self in the individual ego. Here again Jung's myth frees the individual from religious addiction to one or other version of the self and relocates the true self with the individual prior to allegiance to one or other specific religion. For he makes the point explicitly that the figures in whom the archetypal self concretizes in religious or cultural form are relative expressions of the archetypal self's inexhaustible precedence as potential. Such a position flatly contradicts affirmations made by the various monotheisms and, indeed, by most religions that theirs is the only legitimate version of the self. Yet the religious claim to represent an exhaustive or even highly privileged expression of the self continues to have great currency. An outstanding example is to be found in John 14: 4, which reads, "I am the Way, the Truth and the Life. No one can come to the Father except through me." If this proclamation is taken as literal and personal it would mean that the self is exhaustively and exclusively incarnate in the person of Jesus. Only if the statement is elevated to a gnostic level and the I becomes the I of the self as distinguished from the ego can the statement be saved from the literal interpretation that has worked such damage between the Christian and non-Christian worlds throughout the centuries. Thus reconceived John 14: 4 would mean that the only way to the truth and life of divinity is through the self as it becomes incarnate in consciousness and that this is true of all religions and indeed of every life lived under the growing suasion of the self whether in or beyond a specific religion. The foundations for a now much needed tolerance, and more, a mutual appreciation, between communities bonded by diverse manifestations of the self and turned against each other by these very manifestations lie in Jung's very clear statement, "Hence in its scientific usage the term 'self' refers neither to Christ nor to the Buddha but to the totality of the figures that are its equivalent, and each of these figures is a symbol of the self" (Jung 1968a: 18). Jung's affirmation of the relativity of Christ as one among many symbols of the self is one he made throughout his work. It is nowhere more explicit than when he writes, "Is the self a symbol of Christ or is Christ a symbol of the self?" He answers simply, "In this present study I have affirmed the latter alternative" (Jung 1968c: 68). Nor did he abandon this alternative in any of his other works.

Fundamentalism from a Jungian perspective

The foregoing lays the basis for a Jungian understanding of fundamentalism and the pathology of religion as currently the greatest single threat to human survival. There may still be time to work with the ecological threat. Time may be running out in humanity's efforts to survive its religions. They could end the joint human project through conflicts between their particular concretions should they ever move to the use of all available weaponry in the solution of their conflict. The fundamentalist psyche is characterized by three dominant traits: externalism, literalism and historicism. Each is actually an aspect of the other but each is worth looking at individually. These traits also raise the question as to the reality of the distinction between fundamentalism and non-fundamentalist belief. Members of all traditions will make the distinction in an attempt to show that the poverty of funda-mentalist thought and the horrors of fundamentalist action are extreme expressions of a more moderate belief. Yet, though they hide behind a more sophisticated intellectual disguise, a closer examination reveals that these so called more moderate expressions of orthodoxy are to some great extent contaminated with the same traits as fundamentalism itself.

Externalism, literalism and historicism are forms of the objectification of deity beyond the psyche and so the reduction of divinity to a person, entity or object over against the human. Externalism is the dominant trait of the fundamentalist mind and includes the other two. Jung relies on Meister Eckhart to describe externalism when he writes of those "who put nothing into their own souls and have 'all God outside'" (Jung 1968a: 9, 11). The projection of God beyond the soul robs the soul of its life and denies to the individual the fullest experience of the archetypal basis of divinity and of the divine figures now existing beyond the soul dead to the experience of the divine within it. Jung depicts this loss of soul as a debilitating kenosis, a depressive emptying out of the life of the soul in the creation of divinities beyond her. He writes with Christianity in mind but with a meaning applicable to all the transcendent Gods, "Too few people have experienced the divine image as the innermost possession of their own soul" (Jung 1968a: 12). In the critique he leveled against the theology of his father and the clergy in his immediate family, Jung writes of their religious insensitivity to human interiority and immediate religious experience such as his own. They held and were held by the formal certitudes afforded by their "blind faith" (Jung 1965a: 73f). As he takes up this critique in his more studied work, Jung describes the same syndrome of a faith divorced from experience and depth. "With a truly tragic delusion these theologians fail to see that it is not a matter of proving the existence of the light, but of blind people who do not know that their eyes could see" (Jung 1968a: 13). With theologian or anyone, the consequence of externalism is to empty consciousness of the soul's natural sense of the sacred within as the basis of the sense of the sacred beyond it without which no humanizing relation to the sacred is possible. Such externalism always implies an invasion of the soul and psyche by a power foreign to it. In short if the soul were not naturally related to the divine it could never seek nor receive the divine as a nonintrusive presence (Jung 1968a: 11). In the face of charges of a reductive psychologism Jung's defense remained throughout his life, "I have been accused of 'deifying the soul'. Not I but God himself has deified it!" (Jung 1968a: 13). But this God is not a God beyond the soul but the soul's own life alienated from it when God is understood as beyond it.

The spiritually debilitating consequences of externalism are tragically apparent in the related pathology of historicism. In its Christian variant, historicism reduces the figure of Christ to a past historical figure and not a present psychic force. The imitation of Christ becomes the slavish reproduction in the individual's life of the details of a past life instead of the ongoing rhythm of archetypal death and resurrection in the now of psychic life. As Jung diagnoses it, historicism turns the Christ figure into "an external object of worship, and it is precisely this veneration for the object that prevents it from reaching down into the depths of the psyche and giving the latter a wholeness in keeping with the ideal" (Jung 1968a: 7). Such externalization leaves the individual removed from all but the most pallid impress of the power of the image of Christ or any other religious figure largely divested of its transformative power because removed from the depths of the human subject which is both its origin and referent.

Finally literalism combines with historical externalism to look upon the lives of religious figures through literal accounts of past events and not symbolic expressions of the unconscious which creates these figures and their deeds as triggers to their reenactment in the internal forum of the living psyche. Revelation, the poetry of the soul's deepest movements, becomes a recounting of history as past event and its power to mediate transformative life is all but lost. Even when modern biblical scholarship reached an agreement that the historical life of Jesus can never be gained behind the myth that has given his story whatever staying power it has, the hankering after personal or biographical details continues. In this thinly disguised literalism biblical scholarship squanders the spiritual substance of what it studies in misguided efforts to find the historical Jesus who never existed except in the myth and symbols that grew around him as the basis of humanity's continuing fascination with him. Jung's indictment of the failure of modern "spokesmen of religion" to address the question of why there is symbolic biblical discourse at all still stands (Jung 1966a: 227). If such spokesmen were to address the improbability yet perseverance of symbolic expression and its truth the search for the historical Jesus would turn into a deeper appreciation of the symbolic Jesus. The depths of the soul from which such symbols proceed to consciousness would be recovered from their literal religious overlay and the spiritually coarsening effect of a blind faith in what Jung calls "sacrosanct unintelligibility", and "preposterous nonsense" would be greatly alleviated (Jung 1969e: 109, 110). And yet it must be acknowledged that, even when symbol and myth are stripped of their spiritual vitality as archetypal expression through the processes described above, they continue to exercise a truly possessive power over their victims in reducing faith to collective unconsciousness in the communities they possess. For they provide the instant truth and mass identity so appealing to the human lust for saving certitude as an anodyne to the authentic agony of doubt and ambiguity hanging over the human situation. Though it appeals to this basest of human instincts, the need for instant certitude and the collective assurance of being chosen, fundamentalism, is for that very reason likely to continue its present growth and increasing threat to humanity.

Currently we are faced with an even greater threat than religious fundamentalism though this threat is for Jung but a variant of its predecessor. This form of fundamentalism is political fundamentalism, the fundamentalism that informs the "isms". In Jung's analysis, like religion itself, political fundamentalism is an expression of archetypal power. In so identifying its roots in the psyche Jung has given us the key to its defeat. In a certain deepening of sociology and political science it is helpful to identify the archetypal basis informing the political religions which Jung describes as ranging from paradise regained in socialist utopias (Jung 1964b: 537) to life under a benign father in the fascist alternative (Jung 1964a: 190). But beyond archetypal sociology or political science Jung also provides what probably is, in the end, the only prophylactic against infection by political or religious fundamentalist faith when he writes, "*Resistance to the organized mass can be effected only by the man who is as well organized in his individuality as the mass itself*" (Jung 1964c: 278, italics Jung's). This statement is of so high a moral order it prompts the question of its human possibility. It elicits the response, "Yes but how many were as well organized as the Gestapo in the second world war and how many are as well organized as the various coalitions in today's wars?" The moral demand and level of consciousness Jung imposes on those who are to oppose fundamentalism, religious or political, are so rigorous and so personal that one is forced to wonder if humanity has the will and time available to save itself from its faiths and especially from those composite faiths in which a background of religious commitment informs a political, and economic absolute imposed at gunpoint as currently in Iraq. Such exponential growth in collective unconsciousness is always mirrored in the exponential growth in loss of life. Facing this problem in his maturity Jung appeals to "leading minorities" of those conscious of the unconscious as carrying the hope of wider collective awareness of the psychic powers that transcend consciousness and control it to the extent they remain unconscious (Jung 1976a: 610, 611). Again, the question as to whether such leading minorities are currently extant or growing remains ambiguous. They would not at this moment in history seem capable of mustering the overwhelming support that faith in all its varying faces still does.

The personal and collective implications of Jung's myth and spirituality

The spirituality attaching to Jung's myth is primarily personal but always with profound collective or societal implications. For Jung challenges the individual to recover one's unique myth through an ongoing dialogue with the unconscious primarily through the continued revelation of the dream. The importance of continued dialogue with the unconscious through the dream cannot be overestimated in Jungian theory or therapy and its social consequences. To neglect such dialogue is to maim Jungian theory and therapy. Effectively the recovery of the individual's personal myth is the only power that frees the individual from an unconscious adherence to the myths into which the individual is inevitably born. These myths, usually layered, would include religion, nationality, ethnicity, social class and whatever else would impact on an emerging ego with archetypal force. As and to the extent the true self as the author of the dream incarnates in personal consciousness and so frees it from its multiple mythical overlay the individual for the first time is enabled to separate from and then face the myths into which one is born out of the power of one's own emerging myth.

This affirmation of the emerging self can take on many forms and be quite wide ranging. The affirmation of the truth of the self may support a fuller appreciation of the symbolic validity of inherited myths which only a heightened experience of one's personal symbology can work. Or this affirmation may be a discerning appreciation in which the conscious self sets the boundaries of a qualified loyalty to one's native myths based on a prior fidelity to the truth of the self. True believers view this option as picking and choosing what elements of a myth, especially religious, suits the individual involved. But grounded in one's own wisdom such picking and choosing may be far from a cherry picking approach. Or the affirmation of the self may be one of a total surpassing of one's inherited myth. This was the case with Wolfgang Pauli, whose material strongly suggested that he came into the truth of the self without the mediation or support of his original but long abandoned mythical inheritance (Jung 1969b: 41; 1976b: 285). Needless to say there may be as many shades of difference in these various forms of the affirmation of the self as there are individuals under-going the incarnation of the self in their conscious lives. Pauli's situation may currently be much wider as more individuals fail to experience the self in their traditional religions and wider more encompassing culture. They are driven to look elsewhere for the truth of the self in personal and collective values still loosely gathered under the canvas of "spirituality". But in whatever form it take, the incarnation of the self in the individual's consciousness provides the basis for the personal and liberating relation to whatever archetypal powers preside at one's birth with their impact on consequent life. Ranging from a deepened appreciation to total rejection of one's inherited mythology, such incarnation then becomes the effective basis of one's personal religion. Whether a practicing relation to a religious tradition continues or not is secondary to the priority of fidelity to one's own truth.

But there is more to a Jungian spirituality than the cultivation of the self in one's personal consciousness. This is so because the accessing of the self implicates a relation to the archetypal powers which also create history and its epochs. And Jung thought the psyche in his time and ours was ushering in a new religious epoch and its supporting myth. This is evident when he compares himself and his psychology to the mind of Joachim di Fiore, a late twelfth century monk, who anticipated the new religious spirit which did indeed come to inform so much of the achievement of the thirteenth century (Jung 1953a: 138). Something like this change is happening today.

Cultural commentators will make the point that the Thirty Years War (1618–1648), was a major contributing factor to the Enlightenment and to contemporary ideas of the secular state as the European mind realized it could no longer entrust the peace to religious forces and so placed reason beyond and above them all (Tillich 1967: 48, 49; Livingston 1997: 10). At that point reason and its tolerance compensated religion. Currently a newer myth seeks to supplant both reason and religion. The religions and especially the monotheisms, religious and political, threaten the future of the species and Enlightenment reason has itself become problematic. In Jung's view the Enlightenment mind, whose historical moment was no doubt necessary and valuable, nevertheless uprooted Western humanity from its native depths by eventually reducing the total human cognitive capacity to reason, then to science and eventually to their dubious child, technology (Dourley 2008: 178–191). In the face of the dual threat of warring religious and political absolutes and a humanity truncated through its entrapment in the wasteland of an increasingly shallow intellectual and technological rationality, Jung proposed an understanding of the psyche, mythic in import, which would reconnect the mind with its roots in the unconscious. Such a myth would breed a religious sense of deeper ingression into the psyche and an accompanying wider compassion beyond the psyche than can contemporary reason and any extant community united by a political or religious absolute. In this sense the individual's surfacing of one's individual myth from the power that gives birth to them all is the greatest contribution the individual can make to a now emerging spiritual sensibility of wider universal sympathy and inclusion. If this universal sentiment of sympathy for all that is, even across acknowledged and respected archetypal divides, is the defining characteristic of the myth the unconscious is currently creating, it cannot be worked by reason, always the servant of myth and not its origin, nor by the extant religions whose limited sensibilities the new myth seeks to supersede. Only the unconscious can breed the sense of the one world, the sense that the source of the totality can be seen through all of its expressions by the mind resonating with that source in the ground of each individual life. And this perception of the unity at the origin of the diversity of archetypal expression is what gives life to Jung's myth. It is most vividly apparent in his move to a quaternitarian mythology.

Jung's move to a quaternitarian future

When Jung moves to a quaternitarian paradigm he sacralizes entire realms of reality whose sacred nature is denied or diminished by the reigning Western myths, especially but not only in their religious form. The deepest reason forcing him to a myth of quaternity was his clear realization that the advent of all religious experience is through the unconscious and that the unconscious is driven to express its full inventory in human consciousness and history. To translate this statement into religious terms it would mean that God, as the creator of all that is, is reflected in all that is and all that is lies as potential within its source. No existent reality of itself is less sacred than another. Some have called this position the principle of plenitude and mean by it that everything that is is an expression of and so points to its origin which in turn seeks the total expression of its potential beyond itself in creation. But on closer examination of Christianity Jung found that only the spirit, the male and figures of the good such as the Christ figure were sacred. And so he asked where is the missing fourth, so evident in creation and strangely absent in creation's alleged creator. In this context the missing fourth was extended in his wider work to become matter, the feminine and Satan (Jung 1969e: 164, 174, 175). Traditional spirituality could only divinize and so honor half of reality. Its values lay in a humanity which was only half there. The missing fourth, the reality of evil, of the feminine, and of material creation, were indeed united but only in their joint exclusion from the Spirit of Christianity's presiding symbol, the Trinity. All variants of orthodox monotheism tend to share in this exclusion. This exclusion meant in practice and fact that the divinity of their source and so of their reality was denied to the feminine, to material creation and to the Satanic. The truth of Jung's evaluation of the exclusion of so much of reality from the sacred is already being seen in movements of its reversal. The widespread cultural sacralization of the feminine and the body witness the truth of Jung's then prophetic vision. However, the union of Christ and Satan to date defies societal and too often personal realization. The failure of this union contributes to and is most evident in the demonization of the other as individual or group. World leaders can still present their adversaries as the axis of evil, especially where they embody a different religion and polity, and be repeatedly voted into office.

Jung's emerging myth would restore the innate sacredness to all realms of creation absent in Trinitarian symbolism. It would then challenge a spirituality which denied their innate sacredness with the questions of whether their exclusion was the cause of its current spiritual pathology and whether it could embrace a sense of their divinity and remain itself? The Spirit of the quaternity would unite the dark with the light Son of the same Father, the female with the male and body/matter with spirit. Can the Christian Spirit do so and retain its historical reality? The question is particularly powerful when asked of monotheistic consciousness. Could it retain its current identity with a growing awareness of the divinity of the feminine, of nature, and of the demonic? If the answer were yes, a further question would follow immediately. If it did recognize and reintegrate these elements as sacred in themselves would this spiritual recovery necessitate the recovery of what it had excluded as heresy in the process of the creation of its now pathologically one-sided corporate self and spirituality? Would it not have to recover a gnostic, alchemical, mystical and pantheistic sense and drink once more from the grail? Jung would seem to think it would have to and to leave open whether it could or would.

The need to recover spiritual health through the recovery of a now healing heresy is but one side of a larger picture Jung draws of the development of religious consciousness historically and presently. He sketches this wider portrait in black and white in his work on Job. Here he draws out the consequences of his understanding of divinity and humanity as "functions" of each other from the outset, now engaged in a joint project of mutual redemption in human history (Jung 1971a: 243). Obviously Jung is here playing with an extended metaphor in which the unconscious is to consciousness as the divine is to the human. When expressed in religious language he is arguing that divinity was forced by its unconsciousness to create human consciousness as the only theatre in which divinity could become conscious of its conflicted proclivities. This is the process he describes as the "relativity of God" meaning that only in human consciousness does God become self-conscious (Jung 1971a: 242). In this process divinity and humanity sacrifice themselves to each other. A distant God must give up all remove and become real in human suffering as the divine self-contradiction is perceived and resolved in the human agony of unifying divine opposites in itself. Humanity and the individual human, on their part, must undergo a never ending cyclical death, a psychic baptism into the pleroma and a return therefrom if the drive of the origin to become conscious through the resolution of its conflicts in humanity is to move forward (Jung 1969d: 425). When he gives his answer to Job, Jung depicts a crucified Christ figure, a symbol of humanity suffering between the yes and a no of divinely grounded opposites, dying in despair as the precondition to a resurrected consciousness in which these lethal opposites would grow closer together in a humanity enriched by their synthesis (Jung 1969d: 408).

Symbolically the death and resurrection of the Christ figure describes the psychodynamic of what Jung calls the transcendent function. The process is wholly contained within the historical psyche and is the only legitimate sense of transcendence as transformative in Jung's work. This dynamic describes the base movement of the psyche both individually and collectively. It grounds the individual's spirituality on suffering whatever aspect of the divine self-contradiction is most prominent in each individual's life. Collectively it also describes the ground movement and meaning of history itself as one of the reconciliation in human consciousness of the eternally unresolved conflict of divine opposites. In Jung's words the death of Christ between divinely based opposites is as "'eschatological' as it is 'psychological'" (Jung 1969d: 408). Jung's meaning here entrusts and burdens humanity with the mutual redemption of the divine and human in a single self-contained historical process. When this sweeping vision is taken to the personal level it means that the most intense suffering in an individual's life is an incarnation in that life of some aspect of the divinity's self-contradiction seeking relief in that suffering and its resolution. To the extent such suffering is well born and issues into a higher consciousness it redeems both the divine who suffers in it and the human who suffers through it. In this Jung joins another twentieth century spiritual innovator, Teilhard de Chardin, when the latter encourages his readers to bring to God "a little fulfillment" (Teilhard de Chardin 1964: 62).

How the mystics did it

These foundational themes in a Jungian spirituality are dramatically evident in his appreciation of certain Western mystics and might well point to a dimension of the psyche beyond the archetypal itself, hinted at but not explicitly charted throughout the *Collected Works*. Jung's appreciation of certain streams of mysticism and their possible relation to both the contemporary religious and political situation will be addressed at length in Chapters 9 and 10. What follows is a brief treatment of this topic in the context of the foregoing exposition of his spirituality.

If, for Jung, the referents of all religious experience and expression are the deeper movements of the psyche, this is true of mystics to a surpassing degree. In Jung's view, "Mystics are people who have a particularly vivid experience of the processes of the collective unconscious. Mystical experience is experience of archetypes" (Jung 1976c: 98). Ironically since Jung obviously underwent such vivid experience personally his own description of a mystic would have to include himself and may explain in part their attraction for him. Historically the mystics to whom he is most drawn are mystics whose experience was characterized by an apophatic moment, that is, an immersion in divinity in which all distinction between themselves and the divine was annihilated in a moment of an all consuming nothingness.

Jung picks up the apophatic tradition with the thirteenth century Beguines and Mechthild of Magdeburg in particular. She and her contemporary, Hadewijch of Antwerp, describe a sexual union with a youthful Christ figure culminating in an identity beyond all difference. Marguerite Porete, burnt by the Inquisition in Paris in 1310, talks of the annihilated soul who became the all through attaining the nothing (Dourley 2004). Contemporary scholarship has now demonstrated the influence of these women mystics on a towering mystical figure in the history of the Christian West and in Jung's work, Meister Eckhart, who died during his trial for heresy around 1328 (McGinn 1998a: 246). Eckhart's paradoxical prayer, "This is why I pray to God to rid me of God", is a prayer to the Godhead beyond the Trinitarian God, the God of creation (Eckhart 1978: 216, 219). It is a prayer to remove all distance between himself and his origin, between the creator and creature, so that he might reclaim his native divinity through a total immersion in the nothingness that precedes all creation and definition. For Jung this experience of identity with the Godhead would describe a movement of the psyche in which "God disappears as an object and dwindles into a subject which is no longer distinguishable from the ego" (Jung 1971a: 255). In this psychic situation, continues Jung, "the original state of identity with God is re-established and a new potential is produced" (Jung 1971a: 255). What Eckhart and the mystics of the apophatic moment are describing as an immersion in the divine nothingness is a moment of the ego's dissolution in what Jung terms the "Great Mother" or "Goddess", who precedes all form and creation and from whom all form and creation derive. In so doing they would seem to go to a moment of total rest or resignation in the source of their being ever present to them in the depths of their personal participation in the universal ground of the psyche. Here again the question of the quaternity arises now in relation to divinity and humanity as contributing to each other's wealth. These mystic travelers would seem to go beyond the compulsive creativity of the archetypal to a moment of rest in a fourth, the God beyond the God of Trinity and beyond the Gods of biblical theism, namely, in the Goddess herself.

Eckhart's journey is completed by the only mystic who appears more frequently in Jung's pages, Jacob Boehme, a self-educated shoemaker, cloth merchant and family man who lived in Silesia from 1575 to 1624. He too went to the nothing, in his idiom, the One or the *ungrund* (Boehme 1911: v, 2). But his return prompted a major revision of the divine human relation in much of subsequent religious and philosophical thought. For he came to realize that contrary to traditional Trinitarian thought, God had not resolved the opposites in the turbulence of divine life from eternity. Rather only in human history could the divine self-contradiction be perceived and redeemed. When Jung referred to "a thought and premonition that have long been present in humanity: the idea of the creature that surpasses its creator by a small but decisive factor", he probably had the image of Job in mind (Jung 1965a: 220). The premonition could equally apply to Boehme and explain his frequent appearances throughout the *Collected Works*. For Boehme's experience surfaces a second quaternity. Humanity completes the Trinity, as creator, in time by working in itself a synthesis that evaded divinity in eternity. In effect the individual and humanity itself become the place of the uniting Spirit where alone the dark fire of the Father and the more feminine light of the Son realize their union. When the quaternitarian implications of Eckhart and Boehme are combined the conclusion can only be that the movement into the psyche to the point where divinity and humanity coincide within is the necessary precondition to the resolution of divinely grounded conflict without. The wisdom gained from the moment of identity with the ground of all within is the deepest basis for compassion for the all beyond. In his alchemical work Jung affirms that the individual's spiritual development culminates in a state of resonance with "the eternal Ground of all empirical being" (Jung 1970: 534). Conscious unity with this ground is the experience of the alchemical *unus mundus*. It is the experience of all that is as transparent to the divine by a mind transparent to its depths. It would be the ultimate form of a universal sacramental sensitivity. Yet such a sensitivity is purely natural or the culmination of natural maturation and functions as the basis of the sacramental sense itself. Such sensitivity of the mutual inherence of the divine and creation is all that alone prevents particular sacraments from degenerating into magic, formalism, lifeless ritual or attempted manipulation of the divine. In this Jung again echoes Teilhard de Chardin's claim that "nothing here below is profane to those who know how to see" (Teilhard de Chardin 1964: 66).

This culminating religious consciousness is for Jung a wholly natural process though it unfolds in time and space in a diversity of religious and cultural expressions and too often in patterns of conflict between the communities it creates in its concretions. For Jung the evolution of religious consciousness is always toward the individual but to an individual who lives, like the mystics, out of the energies of the ever present originating and maternal nothingness. Such an individual may be a solitary individual but such solitude is rooted in the source of the totality and so is never unrelated. The rootedness is all important. Its access through institution or individual quest or combinations of both is secondary. Either approach is authentic only when it serves the rootedness. Jung could give no better summary of the spirituality informing his psychology than when he writes of the fully conscious religion of the modern:

> Indeed, he is completely modern only when he has come to the very edge of the world, leaving behind him all that has been discarded and outgrown, and acknowledging that he stands before the Nothing out of which All may grow.
>
> (Jung 1964d: 75)

This is a stark but richly rewarding spirituality and one which the mystics of the maternal Nothingness would recognize as their own. They would join in the applause for the continuity and formulation Jung gave to their experience for his contemporaries and for today.

Chapter 2

The numinous, the universal, and a myth of supersession

Preamble

The opening chapter made it clear that a Jungian spirituality is grounded in nothing less than a myth of the psyche as all encompassing. As such this myth includes an ontology, an epistemology, a cosmology and a compelling theory on the genesis and evolution of human religiosity. All these sides of the myth rest on the primary dialectic between the archetypal unconscious and consciousness. Most importantly Jung's myth serves as a harbinger of and contributor to an emerging societal consciousness comparable to a collective religious revelation. Jung's understanding of the psyche bears this capacity because he attributes to the archetypal unconscious not only the creation of the divinities but also by extension the creation of the values that they carry as the bases of the epochs that the historical parade of divinities display throughout human history. His contention is that we stand on the verge of a newer epoch and so on the edge of the supersession of the reigning Gods.

At its core Jungian spirituality fosters an immediate dialogue between consciousness and the archetypal dimension of the psyche from which the spirits address consciousness in the transformation of individual and collective life. This divine address is the basis of religious experience universally. Its very intensity makes such experience religious whether expressed in recognizably religious symbolism or not. Jung suggests much of the contemporary mind can understand religion and religious experience only in a discourse which is explicitly and traditionally religious. Hence it largely fails to see political and other forms of social faith as in themselves religious and funded by the same archetypal powers as had funded previous religions. At a more individual level Jung confesses such popular religious obtuseness forced him frequently to accompany those with whom he worked through the impact of their archetypal experience and suffering when such events could not be recognized as religious by those in religious traditions and so subjected to traditional religious perspectives and redress (Jung 1969b: 20, 43, 44). In this his psychology offered relief to such suffering which religion could neither identify as religious nor address from specifically religious resources.

The power borne by archetypal experience Jung described as "numinous" in continuity with the religionist, Rudolph Otto (Jung 1969b: 7). Because it is the power which creates the religions through the primordial energy of the archetypal, the experience of the numinous is as universal a human potential and inevitability as the religions it births. Humanity can evade neither numinous experience nor the flux of religions it grounds in its expressions. In spite of the ambiguous history of religion and its political equivalents especially in their communal form, humanity's inability to jettison its religious experience must be faced and dealt with. Efforts of the Enlightenment and since to divest humanity of its religious sense have been utter failures. In effect any success they enjoy has been purely intellectual and done little to eliminate or moderate religion as it possesses individuals and bonds conflictual tribal alignments. Samuel P. Huntington, the father of the phrase "the clash of civilizations", documents just how thorough a failure the effort to remove religion as a pervasive human determinant has been in a section of his work entitled, *"La Revanche de Dieu"* (Huntington 1996: 95–101). Here he argues that rather than declining, currently religion provides the glue for entire civilizations in conflict. Particular religions threaten universal humanity. The Huntington/Jung interface will be more directly addressed in Chapter 7. Let it be said in passing here that in an age when the question is no longer how to be saved by religion but from it, the facing and humanization of religion's inevitability and current collective concretions remains among humanity's most pressing problems. At the university level departments of religious studies should constitute a section of interdisciplinary work addressed to human survival. There it would function to identify the sources of religion and to parry the threat they currently present to humanity.

Jung contends that the numinous as the core of the human sense of ultimacy is never static in its impact on historical consciousness and its evolution. Currently Jung understands the unconscious to be sponsoring a new societal myth whose numinosity supports the awareness that the human sense of the divine emerges from humanity's own depths with the purpose of expressing in consciousness the totality of the divine potential. In religious terms this would mean that a sense of the sacred is emerging from the profoundly human which would embrace a totality more inclusive than presently reigning religious and political orthodoxies can. These foundational Jungian positions are worthy of closer examination.

The inevitability of the numinous

Jung closely linked numinous experience with his claimed discovery of nothing less than "the psychic origin of religious phenomena" (Jung 1968a:

9, 14). This claim is a bald, all inclusive affirmation that immediate religious experience, and the religions of the world this experience generates, derive from the numinous impact of the archetypal unconscious on consciousness. For Jung such powerful impress would constitute the sole source and agency of humanity's individual and collective religious experience and expression. Jung further identified and located the residual potential for numinous experience in humanity's universally possessed "authentic religious function" (Jung 1969b: 6). This religious function was simply the conscious experience of the numinosity of archetypal powers to be engaged with a religious attention, even scrupulosity, by those who experienced them. Devotion to this experience was particularly focused on tracking dreams as they addressed one's conscious life. In his words, "the careful and scrupulous observation" of the numinous expressions of this natural human function serve effectively as a private revelation (Jung 1969b: 7, 8). Personally, the dream, and whatever other media the archetypal may use to make itself manifest, become the word of God for the individual thus addressed. Collectively, the religious function also creates, usually through exceptional individuals and their immediate following, the great collective revelations whose numinous content compensates society toward its needed balance and stability in the service of the deeper ingression of the archetypal unconscious into historical consciousness. For Jung this process is never ending since it engages the entrance of an infinite creative agency, the collective unconscious, into the finitude of an always developing historical consciousness. Though without end and inexhaustible, the process can nevertheless be tracked. For Jung it continues at the moment in the genesis of a personal and societal mythic consciousness of deeper psychic origin and so of ever wider inclusion.

The consequences of numinous experience thus understood are far-reaching for individual and society. Jung would understand the numinous power of the individual's dream to derive from the same source as do the world's religions, their divinities, and their salvific strategies for humanity. With the sustenance such personal revelation provides, the individual is, at once, both freer and yet forced, in the name of freedom itself, to address whatever archetypal constructions and constrictions create the culture into which one is born. The individual is freer because of the courage to transcend archetypally imposed limitation proffered by a more intense experience of one's own archetypal truth. Yet the very freedom thus conferred also constrains the recipient to honor the sense of an emerging personal truth in the face of individual and collective archetypal restraints or to be maimed or spiritually killed by them. In every life a developing spiritual maturity demands a confrontation with the divinities which control it. In such intimate confrontation the power of the numinous can take the form of endorsement, rejection or modification of one's archetypal inheritance, but will always derive from the power of living into one's unique myth. If the individual's myth cannot be adequately accessed the failure to do so means that its victim will have to live out of a myth not of one's own provenance. Jung refers to such tragedy in a specifically Christian context when he writes of "the victims of the Summum Bonum", devotees of a God in whom there is no darkness (Jung 1976d: 725) and again of "unconscious souls", and "dumb fish" whose suffering is not from the birth of the self but from its absence or repression (Jung 1965a: 216, 220). Christians are not the only victims. All those who cannot write their own sacred scripture directly out of the unconscious are doomed to submit to another's and so live another's myth.

In a more universal sense Jung's appreciation of the numinous would mean that whether God exists or not humanity cannot rid itself of the sense of God. To the individual the numinous forbids atheism and, to society, it forbids a secularity wholly devoid of a religious or ultimate dimension. Atheism is forbidden the individual because no individual life is divested of archetypally grounded concerns, urgencies, goals, and values which take on a numinous aura regardless of their greater or lesser nobility. With Jung the question is never whether individual or society are religious. The question is what the individual or society hold as numinous, or better, what shape the numinous hold on individual and society assumes in any given historical moment. In his appreciation of the inescapable impact of the numinous on individual and society Jung approximates if he does not identify with Paul Tillich's remark that "secular culture is essentially as impossible as atheism, because both presuppose the unconditional element and both express ultimate concern" (Tillich 1964: 27). Jung would locate such "concern" in the numinous invariably active in the reciprocal drive of the self to become conscious and consciousness to accept and humanize its birth.

Again, the prevalence of the numinous in human consciousness is what lies behind Jung's repeated references to the "*consensus gentium*", that is, to humanity's collective pre-rational and non-discursive consent that it is possessed of and by an experienced sense of the divine. In appealing to their archetypal ground, Jung identifies the basis of the foundational endurance in variation of unlikely religious and theological statements and dogmas throughout the millennia (Jung 1968a: 15, 17). Indeed he provides the Vincentian Canon with its archetypal basis and in so doing confers on it a vastly more extensive meaning than it has in its specifically Christian and so limited context. Vincent of Lérins authored the Vincentian Canon in 434 CE as the norm of truth to resolve theological debate within the Christian Church. It read that that was to be believed which has been "believed always, everywhere and by all". In Jung's version, applied to no less a mystery than the Trinity itself, it takes on this form, "The archetype is 'that which is believed always, everywhere, and by everybody'" (Jung 1969e: 117). This statement hardly means that everyone, everywhere and always believed in the specifically Christian version of the Trinity. It does mean that the basis of such belief lies in the archetypal world and manifests in humanity in a variety of expressions of which the Christian Trinity is one. The point is that this and every dogma retains some fascination for humanity because of the numinosity that informs the symbolic expression and its dogmatic formulation even when symbol and dogma lose much of their power to an enervating literalism.

In the context of humanity's universal sense of ultimacy, Jung's analysis of the ontological argument for God's existence, namely, that humanity has an innate sense of God, joins such moderns as Paul Tillich in the affirmation that the argument is not an argument nor does it prove anything (Jung 1971b: 41–43; Tillich 1951: 204–208). Rather it simply points to humanity's universal and unmediated experience of the absolute or unconditioned, that is, of the numinous. On this the formulations of Tillich and Jung again approach identity. Tillich writes in the context of his discussion of the ontological argument, "The arguments for the existence of God neither are arguments nor are they proof of the existence of God. They are expressions of the *question* of God which is implied in human finitude" (Tillich 1951: 205, italics Tillich's). Tillich will base the possibility and necessity of this question on the human experience of an element of the infinite in the finite as the basis of religion itself. Jung writes of the ontological argument in near identical language though it can be assumed he never read Tillich:

> The ontological argument is neither argument nor proof, but merely the psychological demonstration of the fact that there is a class of men for whom a definite idea has efficacy and reality – a reality that even rivals the world of perception.
>
> (Jung 1971b: 41)

Though he does not do it here Jung would have to include himself and his psychology among the class of men for whom an "idea" beyond the senses continued to hold a certain "efficacy". He goes on in these passages to argue that the substance of Anselm's proof that the mind is vested with a sense of God is a *"psychological fact"* hidden by the way it has been intellectualized and rationalized by Anselm himself and as it moved through history. Writes Jung, "The real point is that it [the ontological argument] is a psychological fact whose existence and efficacy are so overwhelmingly clear that no sort of argumentation is needed to prove it" (Jung 1971b: 42). Here Jung contends that "the idea of God" is real, engendered by the psyche and so natural to the mind. However, though his psychological defense of the validity of the ontological argument by showing it to be a psychic fact is strong, it may be somewhat overstated at least for those impervious to the full inventory of psychic truth due to their imprisonment by the senses and by a mentation bound thereto. His elevation of the ontological argument to its psychological truth would seem not to take seriously a different "class of men" whom he refers to here as "sensualists", that is, as wholly dependent on the senses, to whom the deeper psyche remains as foreign as the suggestion that a fully developed human sensitivity includes a sense of God (Jung 1971b: 41). Though Jung is generous to the "sensualists" in his treatment of them here as a type that is real and must be accepted, nevertheless, it is to the conscious and cultural recovery of the human depths on which the ontological argument rests that so much of Jung's late efforts were directed. That these depths remain impervious to the sensualist bears witness to the withering superficiality of contemporary cultural consciousness and its religious sense.

More importantly, Jung's understanding of the numinous would imply that the Gods create themselves or are created in the interplay between the ego, the archetypal unconscious and whatever conscious imbalance, again individual or societal, the divinities address and seek to remedy in their diverse revelations. Jung's thought here contributes to an answer to one of humanity's currently most pressing questions involving survival itself. If the Gods create themselves through the human experience of the numinous has one yet to be created worth a human life? Such a question would be a valuable heuristic prod in furthering the swelling contemporary search for the link between the numinosity of religion and the violence and loss of life religion induces in and between the communities it possesses (Dourley 2003). This issue will be examined in greater length in Chapter 6.

Thus, though it is high among the distinguishing features of his psychology theoretically and therapeutically, the numinous remained for Jung a profoundly ambiguous force. Here again Jung would agree with Tillich when the latter writes about the intractable power of faith, "Our ultimate concern can destroy us as it can heal us. But we can never be without it" (Tillich 1957: 16). Since humanity can never be free of it, the ambivalence of the numinous demands an examination of both its shadow side as well as its potential for the enrichment of human life.

The numinous as threat to the species

Reflection on the shadow side of the numinous engages Jung's political and social psychology and brings it into discussion with contemporary geopolitical thought. Huntington identifies religion as the operative bonding power of contemporary civilizations (Huntington 1996: 95–101, 266–272). Thus bonded by their religions, contemporary and future wars between civilizations are and will be religious wars. To this point Huntington's analysis of the current geopolitical situation coincides with Jung's in identifying the universal threat communities bonded by the numinous pose to collective survival whenever they come into sustained contact with each other. The political side of Jung's thought would affirm with Huntington that archetypal and so numinous bonding is the glue of each culture or civilization. How many cannot help but respond with a religious devotion to the sight of the flag, to the playing of the national anthem, to the mythological background that supports ethnic differentiation or tribal nationalism? More, Jung's social psychology supports a grim psycho-sociological law, namely, the more intense the numinous bonding uniting a community, the tighter is its faith and the less conscious and so morally responsible are the individuals thus bonded (Dourley 2003: 136). Jung explicitly relates the resultant, reciprocal, fear between differently bonded communities to processes of mutual demonization. "This ghastly power [unconscious bonding] is mostly explained as fear of the neighbouring nation, which is supposed to be possessed by a malevolent fiend" (Jung 1969b: 48). It is not difficult to see such fear operative in the interface of contemporary nation-states especially when their nationalism is supported by an explicit or implicit religious power taking their collective uncon-sciousness to the second degree.

Explicit and blatant religion provided the archetypal bonding for the earlier period of Western development culminating in Christendom and its ongoing difficulties with Judaic and Islamic cultures. Again Jung is explicit in identifying historically the archetypal cohesion bonding these religions and the close relation of such cohesion to its shadow manifestations.

> Hitler's enormous psychological effect was based upon his highly ingenious method of playing on the well-known national inferiority complex of the Germans, of which he himself was the most outstanding example. A similar yet positive release of unconscious dynamism was the overwhelming expansion of Christianity in the second and third centuries and of Islam in the seventh century.
>
> (Jung 1976a: 607)

Jung diagnoses the shadow side of these same energies creating religions and political societies among which he would include fifteenth century German "witch hunts" as examples of "epidemic insanity" (Jung 1976a: 607). His overriding point is that the origins of Christianity, Islam, National Socialism and historical witch hunts are instances, for better or worse, of the archetypal numinosity creating and bonding the communities and movements in question. Shorn of their shadow such energies continue to be depicted as the noble power informing faith, patriotism and loyalty to one's motherland or fatherland. The inevitable body count in their wake is rarely directly connected with such dubious virtue.

To continue with the analysis of the Western development, following the Reformation, wars and especially the Thirty Years War (1618–1648) between religious factions, decimated the population of Europe (Livingston 1997: 10; Tillich 1967: 48, 49). These wars contributed greatly to the con-viction that religiously bonded communities could not keep the peace. A similar situation is developing today on a more global basis. It is now becoming evident that neither the so called "world religions" can any longer be entrusted with world peace nor can political reason as a derivative of the Enlightenment. Just as reason surpassed warring Christian factions in the wake of the Reformation, the current quest is for a religious consciousness which surpasses both the extant warring religions and a rather feckless political rationality limited to stopgap measures in the absence of a vision surpassing that of the religious enmity it surveys. At the time of the Enlightenment human hope turned to a more tolerant reason above and beyond conflicting European religious factions. Currently hope turns to a religious consciousness which would surpass both the extant religions themselves and the pragmatic self-interest and relative superficiality of political and military efforts to referee archetypally induced unconsciousness in warring collectivities. This consciousness would ultimately have to rest on the individual's immediate conversation with a deeper humanity at once the source of the extant religions in conflict and, hopefully, of a symbolic and mythic access to a way beyond them.

In his response to the Enlightenment in its relation to the contemporary scene, Jung argues around the following salient points. First he does not disparage the emergence of reason from religious control through the processes begun in the Reformation and culminating in the Enlightenment. In his own imagery the freedom of reason from religious constraint was much like a dragon fight against a consuming mother (Church) and he would applaud the victory of a consciousness free of her coils. Yet he is deeply concerned with some of the consequences of such a victory as they reach into our times. His analysis of the contemporary spiritual bankruptcy of the West suggests that the victory of Enlightenment reason over religious factionalism left the connection of the contemporary Western mind with the unconscious maimed or even severed. For all its very real inadequacies, which did indeed demand its submission to a more benign reason, religion had been a major link with the unconscious to the point of the Enlightenment. The Enlightenment in freeing reason from external constriction could not restore its link with its own depths, nor could traditional religious institutions because their bellicose enmity toward each other and toward Enlightenment reason had contributed so much to the genesis of the Enlightenment in the first place.

At the moment this problem remains for Western religions and the religious sensitivity in Western culture. Through the separation of Church and state religions have been largely dispossessed of their political power, at least in a direct sense, and have lost much of their spiritual credibility in a losing battle with reason, science and secularity unnecessarily perceived as hostile to or divested of their own religions concerns. The institutions continue to take their revealed truth literally and historically and are unable to appreciate the truth of mythical and symbolic expression. They have lost the mind and spirit of the culture in which they exist. Their problem is epitomized in the current debate between creationist and evolutionist. From the Scopes trial to the present, significant sections of the institutional religious mind is fighting a losing battle. Their much deeper problem lies in their clinging to supernaturalist forms of theism, wholly transcendent Gods beyond nature, whose arbitrary incursions into human history described in revealed texts are no longer acceptable to a mature humanity and its emerging spirituality. Here again Jung's proposal of a natural divinity accessible to consciousness would contribute greatly to a vital, societal spirituality no longer attached to a now dysfunctional but still traditional understanding of transcendence.

There is a yet deeper level in Jung's response to the contemporary impact of Enlightenment reason on current consciousness, one which has a wider societal implication. It lies in his conviction that the numinosity formerly attaching to religion transferred to archetypally funded forms of conflicting political faith. Consequently the body count soared with the help of a more efficient technology of killing. In these positions the genius of Jung's political psychology is evident in its ability to identify the archetypal source of all faith as the basis of the continuity between specifically religious faiths, largely discounted by and since the Enlightenment, and their modern continuation in the faiths that inform the political "isms", "so fanatically believed in by modern man" (Jung 1969f: 175). Reason's diminishment of the ecclesial communities did not and could not dissolve the archetypal numinosity which had created them. This numinosity simply moved from religious into political faith. These are the faiths that account for twentieth century and current "epidemic insanity", "mass intoxications", and "mass psychosis" (Jung 1976a: 607; 1968d: 126, 127). They have funded the genocidal impulse in the twentieth century and continue to do so in ours. Their power is most evident in the current wars in Iraq and Afghanistan where the archetypal coalition of a demographically identifiable "Jesus land", democracy, and capitalism intensify exponentially the numinosity attached to each in a religious ecstasy of death and destruction (Dourley 2006a: 78). The resistance to these forces is equally archetypally funded often through more explicit religious and cultural syntheses of religious and political faiths. Their power should serve a new geopolitical wisdom that no policy should ever push an opposing constituency to its foundational religious or political faith because of the insuperable destructive force such intensified collective unconsciousness unleashes. The lesson was there for the learning in Vietnam and again in Iraq. It is daily visible in the Middle East but the mind of faith, religious and political, to date defies humanization of the religious impulse and the lessons of history.

At the more personal level Jungian psychology should also free individuals from archetypal manipulation by making them aware of the powerful suasion archetypal symbols can exercise in the hands of leaders abusing such symbols in creating an unconscious collective religiosity in the service of questionable, often violent, goals. For instance, one might ask, "How many have already died and are dying under the power of the symbol of a new world order?" Jung's response to the use of the numinous in the induction of collective unconsciousness remains true today. *"Resistance to the organized mass can be effected only by the man who is as well organized in his individuality as the mass itself"* (Jung 1964c: 278, italics Jung's). Jung was no doubt prompted to such statements by then recent events in Nazi Germany. Yet it remains true in every period that a primary commitment to the self would render the individual relatively immune to the attractive archetypal and uncritical commitments in every social environment. Responding to the political surroundings out of the cultivation of the self would provide the needed instability to undermine political tyranny and the intoxicated collective unconsciousness on which it feeds. Individuals who cannot be depended upon to immerse themselves in collective certitudes constitute one of the major resources in the contemporary struggle against every stripe of archetypally induced societal unconsciousness.

Nevertheless, though the historical evolution of religious consciousness may currently be leaving political and religions monotheisms in its wake, such evolution has not and cannot outgrow the archetypal unconscious and its drive to become ever more fully conscious in history through its foundational sponsorship of an ever more extensive expression and inclusive embrace of its total potential and of all opposites that lie therein. Put simply the evolution of religion will go on toward that consciousness in which the source of consciousness finds total expression in the unification of its antinomies in human consciousness. If Jung sounds the death knell for the monotheistic mind and epoch, his own myth contributes to the overture of a new personal and societal consciousness informed by a greater profundity and so by a greatly extended compassion. This consciousness would both absorb and supplant the monotheistic myth in all its variants.

New configurations of the numinous in a now emerging myth

As it is honed in his later work, Jung's myth rests on a sense of radical psychic containment wholly revisioning the human relation to transcendence. Such containment would affirm that, within the psyche, the unconscious transcends consciousness infinitely but that nothing transcends the psyche itself. Jung points to the infinity of the unconscious when he refers to it as of "indefinite extent with no assignable limits . . . by definition unlimited" (Jung 1969c: 258). Thus contained, the individual's relation to the divine rests solely on the ego's experience of archetypally induced numinosity as the basis of all religious experience personal and communal. "As the Sufis say, there is no God but the experience of God" (Corbett

2007: 4). The relation of the individual to God becomes the experienced relation of the ego to the archetypal unconscious. To imagine the relationship of the human to the divine as to individual divinities or self-sufficient powers beyond the psyche is hostile to Jung's mature psychology and at the heart of the insuperable divide yawning between his psychology and the monotheisms of Buber and White (Dourley 1994, 2007). These differences will be spelled out in Chapters 4 and 5. The process of the inner dialogue with divinity is comparable to capping the "volcano" (Jung 1969b: 15) that spews the transcendent Gods into their wholly otherness in favor of the inner dialogue with them in processes of their humanization and humanity's divinization (Dourley 2006b).

A redeeming universal sentiment runs through Jung's foundational position on the internalization of the dialogue with divinity which particular religions, because of their very particularity, cannot convey. The numinosity which attaches to the emerging myth combines the individual and the universal, again, at personal and collective levels. It rests on the dynamic of the individuation process itself. Under its impulse the many complexes that make up a personal life move toward a personal integration always combined with an ever extending compassion for the all. The major psychological notes that Jung attributes to processes of individuation themselves describe a unity of opposites, those of personal integration at an individual level and a more universal acceptance, indeed, compassionate embrace of all that is beyond the individual.

Reflecting on these opposites embedded in the experience of the numinosity of the self, one can conclude only that they derive from the immersion or what Jung calls a "baptism" of the individual's consciousness in the universal source of the totality, namely, that transpersonal power Jung describes as the "pleroma", a primordial fullness (Jung 1969d: 425, 428) and elsewhere as the "eternal Ground of all empirical being" (Jung 1970: 534). When put into a personal idiom both referents are to the Great Mother or Goddess. This experiential dissolution in and consequent residual resonance with what Jung, Goethe and some mystics call that nothing out of which the all does grow alone accounts for the ever deepening personal integration and expanding compassion toward which processes of individuation and history are driven by the nature of the psyche itself (Jung 1964d: 75). The intensity of the numinosity such processes bear enable Jung to write simply, *"Individuation is the life in God,* as mandala psychology clearly shows" (Jung 1976d: 719, italics Jung's). The cycle of dissolution in the source as universal power involves a moment of the loss of the ego in the Great Mother or Goddess preceding a return to a greatly enhanced consciousness. In his early efforts Jung described the further reaches of entry into the mother as a "Jonah-and-the-Whale-Complex" to distinguish it from the literalism and relative superficiality of Freud's Oedipus complex, which related the moment of loss in the mother to physical incest (Jung 1966a: 419). The numinosity of dissolution in a primordial creative nothingness with universal extension would thus constitute an essential moment in the cycle of renewal, a moment of the numinosity of the night to be dealt with in more detail in a later chapter (Dourley 2006c). This cycle is by no means lived out by everyone at the same level of intensity but Jung has warned that all are destined to descend into a "a deep pit" in the interests of becoming who they truly are (Jung 1968c: 70). The only real difference for Jung is whether the descent is consciously undertaken as a moment in a cycle of rebirth or unconsciously undergone with a much greater suffering and a likely less gracious outcome. Yet in either case the process is one of a momentary and cyclical identity with a power that is universal and the ground of all that is. Such experience of its nature would sponsor a consciousness of more universal embrace in those who undergo it.

But Jung's psychology, breathtaking in its vision of a recurrent descent into and return from the primordial nothing, is not naive or simplistic. Processes of individuation can only be approximated in finitude because the source of the numinous will always outstrip its incarnation or penetration into the consciousness of any stage of personal or collective history. But neither can such processes be abandoned because of the natural press of the self and its numinosity to ever greater conscious embodiment in individual and society. This psychic situation is problematic. On the one hand lies the temptation to collective idolatry. It is perhaps not only natural but also terrifying that religious and political institutions strive to preserve the inexhaustible numinosity that gave them birth in absolutes in whose name and power murder can be committed. On the other hand, to give up the search for the life the numinous alone affords individually or societally moves to patterns of cynical withdrawal, meaninglessness and ultimately to the loss of the will to live. Idolatrous commitment to institutional or personal absolutes, or the cultivation of insensitivity to the temptation to do so are opposites that share the common trait of the deepest form of self-betrayal, the betrayal of the self. For the self will not be denied consciousness and, yet, is itself profoundly iconoclastic because whatever state of consciousness it does attain will always remain residually preliminary.

Yet as Jung's understanding of the psyche describes this dilemma so also does it address it. His psychology would reduce to gross and now dangerous inanity the claims of individual or institution to an unqualified and universal ultimacy. In this sense his psychology would question the social and individual morality of religious or political monotheism as currently hostile to human maturation, at both personal and societal levels. Effectively he asks if monotheistic consciousness can any longer meet the demands of a social ethic or personal morality. His answer is a resounding "No", an indictment of monotheistic faith, religious or political, as now immoral at this moment in the evolution of morality. At the same time his psychology would endow such claims and their myths with the respect owed their archetypal and numinous but far from all inclusive expression. In this manner his myth breeds a gracious relativity in all religious and political statement and commitment. Such tolerance is now one with which humanity can, and apparently, has to live. And yet such necessary relativity provoked by the emergence of conflicting faiths looks beyond itself. It lives in the hope of a more inclusive myth on the way to an all inclusive myth. This myth would surpass mere tolerance as a forced pragmatic necessity if humanity is to survive its current archetypal bonds and certitudes. Its compassion would transcend even as it included those particular and historical numinous and archetypal concretions now forced by the same unconscious which created them to seek their own supersession.

The path to such a myth is not easy and the alternatives surrounding its birth or failure are stark. Jung identifies them succinctly when he writes: "We are threatened with universal genocide if we cannot work out the way of salvation by a symbolic death" (Jung 1976d: 735). What Jung means by "symbolic death" in context refers most immediately to the surpassing of the Christian symbol based on an all good God and single emissary devoid of a relation to so much of what is. But this symbolic death extends to all symbols that bond communities in mutual hostility and prevent a higher compassion beyond the state of their current animosity. This collective enmity is why the choice humanity now faces is a choice between universal genocide and a symbolic death. It is a choice between religious and spiritual growth or death. In this text Jung is found to be arguing that species wide genocide is inevitable if communities cannot lose their current constricted sense of the numinous for a numinosity which would embrace what they cannot include in their sense of the sacred and this is particularly true of other faith communities. But the extension of authentic acceptance to the other as individual or community will entail a symbolic death, that is, a loss of that faith which excludes the other from full participation in that divinity which grounds and gives rise to all expressions of the numinous, again, through all that is.

In a variation of this same theme Jung contends that a humanity severed from its source and, by extension, the universal compassion this source sponsors will lose the will to live. He writes:

> Nevertheless, when a living organism is cut off from its roots, it loses the connections with the foundations of its existence and must necessarily perish. When that happens anamnesis of the origins is a matter of life and death.

> (Jung 1968e: 180)

In these words Jung strongly suggests that unless an uprooted humanity can recover that numinosity attaching to the native memory and so experience of a common divinity in its depths as the power informing a now emerging myth, then its forgetfulness will prompt the loss of the will to live. In Jung's view such a recovery remained problematic. In his late work on Job, he writes, "Everything now depends on man" (Jung 1969d: 459). This is a bit of an overstatement even in terms of his own psychology. Jung needs to add that everything depends on humanity's response to the archetypal unconscious and the new myth it currently urges. But with these words he puts the ball squarely in humanity's court. In the end the most one can responsibly say is that Jung has given the human community the opportunity clearly to see what is at stake in the fearsome option, forced now by the psyche itself, either to cling to current constrictive faiths and die or to lose them toward a more universal sympathy. In the end we can do little more than hope that the gentle suasion of Jung's mythology with its profound sense of the numinosity of a more inclusive compassion will be a significant contributor to humanity's option to transcend its current faiths and to choose life.

If this option is to be more than a velleity as universally honored in theory as it is dismissed in practice, focused thought must be brought to bear on Jung's position that the archetypal unconscious is the ultimate creator of the myths that make epochs. To elucidate what is at stake here, there is no historical doubt that adolescents were hanged in public in Dickens' time for pilfering handkerchiefs. Today only the more barbaric cultures practice capital punishment. Something changed deeply and rather quickly considering the immensities of history. No doubt very conscious, political activity accounts for much of this change. However, the question remains whether the change could have been worked without an accompanying and enabling sea change in the deeper cultural sensitivity behind the eventual collective receptivity to the elimination of the practice. Jung would locate the origin of that emerging sensitivity and its eventual collective reception in the unconscious without which the odious spectacle would not be seen as such and stopped. To the current monotheistic mind the supersession of their presiding God or political absolute remains as unimaginable as the elimination of capital punishment was to the British and much of the Western mind in the early nineteenth century. Yet Jung would argue that just such a transformation is being prompted by a now widely emerging myth empowered by the common source of all myths. In trying to describe its content and dynamics Jung frequently used terminology borrowed from the Christian myth, namely, that of incarnation. The current challenge to conscious humanity is to understand incarnation not as pertinent to one tradition and describing one historical life but as the process of the unconscious becoming conscious in a humanity increasingly enabled to embrace all that is as the source of all that is becomes more conscious in it. The following chapter expands on this foundational Jungian notion.

Chapter 3

Taking back divinity

Jung on the relativity of God

The opening chapters suggest that a Jungian spirituality engages the archetypal unconscious in an unmediated conversation with the spirits that rise from it to address the consciousness of the conversant. More, this dialogue on an individual plane is at the same time a dialogue with the power that creates the religious and political forms of communal bonding around societal absolutes. These foundational Jungian positions imply that the deepest movement of history is that of the progressive concretion in human consciousness of its archetypal ground. Throughout his work Jung referred to this process as one of "incarnation". In some of his later statements in the same paragraph he will describe the process of incarnation as one of "penetration" and mean by it the same ongoing ingression of the archetypal unconscious into human consciousness (Jung 1976d: 734). Because of the peculiar meaning he gives to it and to its centrality in his psychology, Jung's revisioning of incarnation and its close relation to his thought on the "relativity of God" warrant closer examination.

Jung and the termination of the imagination of the supernatural

The opening chapter made the point that Jung understands the psyche, taken in its totality, to be the sole source of human experience. Even the apparently objective basis of the world of sensation is mediated through "psychic images" (Jung 1969b: 12). This passage could be a simplistic statement that all knowledge begins in the senses feeding the intellect with the potentially knowable regardless of what epistemology might be used to show how sense images, always of the particular, are transformed into universals by the mind. This view would be consistent with the sense bound nature of Aristotelian philosophy and theology especially evident in the work of Thomas Aquinas. But Jung explicitly twice denies that all knowledge originates in the senses in his flat rejection of the Thomistic and Aristotelian first principle, "*Nihil est in intellectu quod non antea fuerit in sensu*" (Nothing is in the intellect which was not previously in the senses)

(Jung 1969g: 492; 1969h: 559). For Jung the reduction of the totality of the knowable to its origin in the senses constitutes a tragic and demeaning limitation of the total human cognitive resource. Such truncation removes the mind from its deeper cognitive capability in the meaning to be found in archetypally informed experience. Consequently Jung must be taken at face value when he makes the blatant metaphysical statement, "Not only does the psyche exist, it is existence itself" (Jung 1969b: 12). In particular the student of religion or of psychology interested in the origins of religious experience must take these epistemological and ontological remarks with a deep-seated seriousness when Jung goes on to deny in these passages the reality of an "Archimedean point" external to the psyche which could address the psyche from beyond the psyche (Jung 1969b: 12). With these words Jung denies the validity of an imagination that would posit a divinity addressing the psyche from beyond the psyche with a body of knowledge usually termed "revelation". In a Jungian context such incursions into the psyche from an agency beyond it would remain ever foreign to it and destructive of it.

Jung's rejection of the epistemic possibility of any agency addressing the psyche from beyond the psyche discredits the biblical imagination foundational to all forms of mainstream monotheistic imagination. The scriptural imagination of the diverse One and Only Gods of biblical repute jointly frame the relation of the divine to the human as that of a wholly other and self-sufficient God first creating, then addressing and finally saving humanity from a position somehow transcendent to it. Though he waffles on the issue, the burden of Jung's extensive writing on religion effectively denies the ontological reality of the transcendent One and Only Gods of the variant monotheisms and the supernatural world from which they arbitrarily invade the human in creative and redemptive enterprise (Dourley 1998). Such moments of unbidden grace reduce grace to the gratuitous. They divest the divine of all compulsion, self-interest or completion in relation to the human even as they strip the human and creation of being needed by the divine and so of any ultimate meaning. Monotheistic accounts and theological reflection on creation authored by these transcendent Gods rarely noted that they have divested creation and human activity in it of ultimate meaning as contributing to the wealth of divinity itself. The depression and anger in those living under the burden of such revelation seeking the origin and validation of life from beyond life is only too understandable from a Jungian viewpoint.

While Jung's psychology undermines the ontological reality of biblical monotheistic divinities and, indeed, of all divinity understood to exist beyond the psyche, Jung equally rejects the possibility of a religion-free humanity. On empirical grounds (Dourley 1993) he claims to identify in universal humanity an "authentic religious function in the unconscious" (Jung 1969b: 6). This function produces the varieties of religious experience and, through such experience, the oft conflicting Gods and their religious communities. It produces such experience with an insistence humanity can neither escape nor easily bring into its service because of the archetypal energy on which such experience rests. A succinct statement of Jung's thought on religion would entail but three sentences. Religion, personal and collective, is inevitable. It can, does and has killed fluently. It could be humanity's greatest resource if understood as a latent human potential seeking its total realization and completion in humanity.

Framing Jung's challenge to human religiosity in these terms does not involve Jung in a contradiction. Religion is inevitable as long as the human psyche retains its current nature and archetypal forces retain their current power. The logic of his psychology consistently affirms that the only legitimate and inevitable form of transcendence is intrapsychic. Jung locates transcendence in the transcendence of the archetypal psyche in dialogue with its spokesperson and center of realization, the ego. In this paradigm the ego is at once creature and cooperative redeemer of its archetypal origin. For Jung humanity is only now becoming aware that the divinities which the psyche has created and allowed to escape its containment must now be identified as creations of the psyche and recalled to their psychic origin where humanity can deal with them consciously for the first time in an atmosphere of a greatly enhanced ethical responsibility. This wholly contained inner dialogue would be a first for the Western monotheisms, at least, in their orthodox and predominantly exoteric constituencies. It might be less a challenge with Eastern traditions with their variants on the equation of self-recovery and the recovery of divinity as two aspects of the same process. In fact much of Jung's psychological project as it touches Western religion was more fully to acquaint the West with the more Eastern *"self-liberating power of the introverted mind"* (Jung 1969g: 484, italics Jung's). All of this is succinctly put when Jung writes, "With us, man is incommensurably small and the grace of God is everything; but in the East, man is God and he redeems himself" (Jung 1969g: 480). Jung makes explicit the current evolution of religion toward a radical all pervasive pantheism which would locate the divine in everything and especially in the human psyche now growing aware of a universal divine presence in itself and nature. With Jung this is a recent and still occurring evolution. "It was only quite late that we realized (or rather are beginning to realize) that God is Reality itself and therefore – last but not least – man. This realization is a millennial project" (Jung 1969d: 402). This realization remains wholly incompatible with more traditional Western conceptions of religious transcendence (Jung 1969d: 385).

This recalling of the Gods to their psychogenetic origin and the responsibility of dealing with them there is the defining characteristic and psychological culmination of Jung's psychology. As the only resource for human consciousness, the psyche creates the experience even of the divine. Like

Otto, and much of twentieth century religionist thought, Jung equates the experience of divinity with the experience of "the *numinosum*" (Jung 1969b: 7). Unlike Otto the origin and referent of the experience of the numinous is not, for Jung, a "wholly other God". Rather a wholly immanental and universal archetypal energy and imagery, creative of the religious experience itself, currently breeds a universal sentiment and embrace toward the enhancement of personal and collective religious consciousness.

Contained within the natural psyche, the substance of the commerce between humanity and divinity is that between consciousness and its intrapsychic creator seeking redemption in its creature, the ego. Jung's sense of radical containment, then, confines the dialogue between the human and the divine to the immediate dialogue of consciousness with its source within the psyche. Jung explicitly extends this confinement to mystical experience as the primordial form of religious experience. Mystics are people who have a particularly vivid experience of the processes of the collective unconscious. "Mystical experience is experience of archetypes" (Jung 1976c: 98). Such experience is for Jung both natural and intrapsychic. Thus understood the experience defeats any distinction between the natural and supernatural in the interests of Jung's vastly extended psychic naturalism which relates humanity to divinity as consciousness to the archetypal unconscious on a wholly intrapsychic basis.

Revisioning incarnation

Within the context of radical containment incarnation takes on a wholly new meaning. It no longer describes the capricious invasion of the human by supernatural divinities at their divine pleasure addressing humanity through patriarch, prophet, judge, messiah or the communities established in their wake. Nor can the reality of incarnation be limited to rather exceptional, indeed unique, human beings. Rather incarnation becomes the process of the unconscious becoming progressively conscious in humanity and its history. As such it demands of every individual the realization of their innate divinity now revisioned as the progressive ingratiation of the self into consciousness. Incarnation becomes a never completed, yet still culminating moment in a dialectical process involving the birth of consciousness from the Great Goddess and the recurring reimmersion of the ego into her in the interest of her ever greater redemption in her child, human consciousness. The self presides over the process in cooperative reciprocity with and dependence on the ego, the sole source of discerning reason in the universe, now vested with the vocation of luring its matrix into ever greater incarnation through her progressive expression and self-realization in history.

This intrapsychic dialectic, taken in all its moments, Jung terms individuation, the core dynamic in his understanding of the psyche. Jung provides one of his most vivid portrayals of the process through the prism of his alchemical work. Its ultimate deviation from orthodox monotheistic thought lies in his conception of God as the *filius philosophorum*, God as the son or creature of the alchemical philosopher (Jung 1969c: 263). In Jung's usage the phrase describes a process in which God and humanity create each other in one organic movement contained within the psyche. From its precedence as creator of the ego the self is "something which existed before the ego and is in fact its father or creator and also its totality" (Jung 1969c: 263). This side of the dialectic is compatible with monotheistic imagery of a God external to the psyche creating humanity and human consciousness from beyond, though, for Jung, even this movement simply describes the emergence of the ego from the unconscious.

The second moment in this dialectic offends orthodox religious monotheism and is incompatible with it in all its forms. For this second moment describes the incarnation of the self in ego consciousness worked by the ego's response to the need of the self to become conscious in it. The self is then a child of the ego's efforts to usher it into consciousness. Writes Jung, "This is why the alchemists called their incorruptible substance – which means precisely the self – the *filius philosophorum*" (Jung 1969c: 263). In these words Jung is effectively saying that the ego's role in its reciprocity with the self is to proffer to the self a needed cooperation, even provocation, without which the self could not become conscious in the individual and the individual could not approximate that "more compendious" or "supraordinate" personality as the carrier of divinity made conscious as the substance of incarnation (Jung 1969c: 258).

As stated the first movement in this cycle is quite in accord with the traditional imagination of creation. Just as an external God is imagined in all three monotheistic traditions to create the human from nothing, Jung's internalization of this image would have the self giving birth to consciousness as the first moment of individuation. But the second moment in this process is far from traditional and is frankly heretical. For the self as the son of the philosopher, born into the alchemist's consciousness through the alchemist's efforts in the opus, the work of a lifetime, implies, when translated into a religious idiom, that an unconscious God, or God as the unconscious, creates consciousness to become conscious in it in cooperation with consciousness itself. Clearly in this second moment divinity is dependent first on the existence and then on the cooperative efforts of the ego to become conscious or incarnate in consciousness. Such incarnation is the goal of the alchemical psychic transformation as well as being the psychic basis of the Catholic Mass (Jung 1968f: 396–406). However, the eduction of divinity from its natural potential in the unconscious into consciousness through the efforts of consciousness goes well beyond orthodox understandings of the gratuity of grace and the role of the human in processes of redemption. The role the ego plays in the alchemical process in effectively

rendering God conscious in human consciousness goes well beyond traditional Christian understandings of the priority of the divine in the gracing
of the human and would be equally unacceptable in other monotheistic
traditions.

For in these typical passages Jung not only identifies the major moments
of divine/human reciprocity as the core movements of the natural individuation process, but also contends that humanity is natively aware of
divinity's impulse to become conscious in its creature. Such urgency
becomes the ground experience and meaning of each life at the individual
level and of history at the collective level. In this perspective the reality of a
self-sufficient and transcendent God redeeming humanity through the
conferral of grace, salvation, or privileged status from beyond the human
cedes to the myth of the human slowly enticing its both willing and
unwilling creator into an ever-fuller consciousness realized only in the
human (Jung 1969d: 372, 373, 381). From the perspective of alchemy, and
Jung devotes three volumes to it, the process of individuation is in and of
itself a religious process whose consequence is to make the creator's totality
progressively conscious or incarnate in humanity through the process of the
individual's fuller recovery in consciousness of his or her inhesion in a
natural, native and universal divinity.

The psychodynamic of incarnation revisioned

In its most general sense, then, Jung understands incarnation as God's
progressive achievement of consciousness in the creature through the
expression of the divine potentialities, often in the form of polarities, and
their syntheses in humanity. From this more general sense Jung can become
much more specific on the psychodynamic involved in God's education in
and through history (Dourley 1999). As previously described, in an initial
movement the self works the expulsion of the ego from its source in the
unconscious. The ego, now successfully out of the Goddess or Great Mother
in whatever degree, fully enters into the pain of what moderns call
"existential life". Free from the cosmic womb and an unconscious, infantile
identification with the self, the ego must face the great threats to life. Tillich
identifies some of these in his work, *The Courage To Be*, as death, guilt and
meaninglessness (Tillich 1952: 40–63). Again both Tillich and Jung
document the terror of disintegration, the failure to bring life's opposites
together in a balanced vitality. Worse, the negativities of existential consciousness have to be faced with an attenuated or, sometimes severed
relation to the self left behind in the paradise of a consciousness wholly
absorbed by the womb. From Jung's perspective, even greater than the
existential afflictions Tillich identifies, is the ego's torture between the
legitimate but contradictory sides of deity unresolved in the eternity of

divine life. These divinely or archetypally based antinomies seek their solution in the human created out of divine necessity for that purpose.

Throughout his writing Jung remained deeply impressed by the image of the Christ figure dying in despair abandoned by God between the yes and the no of two thieves (Jung 1968c: 44, 69; 1968g: 255; 1969c: 225, 269; 1969d: 455). For Jung the thieves symbolized the divinely grounded opposites. The ego hangs between them and between any side of the divine self-contradiction seeking reconciliation in the suffering of individuation here well imaged as crucifixion. What Jung is doing, in a religious paradigm for individuation, is universalizing the meaning of a specific symbol, the crucifixion of Christ, to depict that moment, human and divine, when the human ego holds the pain of the divine opposites to the point of its death, let us hope toward a resurrected consciousness unifying in its embrace, the lethal opposites occasioning its preceding demise. Christ here becomes a symbol of humanity suffering the divine self-contradiction to its resolution in human consciousness in a process at once redemptive of the divine and the human. Every human and humanity itself is enriched by the unity of the opposites consequent to the death their suffering induces in their victim. Divinity is made more conscious and real through the human perception and resolution of its contradictory nature in humanity itself. In further describing this death toward a higher unity as both "eschatological" and "psychological", Jung is equally explicit in affirming that the resolution of the divine self-contradiction in the human is the base meaning of individuation and the direction in which human history, personal and collective, moves. In this his psychology contains a full blown philosophy of history.

All of this is evident in Jung's description of the Christ figure dying in despair between the opposites of affirmation and negation.

> Here his human nature attains divinity; at that moment God experiences what it means to be a mortal man and drinks to the dregs what he made his faithful servant Job suffer. Here is given the answer to Job, and, clearly, this supreme moment is as divine as it is human, as "eschatological" as it is "psychological".
>
> (Jung 1969d: 408)

Thus understood, the second moment of incarnation as individuation involves the suffering death of the ego and its reimmersion in the Goddess from which it had been born. In a revealing passage Jung identifies the dissolution of the ego in its source as a wedding "with the abyss" and as the goal of the mystic and hero alike. "This piece of mysticism is innate in all better men as the 'longing for the mother,' the nostalgia for the source from which we came" (Jung 1966b: 169). Yet marriage with or death into this abyss is fraught with peril, for the hero or mystic must return from the possibly devouring mother with the prize of a consciousness renewed in its energy and extended in its empathy through the moment of death into the source of the all. For Jung the return completes the cycle of individuation, of birth, death and resurrection to be undergone in any life, "not once but many times" (Jung 1966b: 170).

This cycle is closely related to the rhythm he elsewhere describes in more formal psychological language as that of the progression and regression of libido from and to its source in the collective unconscious (Jung 1969f: 32–40). In some passages, inspired by a commentary on Goethe, he relates progression and regression to the diastolic and systolic movement of blood out of and back to the heart. Progression, the diastolic moment, describes a libido which extends outward to the totality. Regression, the systolic moment, recalls such universal libido to its source in the psyche. Both moments are essential in processes of individuation (Jung 1969f: 37). Elsewhere Jung extends this analogy to the mystics' journey to identity with and return from the furthest realms of divine life (Jung 1971a: 253). Here the themes of suffering are less explicit though not unmentioned. Rather there comes to the fore the recurrent pattern of the ego's movement from and return to its source as modeling the ongoing flow of psychic energies. When enacted by certain mystics, this cycle describes the basic movement toward a human consciousness progressively more capable of uniting in itself the opposites latent in divinity awaiting their conscious differentiation and mutual embrace in humanity. Jung would thus argue that immersion in the source of libido in itself enables those who return from it a greater unification of opposites in their subsequent psychic life as the basis of reconciliation of societal forces beyond themselves. The reason for this may well be that a moment of identity with the source of consciousness within the psyche is also a moment of identity with the source of the opposites that split consciousness when they become conscious. That the individual could better unite these opposites on return from this moment of identity would follow from the experience of having gotten to the archetypal source or even beyond it of whatever form the opposites take in the individual's concrete life. From the experience of this deepest ingression into the unconscious a greatly enhanced empathic consciousness would naturally follow the traveler back to surface life. The momentary death of the ego to the conflict of opposites from a psychic depth beyond even the archetypal source of such opposites would contribute to the ability to bring together warring opposites not only on a personal level but also, through such individual resolution, in the surrounding society. The final chapters will address the societal and political impact of such in depth religious experience in the context of revisioning the social worth of mystical experience.

This possibility and goal of perceiving reality through a deeply rooted resonance with its ground informs Jung's interpretation of the alchemical symbol of the *unus mundus*, the one world. The symbol speaks to a consciousness uniting in itself all strata of the psyche; body, soul and spirit, consequent to a preliminary rigorous purification so intense as best to be imaged as death (Jung 1966c: 269). Jung equates this consciousness with the *corpus glorificationis*, the glorified body reserved by Christian orthodoxy to the resurrected body in its post-temporal heavenly state (Jung 1970: 535, 542). In these passages Jung does not conceive of the glorified body as describing a post-temporal state on the far side of death. Rather he is contending that the alchemist worked to the experience, however ephemeral, of the glorified body in the present body as the culmination of the alchemical process in the here and now of time and finitude. Describing the unities worked by the alchemist, he writes, "By sublimating matter he concretized spirit" (Jung 1970: 536). The intent of this brief statement is to argue that the soul united with spirit in the body purified through the alchemical process culminates in a perception of the surrounding world as transparent to and reflective of its underlying divine unity. Switching images but not intention Jung will also describe the culmination of alchemical transformation as the "one day" usually understood as the day of original creation recaptured in the end of time in paradise regained. For Jung the experience of the one day like the *corpus glorificationis* is not delayed till death, nor is it a past lost state. Rather it describes, again in however a passing manner, the experience of Eden as the present culmination of the alchemical process in the here and now (Jung 1970: 505).

Jung can give a more precise psychological content to the aforementioned experience of the *unus mundus*. It would be one in which the individual ego entered into a possibly resident vibration with what Jung calls "the eternal Ground of all empirical being" (Jung 1970: 534). This eternal ground is at once the ground of both the individual psyche and of the empirical multiple. Union with it would enable consciousness to perceive all of reality as an expression or manifestation of its divine ground. This experience describes a culminating theophany, the appearance of the divine through the mind of the beholder in all that is beheld as transparent to its source. In a more primitive and dangerously literal religious idiom the human would perceive reality through the eyes of God or God would use human eyes to see itself in nature and human nature. The obviously religious and yet wholly natural implications of such consciousness led Jung effectively to equate alchemical and mystical experience evident in his statement, "the mystical experiences of the saints are no different from other effects of the unconscious" (Jung 1970: 546).

In his fuller elaboration of the psychology of alchemical epiphany, Jung further illuminates how individuating consciousness united the previously mentioned two psychological traits that would seem to be incompatible. He contends that the process leads to the personal integration of the individual through the stabilization of the many complexes that make up the individual as the ego comes into ever greater fidelity to the self. At the same time this experience relates the individual, with ever broadening embrace, to the world beyond the ego through the ego's increasing consciousness of their common ground. Jung sums up the dual effect of personal integration and a more universal relatedness in these lines:

> By "composing the unstable," by bringing order into chaos,
> by resolving disharmonies and centring upon the mid-point,
> thus setting a "boundary" to the multitude and focusing
> attention upon the cross, consciousness is reunited with the
> unconscious, the unconscious man is made one with his centre,
> which is also the centre of the universe, and in this wise
> the goal of man's salvation and exaltation is reached.
>
> (Jung 1969c: 292)

The passage makes clear that the moment of unity with the common ground of individual consciousness and the whole of nature works a mysterious unity of opposites – the personal integration of the individual and an enhanced relation to the all beyond the individual. Personal integration and extended relation to the whole become complementary aspects of the experience of the common origin of individual and totality from the universal underlying psyche in which both participate.

The mystical background

As is now evident, many aspects of Jung's understanding of the psyche are not compatible with the theological imagination of a transcendent self-sufficient divinity approaching the psyche from beyond it. Yet Jung was greatly drawn to significant individuals in the Western Christian mystical tradition both for personal sustenance and as spiritual ancestors who had gone before him in their experience of the intimacy of the divine in its native intersection with their humanity and all of nature. A fuller discussion of the larger sweep of Jung's appreciation of the mystics follows in Chapter 10. In the context of this chapter's focus on the dialectic between divinity and humanity, unconscious and consciousness, two such mystics stand out, namely, the two mystics who appear most frequently in Jung's corpus, Meister Eckhart (c.1260–c.1328) and Jacob Boehme (1575–1624). An examination of Jung's appropriation of their experience raises the evolutionary and historical possibility that substantial currents in the Christian mystical tradition itself, at least since the thirteenth century, carry a progressively explicit experience of divinity toward an appreciative undermining and transcendence of the Christian myth itself. One would then be faced with the paradox that certain discernible streams in the history of Christian mysticism urge Christianity's current self-transcendence toward a mythical consciousness questionably consistent with its more traditional orthodox imagination. Such a surpassing of Christianity inspired by its own mystics would cast considerable light on the current turn to gnostic, hermetic, Eastern and mystical spiritualities which have in common the recovery and enhancement of humanity's unmediated experience of its native divinity. Much of the attraction to these spiritual traditions might be explained through the various scandals which continue to plague Christian institutions. But even if they were relatively scandal free, the question arises whether such institutions could effectively address the apparent contemporary need for a spirituality based on a more immediate and gripping experience. At least in his seniority Jung sought through his psychology to foster traditions of such immediacy and through them to restore to a pathologically superficial society a more compelling sense of it own depth and so of God.

A chapter will be devoted to Jung's dialogue with Fr. Victor White O.P. In that dialogue Jung quite simply states that the same Spirit, the Paraclete, which created Christianity, now prompts Christianity beyond itself (Jung 1953a: 138). In this letter Jung does depict himself as a modern Joachim di Fiore (c.1135–1202). The original Joachim foresaw in the late twelfth and early thirteenth centuries the onset of a new age of the Spirit, which to some extent did occur in the thirteenth century. Jung, in this letter, sees himself and his psychology in the twentieth century, doing for the future what Joachim did for the thirteenth century. This letter would confirm that Jung himself saw his psychology as a force contributing to the birth of a new societal myth appreciative of its Christian precedent but surpassing it through the assimilation of elements foreign to current orthodoxy yet endemic to the experience of its own mystics. Their contribution to the dawning of a new mythic consciousness can thus be seen as a major factor in Jung's appreciation of certain specific streams in Western mysticism.

Meister Eckhart and the relativity of God

Jung confesses that he found personal inspiration in Meister Eckhart's sense of resignation and "letting go of oneself" (Jung 1967a: 16). Jung also pays him great tribute for his sensitivity to what moderns would call "the unconscious" six centuries before it was subjected to more formal identification and investigation (Jung 1968h: 194). Of greater importance, beyond the personal level, Jung uses Eckhart to illustrate his own understanding of the intimacy of the divine to the human in their intrapsychic reciprocity. In these passages Jung makes it explicit that he contains the relation of the human to the divine in the relation of consciousness to archetypal powers. Here and elsewhere Jung elaborates this relation through his conception of the "relativity of God" (Jung 1971a: 241–258).

Claiming Eckhart's experience as an historical precedent, Jung grounds his understanding of God's relativity on the perception of the divine and the human as "functions" of each other within the containment of the psyche. In this framework, writes Jung, God no longer exists "outside and beyond all human conditions but as in a certain sense dependent on him [man]" in so intimate a manner that "man can be understood as a function of God and God as a psychological function of man" (Jung 1971a: 243). To remain ignorant of God as a function of the human is to remain ignorant of the approach of the divine to the human from within the psyche. Such ignorance constitutes "a complete unawareness of the fact that God's action springs from one's own inner being" (Jung 1971a: 243). Jung's position here is simply a variation of his denial of an Archimedean point beyond the psyche from which the psyche can be addressed. Here he is more forceful. Those who understand religious experience as originating in an agency or agencies beyond the human psyche are ignorant of the nature of religion itself.

Jung read Eckhart accurately on these points. An independent reading of Eckhart furthers a religiously critical appreciation of the intimate inner dialectic between the human and the divine on which Eckhart's experience and work rests. It is to this wholly immanental dialectic that Jung gives psychological substantiation in his appropriation of Eckhart. Drawing on his own immediate experience, Eckhart distinguished two dimensions of deity, the Godhead (*Gottheit*) and its derivative, God as Trinity and creator (*Gottes*). For Eckhart the distinction is clear. He writes, "God and Godhead are as different as doing and non-doing" (Eckhart 1857a: 143). In his deepest return to God, in the moment of breakthrough to the Godhead, Eckhart achieves a total identity with God beyond all differentiation. He writes, "for in this breaking through I find that I and God are both the same. I am what I was, I neither wax nor wane, for I am the motionless cause who is moving all things" (Eckhart 1857b: 221). The recovery of this unqualified identity with the divine is the basis of Eckhart's doctrine of resignation for here he rests in identity with the Godhead beyond need or compulsion to any activity or external expression whatsoever.

This moment in the cycle describes the furthest ingression into divinity and so into the unconscious. It is followed by a return to conscious life as a creature once more distinct from its creator. As a creature Eckhart stands before the Trinity as his creator in a position of otherness and separation. He describes this consciousness in his famous passage that when he came out from God all creatures spoke of God but none were happy or blessed (Eckhart 1857b: 221). In these words Eckhart anticipates the nineteenth and twentieth century sense of alienation common to significant streams in philosophical idealism, romanticism, and existentialism. At the core of this sense of alienations lies the conviction that to be other is to be alien and the greatest form of alienation is that of the creature from its source.

This pain of alienation from his source as creature over against creator lies behind Eckhart's strange prayer, "I pray God to rid me of God" (Eckhart 1978: 216, 219; see also 1857b: 219, 220). This is a prayer that the alienating otherness of God as creator be removed so that Eckhart may return to his native identity with the Godhead beyond all otherness including and especially that which prevails between creator and creature. Obviously Eckhart is describing a cyclical process of moving from the consciousness of the surrounding world of the multiple, of others, and of God as other, to an identity with the source of both individual consciousness and the multiple to be found in that nothingness beyond all multiplicity.

What Jung, in effect, is doing in his main treatment of Eckhart is using Eckhart's experience of a cyclical and recurring identity with and distancing from the Godhead to describe individuation as immersion in and egression from the unconscious. Jung's conception of the relativity of God, as developed in these pages on Eckhart, effectively describes the ego's dissolution in a moment of identity with its source preceding a revitalized engagement with the surrounding world. Effectively ego and God dissolve into each other. As Jung puts it explicitly, "God disappears as an object and dwindles into a subject which is no longer distinguishable from the ego" (Jung 1971a: 255). In the ego's recurring death into and return from this moment of identity with divinity, divinity becomes progressively incarnate by becoming self-conscious in human consciousness thus recreated in its return from the womb of the all.

In other significant passages on Eckhart, Jung links him with the gnostics on the basis of their common experience of the divine as the ground of their interiority. Again in these passages Jung refers to a state of consciousness or unconsciousness in which divine and human subjectivity become one. In a paradoxical phrase worthy of Eckhart himself, Jung writes, "As the Godhead is essentially unconscious, so too is the man who lives in God" (Jung 1968h: 193). Obviously the ego moves back from this moment of total self loss in its origin to an enhanced consciousness engaging the world. Nevertheless it was a moment that Jung greatly appreciated in the dynamics of individuation most evident in the more radical nature of certain kinds of mystical experience.

Elsewhere he links Eckhart to Zen Buddhism with its emphasis on the power of the "non-ego-like self" pervading the ego as the self takes the ego into its service (Jung 1969i: 543). In the context of his discussion of Zen and Eckhart, Jung deplores the fact that a Zen-like consciousness of the self as the basis of a personal experience of divinity remains foreign to the Church whose function it remains, "to oppose all original experience, because this can only be unorthodox" (Jung 1969i: 553). In a passing remark, predicting the currently increasing cultural search for a viable spirituality no longer in religious institutions but in therapy, Jung states that only currently emerging forms of psychotherapy, and here he would certainly include his own, carry this Zen sense of interiority in contemporary civilization (Jung 1969i: 553, 554).

The substance of Jung's appropriation of Eckhart, then, lies in Jung's identifying the human relation to the divine as wholly intrapsychic and located in the interplay between ego and unconscious under the auspices of the self. This makes divinity as dependent on humanity for its incarnation in consciousness as is the human on the divine for the initial creation of consciousness. In appropriating Eckhart's experience of the breakthrough Jung broadens orthodox theology and psychology by pointing to a moment of total identification of the human and the divine, the conscious and unconscious. In doing this he makes Eckhart's experience a wholly natural recovery of that point endemic to humanity and divinity where they coincide in the depths of the human. He clearly points to the fourth dimension within deity and the psyche, both to the God beyond the God of Trinity, creation and differentiation and to a dimension of the psyche, muted but present in his writing, beyond even the archetypal with its compulsion toward conscious expression. Could Jung have been referring to this dimension of the psyche beyond even archetypal energies when he writes of archetypal, experience and expression, "There is nothing to stop their ultimate ramifications from penetrating to the very ground of the universe. We alone are the dumb ones if we fail to notice it" (Jung 1969e: 200)? If this is implied in this statement, it also would be implied that this "ground of the universe" is the nothing, the abyss and the Great Mother, herself formless in her depths and yet the source of all form that structures mind and reality beyond the mind and makes their interplay possible (Dourley 2006c).

Jacob Boehme and history as God's completion

Jung's identification of an intimate mutual dependency between the divine and the human in Eckhart becomes much more pronounced in the mystical experience of Jacob Boehme. It is not surprising, then, that foundational motifs in Boehme are even more present in Jung's understanding of the psyche than those of Eckhart. Boehme, like Eckhart, is very aware of a moment of total identity with the divine or with what he terms the "*ungrund*" preceding a return to the "very grossest and meanest matter of the earth" (Boehme 1911: sec. 8, v). Yet it is in the return from this identity with the divine to the squalor of existence that Boehme's mystical experience is most unique. It justifies Jung's claim to see in Boehme a spiritual predecessor whose experience describes this foundational dynamic of the archetypal psyche achieving full self-realization only in historical consciousness, personal and collective.

For Boehme's experience led him to the conviction that the opposites as grounded in the divine life are not reconciled in eternity as orthodoxy would have it. The central symbol of Christianity, the Trinity, can be read to mean that the opposites within God are united in eternity as the precondition and ultimate resource for their unity in time. This would be particularly the case with a modern such as Paul Tillich. He would contend that humanity's deepening inhesion in the integration worked in the Trinity eternally is the most profound resource in the integration of human life in time (Tillich 1951: 249–252; 1963: 283–286; Dourley 1995b). Boehme's experience contradicts the eternal resolution of conflicting opposites in intra-Trinitarian life. Rather an unconscious divinity that can neither perceive nor reconcile the opposites inherent in its own life is forced to create human consciousness as the sole agency which can perceive the divine self-contradiction and respond to divinity's plea to resolve its conflicted life in humanity.

This essential aspect of Boehme's experience is picked up and amplified by Jung both in his autobiography and *Collected Works*. In his autobiography he recounts a series of dreams he had in later life in which his minister father figured prominently. In one dream Jung reflects on his refusal to follow his father in touching his head to the ground in deference to Uriah. In the dream context Uriah is a symbol of the betrayal of human fidelity and autonomy to a wholly transcendent God and his chosen king. His father's dream subservience to Uriah continues such a betrayal. In Jung's opinion his refusal to divest himself of his consciousness in deference to such a God reflects what humanity long has known, namely, that "by a small but decisive factor . . . the creature 'surpasses its creator'" (Jung 1965a: 220). Jung does not document this remark and leaves unidentified instances of a human wisdom understood to surpass the divine. In his amplification of this dream he does, however refer to Job (Jung 1965a: 220). Earlier in his autobiography he confesses to "the greatest inner resistances before I could write *Answer to Job*" (Jung 1965a: 216). His resistance was probably to the radical nature of this work which he sensed would be incompatible with orthodox theological thought and imagination. In this work Jung makes it very clear that divinity is a living antinomy or self-contradiction seeking resolution in a superior human consciousness it is forced to create for that purpose (Jung 1969d: 369, 377, 406). This truth is first perceived by Job and enacted by the Christ figure whose human suffering is of the divine self-contradiction toward it resolution in the human in a process at once redemptive of the divine and the human. When translated into religious terms, the process describes the never ending birth, death and resurrection of consciousness in its commerce with its source.

Jung could equally well have appealed to Boehme to make all of the foregoing points. In the subsequent history of the West, Boehme was identified by Hegel not only as no doubt a mystic but also as the father of German philosophy because of his experience of divinity driven to manifest itself in all of nature including human nature (Hegel 1990: 119, 120). Hegel worked Boehme's mystical insight into the substance of his grand essentialist view of God's self-realization in history culminating in the death of

Christ, symbolic of God as other, to the Spirit immanent in history now understood as working the unity and mutual redemption of humanity and divinity as history's ongoing base meaning. Only late in life did Jung acknowledge affinities between his psychology and Hegel's philosophy (Jung 1959b: 502). The common ancestor of Jung and Hegel is Boehme, making of Jung Hegel's psychologist and of Hegel Jung's philosopher.

Before leaving this point, it should be noted that some current Boehme scholarship identifies in Boehme a remote but real source of modern utopian movements and their compulsive attraction (Walsh 1983: ix, 1–3, 108, 111). The idea of acting on behalf of the realization of divine consciousness in history has proven genocidal in the twentieth century. Jung's response to this fact might well be that humanity must face and integrate the power of the archetypal world as it seeks incarnation in historical individuals and communities. Inflation, especially in the form of archetypally possessed communities and individuals, is a real but unavoidable danger in human history. In this position Jung contributes to the understanding of the systemic genocidal potential in all forms of monotheism, religious or political. As stated earlier the ultimate defense against such possession, for Jung, remained the individual's conscious fidelity to the self. *"Resistance to the organized mass can be effected only by the man who is as well organized in his individuality as the mass itself"* (Jung 1964c: 278, italics Jung's). Whether or not such challenging and individual fidelity to the self can finally offset political and/or religious fundamentalism and its archetypal appeal remains to be seen. It remains in the interest of secular and religious fundamentalism to abort the experience of the self in individual consciousness as a residual threat to the collective.

In any event his appropriation of Boehme should make it evident that Jung's psychology is hardly apolitical. This issue will be addressed at greater length in Chapter 6. One might indeed argue that becoming conscious in a Jungian sense is a political activity and not infrequently a subversive one. Processes of becoming conscious in a Jungian sense always foster an enhanced sense of the archetypal powers determining collective consciousness. Becoming conscious, thus understood, might always initiate a certain corrosion of societal determinants since the self always sponsors a more inclusive ingression of the unconscious into personal and collective life. In this sense Jung's understanding of the hieratic, the holding holy of a personal or collective order, is always subject to the psyche's iconoclastic demand that the presiding order be dissolved toward patterns of a more profound human sensitivity of wider inclusion.

In the return of consciousness to the surrounding world from an unqualified identity with a primal featureless ground, two conflicting opposites emerge as foundational. What tradition has termed the Father appears in Boehme's experience as a dark burning fire, an angry, masculine figure of immense power based on the primacy of unrelated self-affirmation. In fact

Boehme identifies this principle as the hell into which the fallen angels were plunged when they refused the outward movement of God into a self-completing manifestation in the human (Boehme 1911: 9–10; 1958: 7–8). Over against this dark side of God the second principle is an androgynous Christ figure (Stoudt 1957: 284) whom Boehme will, on occasion, relate to the feminine in the person of "Sophia, as the Bride of Christ" (Boehme 1978: 154). In contrast with the Father, the Christ figure is imbued with the warming light of consciousness and communicability. With Sophia, functioning here as an outgoing Spirit, the divine life manifests in all that is. It stamps or signs nature and self-consciousness human nature with the darkness of the Father and the light of the Son. In alchemical terms, and Boehme was familiar with alchemy, the Spirit or Self as the unifier of opposites is thus challenged to work a tincture of dark fire and warming light in uniting Father and Son not in eternity but in human consciousness engaging and engaged by eternity in time (Boehme 1911: 47–49).

At this point what distinguishes Boehme and aligns him with Jung comes strongly into play. For only in the theatre of human consciousness can the divine opposites be perceived and reconciled. Thus the resolution of the divine self-contradiction occurs, to the extent it does occur, simultaneously in both divinity and humanity in a single organic process. Boehme depicts the suffering undergone as the Spirit works the unity of divine opposites concurrently in human and divine consciousness as a "crack", or "shriek" like a "flash of lightning" splitting open "the dry hardness of death" (Weeks 1991: 117, 124–126, 180). This bringing of God to conscious birth by uniting divinity's antinomy in human consciousness describes a point in which divinity and humanity jointly undergo the agony of redemption in each other. Boehme lends substance to Jung's remark that the entire world is God's suffering undergone in the human as the price of wholeness. Writes Jung of this universal suffering, "The whole world is God's suffering, and every individual man who wants to get anywhere near his own wholeness knows that this is the way of the cross" (Jung 1969e: 179).

On the theme of suffering, Jung points to Boehme's mandala in his works (Jung 1968i: 297). For Jung not only Boehme's but also all mandala imagery depicts the redemption of the divine in the human. The mandala's cruciform nature focuses on the individual's suffering toward the pain of the personal centre which is also the centre of the universe, God, holding together the hosts of opposites on the periphery (Jung 1969c: 284; 1969e: 155). The closer the individual draws to the centre, the more does that individual feel the human and divine tension of holding centeredness against fragmenting extremes. To unite the opposites of the divine ground of life in personal life and consciousness is the deepest meaning of the suffering that attaches to individuation and for Jung is the substance of incarnation revisioned. Describing the pain of individuation, he writes, "self-realization – to put it in religious or metaphysical terms – amounts to

God's incarnation" (Jung 1969e: 157). The passage equates the realization of the self in consciousness as the truth of incarnation without qualification.

In giving new life to Boehme in the twentieth century, Jung has contributed to humanity's dignity and importance at both the individual and collective level. Individually he has shown that the deepest suffering in each life is some side of divinity's suffering its own unresolved conflict toward resolution in that life. The individual's bearing of this suffering culminates in a consciousness in which the opposites which occasioned it embrace in a sympathy more inclusive of the human totality. This extended empathy is the heart and goal of what Jung describes as the transcendent function. The dynamics of the psyche itself are such that the consciousness born of the suffering of opposites transcends and includes the opposites that gave such consciousness birth (Jung 1969j: 90). Thus the individual's response to the suffering of opposites in each individual life, especially where it is done in conscious dialogue with the self's most intense expression in the dream, confers a higher consciousness on divinity now increasingly incarnate through the uniqueness of the individual's developing myth which emerges through the dialogue itself. At the heart of this myth will always be approximations of the unification of divinely grounded opposites unreconciled in divine life itself.

This dynamic is also at the heart of Jung's shift to a quaternitarian cosmology. Christianity's current suffering toward its own supersession by a myth of greater depth and so inclusion is toward a Spirit working a richer synthesis of opposites than does or can the Spirit of Christianity. For this more encompassing Spirit would unite the spiritual with the bodily, the male with the female and the dark and light sons of the same father, Christ and Satan, with each other (Dourley 1995a: 239). In doing so the emerging myth would recover the divinity of the body, of the feminine and of the demonic, all denied or given a diminished status in the Christian myth and its monotheistic sister myths. Boehme, like Jung, was explicit in locating evil in the divine and implies strongly that God becomes aware of the divinity of evil only as it is perceived and experienced in the human (Berdyaev 1958: xxv–xxix; Weeks 1991: 105, 180). The unifying Spirit at work in the thought of both Boehme and Jung would demand the unity even of the opposites of good and evil as a characteristic of the myth now appreciatively supplanting its Christian precedent.

In the end then, Boehme extends Eckhart and completes Jung's understanding of the psyche's foundational cycle, not by denying the moment of identity with the divine at the core of Eckhart's experience, but by extending this moment to its culmination in time and history in the resolution of God's unresolved tensions in human historical consciousness. Where Eckhart sees the fourth in the Godhead beyond God, Boehme adds that the God beyond God becomes real only in human consciousness and Jung incorporates the truth of both mystics in his understanding of the psyche.

Moving internally Godhead is the fourth in the divine, the residual and natural point where humanity and divinity coincide. Moving from this point to incarnation in the world, humanity is the fourth dimension of divinity where alone the eternal conflict of Father and Son, and of all divine opposites, is resolved, to the extent it is resolved, in the human.

If Eckhart and Boehme are combined in the full amplification of Jung's reception of them, the psyche is extended in two directions. Eckhart describes a moment of identity of ego and unconscious through the total dissolution of the ego in the unconscious, by implication beyond even the archetypes and their compulsion to become conscious in history. Boehme appreciates and has undergone Eckhart's moment of identity with the *ungrund* but insists that the moment must serve the unification of divine opposites in existential consciousness. In the end, identity with the Godhead beyond God becomes real and incarnate only in the human as the manifestation and completion of that identity. The deepest ingression into and even beyond the archetypal stratum of the psyche culminates in an enriched, balanced and empathic human consciousness in everyday life. Because one moment in this cycle is of the infinite, the ego's immersion and loss in the divine fullness, the cycle can never end. Yet because the divine fullness demands realization in the human, the cycle can never be evaded. The agony and ecstasy of humanity lies in its never ending task to be a vessel of the divine pleroma in its always to be surpassed incarnation in the historically human.

Conclusion: Jung and post-modern mysticism

Jung lived before the advent of post-modernism but his appreciation of mystical experience would find a significant resonance in work focusing on the recovery of a viable mysticism in a post-modern context. Don Cupitt, a Cambridge theologian, is a leading figure in this area of scholarship. As his thought progressed, he came to an appreciation of the immediate and experiential nature of mysticism which, he claims, the mystics entered largely through their writing (Cupitt 1998: 11). It is difficult to define precisely what he meant by taking this tack. It could be that only in its being written was the mystics' experience made fully conscious and compelling, though at times he seems to mean more than this. This issue aside, the later Cupitt's understanding of mystical writing had a political and subversive role to play within Christianity, a role that could extend into broader society (Cupitt 1998: 56). Effectively it dissolved the reality of God as an absolute metaphysical other. Here Cupitt shares an obvious affinity with Jung's conception of the relativity of God as a God whose completion is in the creature. In dissolving the objective metaphysical God, the mystic was free and freed others from the power structure of the Church based on such ontological objectivity. If access to divinity is primarily through human interiority the Church and every religious institution would no longer be able to claim it mediated a wholly transcendent divinity unless it understood such mediation as reconnecting consciousness with preceding native divinity.

Cupitt describes the Church as a sacramental and orthodox machine, hierarchically structured to produce a salvation or happiness which it cannot produce in this world or the next because of its insistence on a never-ending dualism between the divine and the human (Cupitt 1998: 50, 51). In extending the orthodox dualism between the creator and creature into eternity Cupitt has a good point. For example, Thomas Aquinas images humanity's blessedness in terms of a "beatific vision". The imagery itself is self-defeating since vision implies a duality between the seer and the seen. The beatific vision would make this dualism eternal. As such it would describe a state of ongoing alienation which could hardly be termed "beatific". For Cupitt the mystic sought a more immediate happiness in the here and now beyond such dualism, a happiness traditional dualism could neither imagine nor foster in the here or hereafter (Cupitt 1998: 54–56).

Such subversion is a dangerous enterprise because it works to corrupt the absolute power of the Church and of the God of happiness the Church allegedly mediates but never delivers as the basis of its power and of the clerical industry devoted to the maintenance of such power. In contrast to ecclesial spirituality, the mystic wants and attains the happiness indefinitely postponed by the Church in the present through an identity with the divine in which all dualism is defeated. Thus the mystic is writing in such a way as to destabilize the institution but must protect himself or herself with what Cupitt calls "a plausible deniability" in the face of possible brushes with the inquisitor, who may glimpse what is truly going on and being said (Cupitt 1998: 120). This ploy enables them to point to their orthodox and usually lengthy and boring pious statements which surround the more corrosive elements in their writing. Cupitt mentions Eckhart's extensive defense during his various trials as an example of such plausible deniability (Cupitt 1998: 120). What Cupitt is actually arguing is that only the seditious elements of mystical writing are to be valued. The more traditional piety expressed therein and often at great length serves as an elaborate disguise of their true meaning and worth.

What Cupitt shares with Jung in their appreciation of mysticism extends beyond their common admiration of profound and immediate religious experience bought to fruition in and through archetypally inspired language and writing. They both are affirming that the mystical experience corrodes the notion of God as an objective other and that this corrosion demands a moment when all dualism cedes to unqualified identity between God and soul. Cupitt calls this a "double meltdown" of God and the soul into each other (Cupitt 1998: 118–122). "When the writing does succeed in melting

God and the soul down into each other, the effect of happiness is astonishing" (Cupitt 1998: 121).

Cupitt's double meltdown, read through Jung's appreciation of Eckhart and Boehme, would describe that moment when ego and unconscious are one. The soul returns to its maternal origin and, reborn from it, becomes the vehicle of an ongoing and deeper incarnation of its sacred source in its subsequent consciousness. Read through a mystical paradigm, the complete process describes that of individuation itself. In the consequent elaboration of the experience of that point where God and the human naturally coincide theology and depth psychology also coincide. Religious and psychological experience and expression become one. Everyone involved in the process Jung terms "individuation" is participating, in an admittedly endless degree of variation, in the dramatic journey so vividly described in the writing and experience of the mystics.

Nor is Cupitt alone in his efforts to revision a viable contemporary mysticism as the basis of a revitalized religious spirit. Lionel Corbett seeks to make Jung's understanding of the religious function the basis of a contemporary religiosity based on the individual's experience of the psyche as the source of the numinous (Corbett 1996: 11–38). As seen in Chapter 1, Corbett is sensitive to the question of whether the psyche is "cause" or "transmitter" of the experience of the divine. The issue he raises is central to the discussion of Jung's understanding of the relativity of God. The issue is whether there is an objective God beyond the psyche. In this case the psyche would mediate the divine. The counter-position is that the psyche is the origin of all experience including religious experience (Corbett 1996: 6–8).

As Jung's mind develops into its seniority, it moves in his later major statements such as his alchemical work and his work on Job to contain the experience of God within the psyche. Put briefly, the psyche would seem capable of generating the experience of the divine and the manner divinity and its activity toward humanity are imaged in consciousness. The numinous latency of the archetypal as it impacts on consciousness accounts fully for the human experience of the divine. Humanity is currently becoming aware of this and turning the dialogue with the divine into the dialogue with the archetypal. Corbett's position is slightly different. He looks upon the question of the reality of God beyond the psyche as beyond human resolution, as Jung occasionally will. As such the question is moot as long as it is realized that the psyche is, at least, the sole mediator of numinous experience and that the experience is the basis of humanity's sense of God. Nevertheless suggesting that the issue is philosophically irresolvable and so, psychologically and therapeutically irrelevant, does not prevent Corbett from accurately pointing out that many Jungian analysts still cling to the idea of a God beyond the psyche who presumably could engage humanity in ways other than through the psyche. Corbett is correct in pointing to the unresolved dualism between psyche and the divine that this position entails and to the unconscious Jewish/Christian bias which informs it (Corbett 1996: 42). Corbett, too, moves beyond general references to mysticism and identifies Eckhart and Boehme as among Jung's predecessors in establishing that divine/human intimacy Jung locates in the psyche itself. In so doing Jung forbids arbitrary divine incursions into human affairs and history from a godly self-sufficiency beyond both (Cupitt 1998: 35, 200). Corbett (1996) argues that the fostering of such intimacy is and will be foundational in contemporary and future religion and the spiritual practice it engenders.

It has become a sociological fact that in Western culture and perhaps beyond, ecclesial religion, what Cupitt (1998) calls the orthodox machine, is becoming increasingly religiously insipid. It continues to lose its spiritually and intellectually sensitive membership even as its total numbers can swell through its appeal to a growing fundamentalism, ranking such institutions among the most serious current threats to humanity's survival. In this societal context Jung's revisioning of mysticism and incarnation would address a number of constituencies and align his thought with the growing influence of a variety of esoteric traditions, East and West.

For those who once could, but no longer can, access their divine depths through the institution, Jung's perspective offers the radical option of unmediated conversation with divinity in and through the psyche. For those for whom the symbolic and ritual sense has died even as they remain in a religious community, the experience of the self incarnating in consciousness could restore a living meaning to their accustomed symbols and rituals. For those without any history of membership in a religious community or conscious relation to religion as traditionally understood, Jung's understanding of incarnation could reconnect the individual with their native divinity and greatly enrich their lives even if such wealth were not understood as a religious reality. Should this happen in significant number, the so called secular world could recover a humanity at once more sensitive to its own creative and life-giving depths and more encompassing in its sympathy for the totality of humanity. Religion and secularity would no longer be opposites. Rather a religious secularity would result expressive of the basis of the religious in the profoundly human and so imbued with a wider sympathy for all.

All of these situations, or combinations of them, share this in common with Jung and his esoteric sympathies. Those in them live directly out of the unconscious in institutional or non-institutional contexts. They are participants in the incarnation of the source of consciousness becoming incarnate in their personal consciousness as the conduit to a now emerging societal religious sensitivity blurring the lines between the religious and the secular. In a strange passage, reminiscent of Cupitt's remarks on the need of the mystic to cloak their intention in a plausible deniablity, Jung claims that in his time the repression of the gnostic experience of the divine is being lifted creating the conditions for its flowering in contemporary culture. "It would not seem to me illogical if a psychological condition, previously suppressed, should reassert itself when the main ideas of the suppressive condition begin to lose their influence" (Jung 1969b: 97). The current revivified interest in mysticism and esotericism at the academic, religious, psychological and personal levels confirms Jung's suspicion that religious communities which could not inform their thought and practice with a gnostic/mystical element, or equivalent esoteric sensitivity, have lost their spiritual credibility and so, paradoxically, the power to suppress the very energies needed for their own renewal. With the mitigation of ecclesial suppression the spirit of the self, freed from institutional constraint, would flow more freely into a universally available and deeper religious sensitivity even within institutions thus freed. Jung anticipated this development in contemporary religious consciousness when he wrote of the growth of a more direct and personalized experience of the self:

> No one can know what the ultimate things are. And, if such experience helps to make life healthier, more beautiful, more complete and more satisfactory to yourself and to those you love, you may safely say: "This was the grace of God".
>
> (Jung 1969b: 105)

His psychology contributed greatly to a widening sense of a natural grace and the readily available means of access to it.

Chapter 4

Martin Buber and the lunatic asylum

[W]hen, for example, I speak of "God" I am unable to refer to anything beyond these demonstrable psychic models which, we have to admit, have shown themselves to be devastatingly real. To anyone who finds their reality incredible I would recommend a reflective tour through a lunatic asylum.

(Jung 1976e: 666)

The preceding chapters depict Jung's psychology as itself a myth, no doubt in alliance with other contemporary perspectives, superseding and so appreciatively undermining all religions and their spiritualities reliant on a divinity understood to be, at least potentially, wholly other than the human. Jung would ground the origin of all the religions and their spiritualities in the immediate commerce of consciousness with the archetypal unconscious. This perspective strongly suggests that monotheistic consciousness is hostile to the current evolution of the human religious instinct, anti-social in its limited empathy and so of questionable morality in the face of the broader inclusiveness currently urged by the present movement of the deeper psyche.

Not surprisingly those wedded to traditional religious dualisms could not imagine divinity as a dimension of humanity because such imagination would deny one of the polarities in such dualism, namely, a transcendent self-sufficient divinity. So they took umbrage with the intimacy and mutual need Jung's myth establishes between the divine and the human. This was especially the case with those skilled in religious and theological thought who could clearly understand the further implications for their religious traditions in Jung's understanding of the psyche's role as the sole source of religious experience. Most prominent among the many who dialogued with Jung on the religious issue were Martin Buber, the Jewish thinker, and Victor White, O.P., a Catholic and Thomistic professor of theology at Blackfriars, Oxford. Both, though of different monotheistic traditions, clung to the necessity of a wholly transcendent God demanded by their differing faith commitments. Their exchanges with Jung proved their religious thought incompatible with Jung's understanding of the religious nature of the psyche. Jung's conversation with both was really one conversation with two variants of the same myth, the myth of a wholly other God addressing humanity from beyond the human. An analysis of the incompatibility of this position with Jung's psychology clarifies the radical and truly innovative dimensions of Jung's myth as it touches on religion, spirituality and the current maturation of the religious instinct, at least, in the West.

In February 1952, Buber published an article in the German magazine *Merkur*, which initiated his interchange with Jung. The article was translated as "Religion and Modern Thinking" and appears along with Buber's reply to Jung's response to Buber's initial attack in the collection of Buber's essays entitled *Eclipse of God* (Buber 1988a, 1988b). In this article Buber links Sartre, Heidegger and Jung as three moderns of some intellectual substance who have jointly contributed to the mid-twentieth century eclipse if not denial of the God who could meet Buber's job description of such a role. The extent of the trio's eclipsing of God varies with the individual ranging from Sartre's atheism to Jung's even more insidious gnosticism. The documents involved in the interchange are accurately footnoted on the first page of Jung's reply to Buber (Jung 1976e: 663, fns. 1, 3).

Though it has many faces, Buber's indictment of Jung as a collaborator in divinity's current demise rests on the charge that Jung's psychology is a full blown modern form of gnosticism grounding a psychologism which reduced humanity's experience of divinity to the experience of the self. In 1916 Jung had indeed written a piece of gnostic poetry entitled *Septem Sermones ad Mortuos* (*Seven Sermons to the Dead*) (Jung 1965a: 378–390). This early poetry, a piece Jung refused to include in the *Collected Works*, is for Buber prima facie evidence of Jung's gnosticism, though Buber also rests his case on other of Jung's writings. It is interesting to note that at the time of his initial attack on Jung's gnosticism, Jung's gnostic poem had not yet been published. Gilles Quispel, the noted scholar of gnosticism, has remarked that an attack on a private and unpublished work is questionably ethical and certainly "not becoming" (Quispel 1992: 224).

Jung's reply to Buber will be taken up in some detail later in the chapter. At this point let it simply be noted that in his reply to Buber Jung was to describe this piece of poetry as "a sin of my youth" (Jung 1976e: 663). In so describing this work, Jung seems to be needlessly defensive and less than fully candid. His reply tends to diminish the value of this early poetry in itself and to dismiss its undeniable affinity with so much of the spirit of his later psychology. For it becomes obvious, as his reply to Buber continues, that Jung is indeed a gnostic if the term refers to one who would identify the experience of God with that of human interiority, in Jung's case with the immediate and interior experience of the numinous impact of the archetypal psyche on consciousness. Such experience and the images it bears are the basis of what Jung so frequently calls his "empiricism". The term is accurately used if such empiricism includes the experience and its imagery that induce the sense of God in all its variants in universal humanity.

Effectively Jung made his and his patients' personal experience of such numinosity and its imagery the psychic basis of the possibility and necessity of human religious experience itself. More, he attributes the origin of such experience entirely to the agency of human interiority (Jung 1971a: 243). In this peculiar and very precise sense Jung is unquestionably a gnostic. He might here have bowed to the accuracy of Buber's accusation and responded, as he does elsewhere, that the loss of a gnostic sense was precisely at the heart of the insipid state of Western spirituality which, in turn, contributed to the malaise of now widespread societal superficiality and meaninglessness. Jung frankly confesses that the current emergence of a gnostic impulse from its Christian suppression would serve the reviviscence of Christianity and its symbols themselves: "It would not seem to me illogical if a psychological condition, previously suppressed should reassert itself when the main ideas of the suppressive condition begin to lose their influence" (Jung 1969b: 97). Jung was effectively to acknowledge his "enthusiasm" for the Gnostics when he describes them as "the first thinkers to concern themselves (after their fashion) with the contents of the collective unconscious" (Jung 1976e: 664). This enthusiasm remains all too apparent throughout his works though sadly and strangely subdued in his dialogue with Buber.

Though he appears uncharacteristically defensive in the face of Buber's accurate analysis of his gnosticism, other and current commentators are far less so. In defense of both gnosticism and Jung's appropriation of it, and in the context of Buber's attack, Quispel writes, "Gnosis is a splendid cause, not an insult with which to slander and slay an accomplished researcher" (Quispel 1992: 224). Elaine Pagels in her groundbreaking work on gnosis devotes a closing chapter to gnosis as a form of self knowledge which is knowledge of God. In it she cites Jung approvingly as raising Valentinus' gnosis to the level of psychoanalytic consciousness (Pagels 1981: 160). More recently Murray Stein writes on the intimacy Jung establishes between the self and divinity:

> This is what could be considered a postmodern, post-rational rendition of an ancient Gnostic idea that the human soul is a spark of the divine luminosity housed within the material world, so in that sense Buber was quite correct in calling Jung a gnostic.
>
> (Stein 2008: 314)

With these authors of substance there is no reluctance relating Jung and his psychology to gnosticism. Indeed, without an appreciation of its gnostic spirit and core, an understanding of Jung's psychology would be reduced to a truncated intellectual exercise guaranteed to miss the point.

In fact the major difference between the experience underlying Jung's psychology and ancient gnosticism is Jung's highly conscious and psychologically sophisticated identification of the psychodynamics of gnostic and, by extension, of religious experience through his archetypal theory. The experience itself would be identical for both Jung and the gnostics. The difference would lie in Jung's analysis of the experience. Whether the gnostics uniformly and clearly located the origin of their experience in what today would be called the archetypal unconscious is less clear and may be ultimately a question beyond resolution. What Jung offers the gnostic, ancient or contemporary, is the ability to understand the gnostic experience as it is undergone in such a manner as not to destroy the experience through intellectualizing it but rather to enhance it by recognizing its inner dynamics and the depths from which it proceeds to consciousness. Whether subjected to critical analysis or not such experience is the only form of religious experience that does not demean humanity by imposing a divinity foreign to it on humanity. The reasons for orthodoxy's resistance to it reduce to a few in number. Gnosis implies an intimacy of divinity to humanity incompatible with any form of supernatural dualism and the theism that supports it. Such supernaturalism is at the heart of the biblical myth in each of its three major variants. Gnosticism thus divests institutional agencies of their claim to mediate salvation by making of such salvation a purely natural potentiality and actuality when and to the extent the potential is realized. And finally, and probably most importantly, most ecclesial agents of such mediation, the generic priestly caste, are probably religiously incapable of the experience and so appreciation of the core of gnosis. They understandably fear what they have never felt and have difficulty understanding.

From Buber's perspective, and indeed from that of anyone holding a supernaturalist position, gnosticism is in and of itself a form of reductionism because it denies to divinity the possibility of a total transcendent remove from the human psyche from which remove it addresses the psyche which it first creates as the sole source of the experience of the divine. Thus for Buber, Jung's psychology, as a form of gnosticism, far too intimately related the divine and the human. In doing so it vested the human with an illegitimate knowledge of the religious mystery beyond the licit boundaries of human experience or knowledge. Buber's was a well-stated variant of the charge of reductionism frequently made in more than one form against Jung's psychology. It was to these various charges that Jung referred when, with some impatience, he writes, "Anyone who dares to establish a connection between the psyche and the idea of God is immediately accused of 'psychologism' or suspected of morbid 'mysticism'" (Jung 1969g: 482). Buber was one of the accusers.

Yet there are difficulties with Buber's charge. To accuse another of a gnosticism which outstrips "with sovereign license" not only the boundaries of psychology but also those of a legitimate experience of deity implies that

Buber himself knew precisely where the legitimate boundaries of human knowledge of the divine lie (Buber 1988a: 78). One wonders how Buber gained access to these boundaries and to his certitude that Jung had over-stepped them. Setting the boundaries of humanity's duly licensed knowl-edge of divinity is a difficult task, especially when one sees humanity and divinity as opposites with no point of native intersection. In Tillich's terms the knowledge of God as so wholly other makes of God a divine "stranger" (Tillich 1964: 10). The question then arises as to how Buber knows of this "stranger", where the boundaries are between the stranger and the human and how and what this "stranger" communicates with humanity. Buber's setting the boundaries of human experience in relation to this transcendent stranger would seem to demand of Buber a possession of a surpassingly lucid knowledge of the nature of divinity, of humanity, of their difference and of what transpires in their knowing each other. Such clarity would ground the unwavering confidence he shows in this essay in his ability to draw the borders between the divine and the human natures and their respective noetic capacities and so to know so well the cognitive protocol operative when the divine and human communicate, a protocol which Jung had obviously violated. If Jung's approach was with sovereign license which violated due boundaries, the question arises as to who issued Buber the license enabling him so clearly to establish them.

Indeed, when Buber does lay out the nature of God and the duly licensed relation of humanity to this God, his discourse seems all too familiar. Buber variously describes this divine being as "that Absolute Other, the Absolute over against me" and "One who is experienced or believed in as being absolutely over against one" (Buber 1988a: 68, 78). More light is shed on the nature of such deity in Buber's reply to Jung's response to Buber's initial attack. Here this deity is clearly a transcendent one who shares nothing by nature with the human psyche or, indeed, human being. This absolute "One" becomes "a super-psychic Being", described later as "an extra-psychical Being" (Buber 1988b: 134, 135). Buber's central concern is to preserve the religious doctrine that God as Being exists "independently of the psyche of men" or of what he calls "the human subject" (Buber 1988b: 133–134). His well-founded fear is that Jung's psychology denies such transcendent independence making of it "the religion of pure psychic immanence" (Buber 1988a: 84). In his remarks on immanence Jung would have to credit Buber with considerable accuracy of his reading of Jung's psychology. In the end it is this transcendent Being existing beyond the psyche with no necessary experiential and natural link to the human whom Sartre, Heidegger and Jung conspire against with admittedly differing strategies and degrees of denial.

Sartre's is a blatant atheism. Such denial rests on depicting the relation between God and the human as that of a divine being who reduces the human subject to an object and in so doing violates the dignity and freedom of humanity. This is the divine voyeur who can watch people in the bath-tub. On this point Buber's is a fair description of one of the main platforms in Sartre's atheism. But Buber then accuses Sartre of misunderstanding the divine–human relation as a subject–object relation, which for Buber it apparently is not. Buber remains somehow confident that he can make this charge against Sartre and extricate his own understanding of God from a subject–object model. Apparently he can do this in spite of his professed understanding of God in this very work as a divine supra-psychic and extra-psychic Being to whom humans relate as to a Thou who well might remain, at least potentially, a stranger to the human psyche and its experience. Buber is on shaky grounds when he accuses Sartre of involving God in a subject–object structure and then structures his own I–Thou relationship on the same insuperable dichotomy.

Making one of the terms in the relationship an Absolute does little to advance his cause and extricate himself from the contradiction in his argument. What he accuses Sartre of doing, namely making of God an object over against the human subject, is precisely what he makes of his own God in his attack on Jung later in the same article. It would seem that the solution of Sartre's problematic would demand of Buber a more sophisticated ontological strategy than simply capitalizing the archaic form of the second person singular as an absolute divine Thou relating to the first person singular as a human subject. He is obviously driven into this impasse by his religious need to extricate his deity from the confines of the psyche and to place him over against the human subject in whose psyche Jung had too strictly confined him. His proclamations in his rebuttal of Sartre are not convincing. He seems to concede to Sartre that, if God is the Absolute Other, this is an affront to human freedom and dignity. But he asks Sartre, "But what if God is not the quintessence of the other but rather its absoluteness?" (Buber 1988a: 67). Whatever the basis is of whatever distinction Buber makes here remains unclear and unconvincing. Sartre's reply to this gambit could be, "God as absolute other would simply make matters worse." For in Sartre's logic, God as absolute otherness could relate to humanity only as that to which humanity was absolutely alien in a relationship of absolute alienation. Indeed this sense of alienation from God was first surfaced by Meister Eckhart in the fourteenth century and is at the heart of Eckhart's prayer to God to free him of God. Nor is Buber's case enhanced when he continues, "God can never become an object for me: I can attain no other relation to Him than that of the I to its eternal Thou, that of the Thou to its eternal I" (Buber 1988a: 68). How the relation of the I to the Thou, eternal or temporal, escapes a subject–object relation on the part of either remains obscure.

What Buber needs here is a responsible philosophical statement which would elucidate precisely how capitalizing the archaic form of the second person singular evades the divine demeaning of humanity by reducing it to an object over against an all powerful divine subject, a demeaning so much at the heart of Sartre's concern. For Buber does concede to Sartre such diminution occurs when the divine–human relation is considered to be one that exists between an all powerful divine subject whose invasive otherness reduces humanity to its object. Yet one suspects that no such philosophy would be forthcoming from Buber because the imaginal background of his religious thought is simply that of the human subject's relation to a divine person termed a Thou whose transcendence precedes humanity and can and must, in principle, exist wholly independently of it. To avoid this implication would entail showing how divinity and humanity naturally share a point of common being which makes possible and inevitable their relationship. But this demonstration would have to rest on a conception such as God as the ground of being or depth of reason and engage a vital pantheism in which the difference of divinity and humanity would proceed from a primal identity. However, this ontological intimacy of the divine and human would eclipse if not corrode the all too familiar traditional conception of a transcendent God addressing humanity from beyond, a traditional dualism which the poetically evasive I–Thou of Buber's thought serves to cloak. If it served no other purpose the dialogue with Jung removed the cloak to reveal the "Thou" as the all too well known Yaweh, the first among his later monotheistic successors. In the end Buber's near poetry simply serves his theological ideology.

The problem of going beyond the understanding of deity's relation to humanity in terms of a subject–object relation has been a serious one in nineteenth and twentieth century philosophy and theology. The more remote origins of the problem can be traced to Hegel. He saw clearly enough that reading the Jewish and Christian myths at face value would convince the unsophisticated reader that humanity was indeed faced with a divine personality of immense power, self-sufficient in his own life, whose arbitrary interventions in human affairs could reduce the human individual and entire peoples, chosen or rejected, to helpless objects of an unassailable divine affront (Hegel 1970: 182f.). Reflecting on the violation of human dignity implicit in such a mythology, Hegel identified the deepest roots of human alienation in a consciousness of God as other than the human. In this Hegel was well aware of the formulation of this problem in a more specifically religious idiom by Meister Eckhart in the fourteenth century.

The problematic at the core of Hegel's work remained throughout his life that of the alienation between the human and the divine demanded by such a literal understanding of monotheistic mythology. His philosophy is a sustained effort to resolve this split. In the end Hegel arrived at a philosophical position consonant with the deeper implications of Jung's psychology, namely, that God necessarily creates human consciousness to become conscious in it through the resolution of the divine antinomy in human history. Both arrive at fundamental agreement on this dialectic; Jung from a psychology of interiority resting on opposites in conflict and Hegel from a philosophical engagement with external history and its conflicts.

The twentieth century problem of God as omnipotent subject over against the human as responding object is thus a continuation of central themes in nineteenth century romanticism and idealism. These traditions at least realized the problem, namely, that the denial of a natural ontological connection between divinity and humanity put the twain in such a position that they could never meet except in their otherness in configurations of a test of power and so of alienation and conflict. This is the insight that Sartre exploits when he describes God as a divine voyeur gazing on humanity from an unqualified transcendence. When divinity and humanity are imagined as sharing no point in common either can be free but never both. The supernaturalist lodges this freedom in God; the modern atheist and most secularists in the human. Jung's paradigm of the psyche would heal the split through its foundational assertion that the divine and human are two dynamic centers in one organic, universal psychic process. The synthesis worked by Hegel and Jung is precisely what Buber's faith in a God transcendent to psyche and history could not tolerate because it denies the natural point of coincidence between the divine and the human as the necessary precondition to the defeat of their mutual alienation.

Heidegger, as a co-conspirator in the contemporary eclipsing of God, fares no better when Buber turns to him from Sartre. Buber again is fair in pointing out that Heidegger has refused to submit to being classified as an atheist. But this is of little consolation to Buber. For Heidegger's sense of divine transcendence fails to meet Buber's requirements and may be even more insidious than Sartre's because there is a certain sense of transcendence retained in Heidegger's thought. Buber is both profound and accurate in reading Heidegger's philosophy as a certain combination of Parmenides' understanding of being as beyond or prior to form with Hegel's understanding of "the original principle which attains self-consciousness in the human spirit" (Buber 1988a: 71).

Buber sees clearly that Heidegger's position also implies that the ultimate, under whatever name, seeks its own completion in historical human consciousness. It is not far from this position to the understanding that human consciousness is in organic and ontological continuity with its source and is indeed the organ through which that source seeks its self-consciousness and so completion. Though Hegel worked out this proposition in terms of divinity realizing itself in history through human conflict, it would take little to internalize the process and to see the individual human ego under the aegis of the self as the seat of that consciousness in which alone the discernment and resolution of the conflict latent in its psychic precedent and matrix could occur. And this is very much what the metaphysic always implicit in Jung's psychology and made explicit in his *Answer to Job* does.

Yet for Buber the implication that humanity and divinity are thus so organically and intimately related denies that arbitrariness which for him must at all cost remain the prerogative of the transcendent. He writes in refutation of Heidegger's understanding of the relation of Being to human consciousness, "The Coming One came of his own will out of the mystery of his withdrawal; we did not cause him to come" (Buber 1988a: 74–75). In fact any such "causing" on the part of humanity is immediately dismissed as "magical" or as a trick of the conjurer (Buber 1988a: 75, 76). Only the God divested of any real need of the creature and certainly of the need to mature in human maturity qualifies as "Him whom we men, basically in agreement despite all the differences in our religious teaching, address as God" (Buber 1988a: 76). Needless to say the initiative in commerce with this God lies with God. This point is compatible with Jung's position that in the commerce with the self the initiative is with the self even though the ego can take action to prompt the exchange. The difference is that with Jung the initiative comes from within. There is also a commendable relativity in Buber's assurance that the one true divine being lies behind all its religious and monotheistic variants. Yet this singular divinity, manifest in historical variation, serves as the basis of Buber's rejection of Heidegger's perception that we live between the Gods unable to relate to our old still reigning myth and, for the moment, unable to birth the new.

Buber concludes his case against Heidegger's suggestion that Western humanity now awaits a new sense of the sacred in whose birth it yearns to cooperate with a reference to Heidegger's conscious and tragic association of such a new consciousness with Hitler and National Socialism (Buber 1988a: 77). One wonders why it was necessary to introduce this material in the polemic against Heidegger's allegedly inadequate conception of transcendence. For surely more than one transcendent and only God has been known to lead the chosen, then and now, to victory over other peoples and lands with the justification that such pillage works God's kingdom on earth. One need only look to Iraq and Afghanistan for contemporary instances of this archetypal phenomenon. Rather than attack Heidegger's admittedly deplorable commitment to National Socialism, Buber might have joined Jung in more acutely analyzing the dangers of the role of the archetypal unconscious in creating collective religious and political commitment to any kind of absolutes, religious or political. These dangers are still evident today in a variety of monotheistic Gods leading their disparate communities against each other in continuity with the spirit of their biblical precedents. In this effort Buber would be greatly aided by Jung's reflection on the role of the unconscious in religious and political bonding leading to just such unfortunate psychic epidemics as that of the Nationalist Socialist period. This issue will be taken up in greater detail in Chapter 6. Thus Buber's legitimate call for a social ethic that could avoid Heidegger's identifying of so questionable an absolute with the then historical hour would surely be better served by a political philosophy and psychology that could show how the sacramental and iconoclastic work together to prevent political and religious idolatry, tribal loss of responsibility and subsequent mayhem. A politic based on Jung's conception of archetypal reality would be better suited to show the inescapable power of human faith as archetypal persuasion working social cohesion through the sacredness of the communal bond in close tandem with the realization that no manifestation of archetypal energy in history, no faith, can be definitive as exhaustive of the potential of its source.

With this archetypal critique the question could then be asked of any monotheistic position claiming an exhaustive purchase on revelation allegedly authored by the sole absolute other whether it could relativize itself and survive. If the answer is no the question could then be asked of this religion whether it is not engaged in a now lethal idolatry and in a consciousness posing a threat to human survival with its claims to an exhaustive and final ultimacy in the face of competing claims. Buber is sparse in his treatment of how the one God, whom he claims all address in basic agreement beneath religious differences, could have created the impression with so many different communities that their revelations were exhaustive and highly, if not exclusively, privileged.

It is little wonder then, in the light of his now obvious thirst for total transcendence, that by the time he gets to Jung in this essay, Buber is prepared to see in his psychology "the new religion, the only one which can still be true, the religion of pure psychic immanence" (Buber 1988a: 84). In this statement meant as an accusation there is considerable truth. Buber never misread Jung. Buber argues that, for Jung, God does not exist apart from the human experience of divinity originating in the movements of the psyche. Buber continues, again correctly, that Jung's understanding of immanence is "metaphysical", embracing philosophical and theological positions, and so breaking down the boundaries between psychology, philosophy and theology (Buber 1988a: 81). On these points, still beyond the grasp of many Jungians, Buber is reading Jung with depth and accuracy. Jung's radical immanence is the core issue in his conflict with Buber. What is at stake in this issue is Buber's insistence that legitimate experience of religious transcendence is in no way dependent on its mediation through the human psyche, or worse, on its origin in that psyche. The true God could break in, accost, disconcert and enrapture the human at any moment in the interests of revelation and salvation (Buber 1988: 75). The source of this inbreaking is the ultimate difference between the two thinkers.

Again Buber, citing Jung's work on Eckhart, is profoundly insightful and correct when he accuses Jung effectively of transforming Kant's forbidden knowledge of the noumenon into the very knowable numinous in the interests of identifying the soul as the origin of humanity's sense of the numinous and so of God (Buber 1988a: 80). But then Buber reveals again the discrediting objectivity of his thought on the divine. He affirms that for him God is as pre-existent to human perception as "the tree before my window" (Buber 1988a: 80). Meeting such a God is epistemologically comparable to throwing back the curtains and discovering the independent existence of the tree outside the window for the first time. Just as the mind did not create the tree neither does the soul create the divine. That God, the tree and Buber might share a common being in a universal divine ground as the basis of the sacred nature of all three seems an option excluded from the discussion, a victim of Buber's need for an objective transcendent God. Jung, on the other hand, would see little epistemic similarity in the perception of a tree and the experience of God. Rather Jung will argue consistently that the experience of God must be psychically generated because such experience has precious little basis in the "objective" phenomenal or sensible world captured by the sensorium. Jung's epistemology which grounds the experience of God in the living structures of the psyche would explain why the sense of God endures though the One has never been caught by the human senses in any residual manner beyond the hallucinatory, valuable though such hallucinations remain for Jung as revelation of the psyche from which they derive. More, the numinosity Jung attributes to the immediate experience of divinity would greatly distance such experience from that of a sensory perception of a tree or any other entity, including a singular God. Buber's reduction of the perception of the divine to the level of the perception of an entity however grand is the target of Tillich's response to such objectification,

> It is obvious that this . . . concept of existence brings God's existence down to the level of that of a stone or a star, and it makes atheism not only possible, but almost unavoidable, as the later development has proved.
>
> (Tillich 1964: 18)

From Tillich's viewpoint reflected in Jung's, Buber's religious thought does not alleviate the eclipse of God. It is a form of thought that has brought it on. A major cause of contemporary atheism is the inanity of contemporary theism.

From Jung's perspective humanity's native sense of the numinous as the experience of the divine is not at all reductionism, for he is convinced on grounds he calls empirical that humanity is necessitated by the psyche itself to undergo both the experience of God and to produce variants of discernibly similar images which accompany this experience. In fact Jung could counter charges of reductionism with the contention that those who make them are unconscious of the unconscious and so unaware of religion's origin in the psyche. Those then become the true reductionists who would reduce the experience of the divine to sporadic interventions from a transcendent beyond throughout personal and collective history. Buber will allow some of Jung's argument. He acknowledges that the One God beyond history and humanity has sponsored a variety of historical appearances. But for Buber such appearances all point to a referent external to the psyche. Jung and instances of mystical thought like Eckhart's studied by the early Buber would locate the One in the psyche as the source of derivative and multiple Gods.

Moreover, Buber, as stated, claims to know where the legitimate "boundaries of psychology" exist and can call these boundaries to Jung's attention when Jung oversteps them. What Buber is doing here is what so many theologians of transcendence do on behalf of the claims of their privileged or exclusive possession of a revelation grounded on such transcendence. They have to deny the psychic origins of their revelation, as well as the attendant radical sense of human interiority and inevitable religious relativism, in order to preserve the supernatural, unique, and final nature of their personally preferred revelation, a preference understood then to be based on faith in an historically identifiable intrusive revelation made by their God of choice or more often of birth. These motives are the true basis of their defense of spheres beyond psychology's domain, spheres that only the believer "licensed" with the privileged cognitive status of faith may enter. Thus Buber has to deny Jung's position of an intrapsychic transcendence of the archetypal to the ego within the psyche itself. He is totally insensitive to the possibility that the traditional understanding of humanity's dialogue with divinity has been so compelling and ineradicable because it is in fact based on humanity's experience of those powers within the psyche which transcend the ego and whose influence is the source of that suasion projected beyond the psyche in the creation of "objective" deity and demon including the monotheistic variants. A tragic consequence of Buber's position is that remaining unconscious becomes the condition of faith and faith must feed such unconsciousness to maintain itself.

Buber's fear of gnostic radical interiority and its implication of the natural genesis of the divine from the depths of the human may be less widespread in today's religious climate. In the 1950s to accuse one's conversant of gnostic tendencies was perhaps an undermining move. In the light of today's discussion this may be less so. The origins of gnosticism will probably be debated indefinitely. Certain streams of more recent scholarship understand gnosticism to be rooted in the Jewish tradition itself (Pagels 1981: xxxvi). Others see it as a Christian phenomenon (Petrement 1990). In positions closer to Jung's spirit, the suggestion is made that Christianity might well have impaired its spirituality when, for institutional cohesion, it removed itself from its earlier gnostic energies (Pagels 1982: 8). In the wake of this scholarship, attributing a gnostic character to an opponent's thought today would be, in not a few circles, more of a compliment than a criticism. Understood benignly gnosticism would point to the individual's experience of the energy of the self which creates the religions. The religions exist then to mediate such experience so often repressed in the interests of a misguided and self-defeating institutional self-preservation and order which has lost the experience to which they owe their origin.

As Buber's indictment of Jung's gnosticism continues it moves to the moral implications of Jung's understanding of the self as a unity of opposites (Buber 1988a: 85f). The opposites that most fascinate Buber are those of good and evil. He could have chosen other sets of opposites that held equal fascination for Jung such as male–female or spiritual–material. For reasons that are ultimately moralistic, Buber dwells on the opposites of good and evil and implies that Jung's psychology, under the rubric of "the integration of evil" would somehow urge the doing of evil, what psychologists would call "acting out", as contributing to the realization of the self (Buber 1988a: 89, 90). In his response to Jung's response he restates his moral concerns by suggesting that Jung proposes a gnostic libertinism like that of Carpocrates as an element of the process of individuation understood as "mystically deifying the instincts instead of hallowing them in faith" (Buber 1988b: 137).

Carpocrates, writing in the first half of the second century and mentioned in Iranaeus' work on heresy, is referred to three times in Jung's *Collected Works* (Jung 1964e: 131; 1969b: 77; 1970: 215). Jung reads Carpocrates as a spokesman for the gnostic insight that the individual must consciously assimilate his or her shadow in the process of individuation. Here shadow refers not so much to evil but to the "more compendious" or "supraordinate" personality and its more extensive sympathy toward which the self always moves, though it can never be more than approximated in the course of a lifetime. No doubt the fuller consciousness, implied here as both an unattainable and unavoidable goal, at every moment in its development would surpass the previous lesser consciousness and empathic embrace of the individual. The thrust of the assimilation of shadow in this context is best caught in the statement sometimes attributed to Carpocrates that nothing human is foreign to such consciousness. Indeed, a characteristic note of the conscious self is that of a sympathy for all that is human and, more, for all that is. Jung is explicit in stating that this embracing wisdom does not endorse licentiousness but rather a fuller knowledge of what is authentically human and as such rightly demands inclusion in consciousness. He writes:

> "No man can be redeemed from a sin he has not committed," says Carpocrates; a deep saying for all who wish to understand, and a golden opportunity for all those who prefer to draw false conclusions. What is down below is not just an excuse for more pleasure, but

something we fear because it demands to play its part in the life of the
more conscious and complete man.

(Jung 1964e: 131)

Jung's reading of Carpocrates in this passage is impossible to interpret as
an invitation to a perverse permissiveness. However, it is consistent with
transcendentalist positions such as Buber's to understand moral impera-
tives as emanating from a divine agency beyond the psyche rather than
from the imperative of the individual self within the psyche. In Jung's
psychology the self functions as the conscience of the individual working
for the balanced wholeness seeking incarnation in each individual life. In
this context Jung will speak of the self as the *"spiritus rector"*, that is, as
the spirit which works against the pathology of one-sidedness toward the
divine balance of opposites in those ever more encompassing totalities so
central to Jung's conception of the human as an image of God (Jung
1971b: 58). Though Buber does refer to conscience in this article, his
externalism prohibits him from understanding the regulating power of the
self as the source of the individual's moral imperative. The experience of
such an imperative rises naturally from the depths of the individual's
psyche and not from Mount Sinai or its functional equivalent in like
theologies of uprootedness functioning in this context to divest the individual of the sureness of one's personal moral instincts grounded in the
psyche. The moral imperative here is to become whole or move toward a
wholeness which, in the spirit of Carpocrates, would not hold anything
human as foreign.

In May 1952, *Merkur* carried Jung's reply to Buber as well as Buber's
rejoinder. Early in his reply Jung takes the familiar approach that he is an
empiricist and as such not a metaphysician (Jung 1976e: 663, 664). But
immediately this poses the problem of what Jung meant by the terms
"metaphysics" and "empiricism". Chapter 1 has addressed these wider
issues attaching to Jungian psychology. Here it suffices to say that Jung
includes within the empirical not only all that the senses and their technological enhancement yield but also the material which he encountered in
his practice as a psychiatrist and therapist in the imagery of his patients. In
this extended sense the empirical would include his patient's dreams,
waking imagery, private cosmologies, delusions, in short, the plethora of
material the unconscious forced on the consciousness of those with whom
he worked. More, since Jung understood the collective unconscious as the
origin not only of the psychological material of the individuals with whom
he worked but also as the origin of both living and dead religions, as well as
the myths, cosmologies and folklore of the world, all this latter material
would also fall under the greatly enlarged category of what Jung terms
"empirical". Webster's dictionary gives its first definition of "empirical" as
"Depending on experience or observation alone; without due regard to

science and theory". If the empirical is extended beyond experiment to experience and observation, there can be little doubt that Jung's psychology resting on a wealth of archetypal expression and experience is indeed "empirical" though such a "database" might remain suspicious in today's more widely accepted sense of the term which would tend to reduce the meaning to the sensibly perceptible and measurable.

Indeed it was largely on the basis of the discernible connectedness between the empirical yield of material from his practice and the imagery which surfaces in the archetypal statements of, for instance, the world's religions, that Jung locates the common generator of both in the archetypal powers of the collective unconscious. A dramatic instance of this is in the symbol of the solar phallus revealed by one of his patients at the Burghölzli psychiatric hospital and expressed in the ancient Mithraic religion (Jung 1966a: 101–102; 1969f: 150–151). Thus if one is to add the "subjectivity" of twentieth century dreams to the "objectivity" of the world religions and mythologies, living or dead, and concede that both are empirical, one must grant to Jung an extensive empirical base for his understanding of the psyche and of its propensities for generating the experience and images of the divine. On these grounds Jung is justified in his claim of an empirical basis for his psychology theoretically and therapeutically. To deny such an empirical base to Jung would deny the simple facticity of the contents of contemporary dreams and of the world's religions and mythologies and their ability to bring a healing meaning to those whom they touch.

In contrast to empiricism and the empiricist he claimed to be, Jung pits "metaphysics" and the "metaphysician" whom he claims he is not. What did he mean by "metaphysics"? His use of the term yields, at least, three senses throughout his work. Occasionally he will argue that metaphysics, as philosophy, is simply a systematized expression of the dominant complex in the philosopher's or theologian's psyche usually unknown to the practicing philosopher. Jung's sardonic depiction of metaphysics as the metaphysician's unconscious expression of the unconscious would explain the apparent permanence of the practice in the face of its consistent failure to achieve any substantial agreement among its adepts. The subtle irony of this position is evident when Jung, citing Nietzsche, suggests that metaphysics thus understood should become the *"ancilla psychologiae"*, "the handmaiden of psychology" (Jung 1969f: 160). By this he implies that just as the theological medieval mind would understand philosophy as the handmaiden or servant of theology informed by faith which alone could reveal philosophy's full meaning to the philosopher, so could contemporary depth psychology explain to the philosopher what complex drove the philosophy in question. In this passage Jung would suggest that analysis or familiarity with the unconscious might well reveal to the philosopher or theologian the complex at the heart of every philosophical conviction or religious faith. This suggestion is certainly to the fore in Jung's interchange with Buber, whose steadfast faith Jung rooted in the unconscious and in Buber's unconsciousness of the psychic source of his own faith.

In a second sense he gives the term, Jung will occasionally refer to his own metaphysical aspirations and to himself as a "philosopher *manqué*" in thinly disguised recognition, never fully acknowledged, of the metaphysical implications of his own psychology (Jung 1935: 194). In this respect Jung could well have admitted that his psychology included a native metaphysics because it does what philosophical metaphysics always attempts to do, namely, identify what is, (ontology) and how what is is known (epistemology). In so far as metaphysics can be understood as concerned with what is and how it is known his psychology does indeed include a latent metaphysic, which requires little amplification to move it to a full blown metaphysic, in the aforementioned sense. Jung, who realized this fact, could have been more candid in admitting it, especially in his dialogue with the theological mind.

But in its third and most frequently used sense which grounds his denials in his discussions with theologians, Jung means by metaphysics a body of knowledge for which there is neither compelling internal or subjective evidence nor external or objective evidence, that is, a body of knowledge for which there is no evidence at all. He derived this meaning of metaphysics from his youthful observations that his clerical father, uncle and cousins, when discussing matters theological and dogmatic, had absolutely no experiential sense of what they were talking about (Jung 1965a: 73). In this sense metaphysics can be related to what he later called the current "sacrosanct unintelligibility" and "preposterous nonsense" of Christian symbols, once the bearers of the energies of the unconscious but now dead at the hands of a murderous intellectualism (Jung 1969e: 109, 110). Metaphysics thus understood can best be described as a blind faith in what it affirms or knows divested of any experiential basis in the human. In his reply to Buber, Jung describes such metaphysicians as those "who for one reason or another think they know about unknowable things in the Beyond" (Jung 1976e: 664). Obviously Jung understood Buber as a metaphysician in this sense and is right in excluding metaphysics thus understood from his works and consciousness.

Jung goes on to explain that, as an empirical psychologist, he is forced to work with the images that are thrown up by the unconscious as the generative basis of the deities that the believer projects beyond the psyche in the supernatural peopling of the heavens and hells of traditional revelations. In flat contradiction of Buber's relation to a transcendental Thou, the numinous powers of the unconscious are for Jung, "everything one could wish or fear for in the psychic 'Thou'" (Jung 1976e: 665). In these words Jung exposes the unbridgeable gap between his understanding of the psychogenetic origins of religion and the religious world view of the metaphysician-believer of Buber's stripe. Jung could not be clearer. For him the dialogue between the I and the divine Thou is the dialectical dialogue between the ego and the archetypal powers of the unconscious. For Buber it is with the transcendental Thou.

In a passage in which he addresses the problematic of this position in a more philosophical phraseology he does not usually use, Jung describes these powers which necessitate humanity's religious experience as "immanent-transcendent" (Jung 1976e: 665). By this he would mean that such powers are within the psyche yet transcendent to the ego and capable of inducing in the ego, especially of the believer, the conviction of the objective existence of powers wholly transcendent to the psyche. When these powers escape containment they become the Gods in the varying pantheons of those who read their myths literally, and who then relate to these Gods or God as to a Thou beyond the human.

To anyone, like Buber, who doubted the reality of these powers as the true generators of religious experience and faith, Jung suggests a trip through an asylum where these powers and the faith they engender are dramatically visible. He writes:

> It should not be overlooked that what I am concerned with are psychic phenomenon which can be proved empirically to be the bases of metaphysical concepts, and that when, for example, I speak of "God" I am unable to refer to anything beyond these demonstrable psychic models which, we have to admit, have shown themselves to be devastatingly real. To anyone who finds their reality incredible I would recommend a reflective tour through a lunatic asylum.
>
> (Jung 1976e: 666)

With this passage Jung unites differing aspects of his understanding of the psychogenesis of religion. Not only do archetypal powers give rise to the sense of transcendence and to the social bonding under the divinities produced by this sense, but also they induce the mass psychoses that follow when collective consciousness identifies with them. Individual, but much more probably, mass or societal psychoses are the instances of the "devastatingly real" to which Jung refers in the above passage. For Jung names the holocaust and other atrocities of the Second World War period as examples of the reality of archetypal possession and the unconsciousness such possession produces (Jung 1976e: 665, 666). Yet along with such atrocities the unconscious as Other is also the source of humanity's sense of "beauty, goodness, wisdom, grace" (Jung 1976e: 666). In the context of his wider work, the sole difference in the manifestation of the inner Other lies in the degree to which individual and community consciously address the power of its divine importunity and so contribute to the responsible birth of the Other into historical consciousness. The alternative is personal or collective possession by the Other in the loss of personal freedom and dignity to whatever personal or collective delusion the Other drives its victims.

Jung's response to Buber moves then to a less subtle but, perhaps, more compelling point because it brings up a problem that is still with us, that is the prolixity of Gods all claiming metaphysical reality and ultimacy and not infrequently pitting their devotees one against another. Jung had already referred to this dark side of deity in his reference to the holocaust and other instances of mass loss of life resulting from communal faith commitments in political form in the twentieth century. Jung wonders about which of these many contending "metaphysical" deities Buber is speaking in this piquant passage:

> Of which metaphysical deity he is speaking I do not know. If he is an orthodox Jew he is speaking of a God to whom the incarnation in the year 1 has not yet been revealed. If he is a Christian, then his deity knows about the incarnation of which Yaweh still shows no sign . . . Consequently I do not permit myself the least judgment as to whether and to what extent it has pleased a metaphysical deity to reveal himself to the devout Jew as he was before the incarnation, to the Church Fathers as the Trinity, to the Protestants as the one and only Saviour without co-redemptrix and to the present Pope as a saviour with co-redemptrix.
>
> (Jung 1976e: 666, 667)

Jung concludes the passage wondering how Buber's God-concept relates to those of Islam, Buddhism, Hinduism and the Taoist traditions.

In the closing passages of his response, he reaffirms that his psychological endeavor deals empirically with the material which comes unmediated from the unconscious. As such it is far from an ersatz eclecticism, "a repulsive theosophical brew" (Jung 1976e: 669). He appeals to philosophers and theologians such as Buber to take note of this point and to forego an uprooted consciousness which removes them from the psyche and its empirical though truly healing expressions and power which dogmas, religious or philosophical, can no longer effect (Jung 1976e: 669).

Nor is his psychology "a new religion," though by his own frequently repeated admissions, it deals with material produced by the powers that produce religious experience and so the historical religions. Nevertheless it does not rely on any revelation received from beyond (Jung 1976e: 669). Moreover, he argues his basic concern and effort in all this is therapeutic. And here he takes up a position that resounds throughout his work and may be called an apology for the recovery of a truly healing religion or spirituality. In a challenge to Buber and to theologians of uprootedness of all persuasions, he contends that since the "word of God" has lost its curative power in our culture, he is forced "to rely on the curative powers inherent in the patient's own nature, regardless of whether the ideas that emerge agree with any known creed or philosophy" (Jung 1976e: 669). These curative powers are ultimately the energies of the self in the service of the suffering ego. Not infrequently experienced as divine by those whom they heal, they constitute for Jung the "modest 'gnosis'" with which his empirical method works (Jung 1976e: 669).

Buber was given the final brief word in the same issue of *Merkur*. He repeats his original charge that Jung oversteps the legitimate boundaries of psychological empiricism especially in his position that the genesis of the experience of deity is a psychological process. For Buber this would mean only that God "was merely a psychic phenomenon" whose independent existence beyond the psyche could not be credibly sustained (Buber 1988b: 133, 134). The need for such a transcendent entity and the literalist cosmology that attach to it are again transparent in Buber's need to ground his sense of deity on the "action of a supra-psychic Being" (Buber 1988b: 134). It is obvious as his reply continues that Jung's response forced Buber to defend himself against the suggestion that his own conception of revelation was somewhat crude or literalistic. He denies that he feels revelation is handed down from heaven "as finished statements" (Buber 1988b: 135). On the contrary he explains revelations as follows:

> Rather it means that the human substance is melted by the fire which visits it, and there now breaks forth from it a word, a statement, which is human in its meaning and form, human conception and human speech, and yet witnesses to Him who stimulated it and to His will.
>
> (Buber 1988b: 135)

Jung himself was thoroughly familiar with such fire. But rather than attribute its origin to a "supra-psychic Being", he located it in the unconscious. It burnt there as the undying "*scintilla*", the spark of divine fire at that point in the human where nature, humanity and divinity share a common point of being. It was for Jung the divine fire in humanity and nature that could not be extinguished and could consume or inspire depending on the response by the ego to it (Jung 1969b: 92, 93, fn. 47). Here the difference between Jung's perspective and Buber's touches precisely on their respective understanding of the dynamics of revelation. Jung locates the fire of revelation touching the mind in the depths of the psyche while a theology of uprootedness locates the fire in a celestial realm beyond the human on whom it then descends.

Buber was also obviously stung by Jung's pointing out to him that a variety of Gods claimed the metaphysical objectivity which he attributed to his own. Buber writes somewhat testily, "I think I was already aware of this and have many times stated and explained it" (Buber 1988b: 136). Here, possibly due to lack of space, Buber proffers no explanation of the multiplicity of one, true and objective Gods all claiming universal allegiance. He leaves the reader with the lingering feeling that a brief word would be a helpful guide to the perplexed in facing so many divine claimants and in discerning the sole legitimate contender among them. Rather Buber simply reaffirms that though there are many images of God, the movement of the faith that produces them is toward "the Imageless", "an existing Being" and "One who exists, and as such is common to men who believe out of varied experience" (Buber 1988b: 136). As previously stated, the latter formulation would be quite compatible with archetypal theory, which would indeed attribute the many Gods to variations of psychic experience and manifestation. However, Buber locates the origin of such diverse manifestation in realms beyond the psyche. He is then faced with two major problems. The first is the perennial difficulty of how such multiple revelations can be graciously received by the human when their origin is foreign or heteronomous to the human. Buber's categories would make of all revelations divine impositions unless he showed their common origin in humanity which his purpose here is to deny. The second is how members of the resultant communities can relate peacefully with each other in the wake of their reception of differing divine claims which always degenerate in those who receive them to exclusive claims to ultimacy. The need for the objective transcendence of a wholly other God pits God as universal creator against God as author of highly particular revelations and makes of all revelation, thus understood, a matter of alienation between a divine and human subject to say nothing of the ensuing relations between faith communities. Nevertheless Buber concludes with the same insistence on the removal to a transcendent heaven of the objective God from the subjectivity of the psyche, a concern which remains the core of the incompatibility of his thought with Jung's.

In the final analysis Buber seems to have little to contribute to the conscious analysis of the disparate images this common experience of divinity produces in humanity and even less to the understanding of the murderous intent such disparate images of deity can spawn between communities caught and divided by them. In the light of this failure, his protestation that though he believes in revelation received from a supra- or extra-psychic being he is nevertheless not a representative of "orthodoxy" has to it a somewhat hollow unconvincing ring (Buber 1988b: 135).

In available letters written after the interchange, Jung adds little wholly new to the debate. He simply repeats his conviction that Buber has little or no appreciation or experience of psychic reality. Such experience would be of the archetypal and autonomous energies productive of that religious experience which Jung closely relates to "gnosis". He continues to see Buber as proposing his God as "the only right one" and feels "these absurdities" of the conflicting Gods must be resolved in favor of humanity (Jung 1952a: 68; 1957a: 367, 368). He writes to Eric Neumann that Buber has not "the faintest idea of what the Gnostic was moved by" which is simply a variant on his theme of Buber's unawareness of the psychic origins of religious experience universally and in himself and his removal from such experience in any way that could go beyond its intellectual and orthodox formulations (Jung 1954a: 147).

However, in his second letter to Bernard Lang on Buber, Jung introduces a new note or at least new imagery to describe his distance from Buber. Here he describes Buber and, by implication, all who would share Buber's understanding of the gift of faith enabling belief in a transcendent God, as confidently convinced that they are the happy possessors of "a 'receiver', an organ by means of which he can know or tune in the Transcendent" (Jung 1957b: 375). The possessor of the organ of belief can then all too easily point to the less fortunate and to their human "deformity or lack of an organ" (Jung 1957b: 376). The organ of faith could thus make its happy possessors somewhat arrogant toward those less organically endowed. More, the possessors of this organ were, in Jung's view, also convinced that the religious knowledge and conviction it provided them somehow had a more public credibility. This organ gave them the facility of a true knowledge, that is, "seeing a thing in such a way that all can know it" (Jung 1957b: 377). For Jung, the contention that what the organ of faith affords its holder is publicly persuasive is simply a matter of claiming a universal validity for one's own faith which can then be imposed on others as the exclusively correct one. The saving sense of the relativity of the God image cedes in such faith consciousness to the imperialism implied in the assertion that one's God is the only one. Appealing as he does so often to Kant, Jung denies that one can have a universally communicable "knowledge" of the noumenal which he implies the organ of faith would provide its holder. On the contrary for Jung the individual must bow to the relativity of the experiential basis of one's belief and affirm that this is the image of God most compelling for oneself or for the community whose tradition influences the experience. Such a commendable relativity prompts Jung's to write, "I 'abhor' the belief that I or anybody else could be in possession of an absolute truth" (Jung 1957b: 378).

Whether Jung knew it or not the notion of "an organ of faith" enabling its possessor to know and assent to what others cannot is not too distant from the Thomistic understanding of the infusion of faith as a theological virtue allowing its happy possessor to assent to a body of revealed knowledge to which others not so blessed cannot. The dualism that Thomistic theology establishes between the natural and supernatural orders is reflected in Buber's need to have a super-psychic being as the author of his faith and its fire. This conception of faith, as well as hope and charity, as infused gifts foreign to one's nature would be familiar to Victor White and to his theology, as will be seen in Chapter 5.

In the context of his discussion with Buber, Jung simply denies on Kantian grounds that such knowledge of God, capable of eliciting a public consensus, is a human possibility. On the contrary he reaffirms a position central to his work that what really lies at the heart of the believer's certitude is not an organ of faith which grants its possessor access to a body of knowledge denied to others. Rather, "What has really happened to these people [believers] is that they have been overpowered by an inner experience" (Jung 1957b: 377). This inner experience would be the unacknowledged archetypal basis of their faith. Once again Jung is suggesting that the believer, and here he includes Buber, is unconscious of the inner agencies that compel belief. He goes on to add that because such experience is never beyond question even by its recipient it easily breeds a fanaticism and "missionary zeal" needed to allay the doubt that such faith brings with it, a doubt that could humanize such faith if allowed to live with it (Jung 1957b: 376, 377).

The source of such experience remains for Jung the numinous impression made by the archetypes on consciousness and manifested externally in the hallucinatory "epiphany" of the divine when this impact escapes the containment of the psyche and takes on the form of an "objective" projection. It is this experience of the archetypal either as a foreign power within the psyche (God speaking to me in my soul) or as a projection beyond (hearing a voice on the road to Damascus) which produces the sense of discontinuous transcendence characteristic of theologies of uprootedness. The temptation to objectify the source of the experience over against the person in whom it occurs is difficult to resist especially in the too often pre-psychological and so pre-conscious world of the believer in whom the experience occurs and of the theologian who, working in the interest of such unconsciousness, adds to it a sophisticated confirmation through interpreting such experience as originating beyond the psyche.

If this line of Jung's reasoning is taken seriously, especially under the pressure of current collective religious and political conflict, it would force the question as to whether faith in an absolute is any longer a form of consciousness that can meet minimal requirements of a social ethic. Belief in a one and only God in the traditional sense would then become the ultimate sin against humanity, surpassed only by the more insidious idea that humanity is capable of cleansing its consciousness of the psychological experience that breeds such absolutes in religious, political or other variants. Jung's critique of Buber would point to the conclusion that humanity cannot live without its faiths but could be destroyed by them if their common origin in the psyche is not acknowledged even by religious leaders as the first step in curtailing their lethal divisiveness.

Given the feeling tone of Jung's reply to Buber, there can be little doubt, in the face of Buber's evenness of writing and self-assurance, who won the debate in terms of literary style and suavity. Nor does the exchange and his references to it in later letters leave much doubt that Jung, on his part, was deeply emotionally engaged in the issues at stake. Buber had touched a tender spot especially in one who denied a philosophical or theological implication in the affirmation that the archetypes and their impact on human consciousness grounded a universal religious propensity as the basis of the religions themselves. Jung could have easily admitted that there was a specifically gnostic metaphysic in his psychology given the extended sense he gave to gnosticism as simply humanity's endemic and pre-discursive sense of God. For Jung gnosticism, alchemy and mysticism were sister forms of consciousness when their commonality was grounded on a living sense and resonance with the depths of the psyche from which the sense of God derives. Had Jung made this more explicit in his exchange with Buber, he then could have asked Buber what was the problem with gnosticism thus understood and whether Buber's experience of the divine fire might not have been a form of gnosticism itself?

On the other hand, the interchange did bring out quite clearly what, in fact, Buber's conditions were for the divinity to whom one related as an I to a Thou. Such a divinity was exposed in the light of the conversation with Jung to be the all too familiar wholly transcendent and monotheistic deity who would somehow be eclipsed, indeed, threatened with extinction, if he were to be understood as a valid and valuable projection of the psyche. The identity of such a deity with the all too traditional Yaweh was exposed. The exchange leaves it very clear that the divine Thou to whom Buber relates the human I is in no significant sense a function of the depth of human subjectivity in the orders of being, knowing or of morality. Whether humanity can survive a plurality of such divinities is currently its major problem. One strategy for survival Jung proposes is a more sustained reflection "on the only question of importance: *what is religion all about?*" (Jung 1952a: 68, italics Jung's).

Going beyond the dialogue with Buber, the processes leading to the creation of a God in principle wholly unrelated to the human psyche was seriously problematic for Jung because of the havoc it worked on the psyche of the believer. Such theologies were hazardous to psychological health because they removed their adherents from the experience of the unconscious itself. The psychologically uprooting processes culminating in Gods wholly other than the human account for the all-prevailing patriarchal quality of the three currently living monotheistic Gods. Their patriarchal quality cannot, in the first instance, be reduced to gender issues. Rather their patriarchal quality attaches to the values they implant in adherents of either gender who worship a consciousness severed from its origin in its divine matrix. Religiously this leads to a relation to wholly other Gods. Humanly it reduces humanity to reason. In effect the divine–human relation is between two centers of consciousness, one of whom is divine. The demeaning effect on the human conversant in this dialogue does not need to be spelled out. Thinkers such as Sartre have done it for us. Moreover, were such one and only Gods fully reflective of the more total unconscious which gives birth to them, their mythologies could not be so wholly divested of the divinity of the feminine, the maternal and the embodied. This divestiture undermines their collective credibility and truncates their believing victims.

Due to its intimacy with the movements of the unconscious, Jung describes the images of deity he found in alchemy to be both male and female in contrast to the Protestant tradition into which he was born and with which, on this particular point, he associates the Jewish. He writes, "But in the Protestant and Jewish spheres the father continues to dominate as much as ever. In philosophical alchemy, on the other hand, the feminine principle plays a role equal to that of the masculine" (Jung 1965a: 202). This passage should not be read literally. It means that theologies of unqualified transcendence remove their victims, male or female, from the broader and more inclusive empathies the deeper unconscious fosters, most importantly from the potentially universal embrace of the Great Mother whose profundity precedes and conceives all lesser Gods of either gender. Again Jung links both traditions through their patriarchal proclivity in the *Answer to Job*, where he writes:

> Yaweh's perfectionism is carried over from the Old Testament into the New, and despite all the recognition and glorification of the feminine principle this never prevailed against the patriarchal supremacy. We have not, therefore, by any means heard the last of it.
>
> (Jung 1969d: 399)

Words written in 1952 pointed prophetically to the deeper issues to be raised by the feminist movement as one of the twentieth century's most significant and continued cultural critiques but still in the future when Jung penned these lines.

Jung is even more explicit in his evaluation of Protestantism in the wake of the Catholic doctrine of the Assumption. No doubt in sharp contrast from the formulators of the proclamation including Pope Pius XII, Jung understood the doctrine symbolically as a recognition of the divinity of Mary and so of the feminine not only as the mother but also as the bride of the Christ figure placing her "functionally on a par with Christ" (Jung 1969d: 399). In the light of this understanding of the Assumption, Jung could write, "The logical consistency of the Papal declaration cannot be surpassed, and it leaves Protestantism with the odium of being nothing but a *man's religion*" (italics Jung's). "*Man's religion*" in this context is again primarily not gender specific. It refers to a state of consciousness in either gender severed from the unconscious and from the realization that maturation of both genders demands the unity of male and female in the psyche of each.

In the mid and latter half of the twentieth century it was considered both fashionable and humorous in certain theological circles to attribute Buber's popularity to his capacity to draw Barthians out of the depression induced by their own theology. In response to the collapse of late nineteenth century Protestant liberal theology with the arrival of the First World War, Barth had again taken up the appeal to a wholly transcendent God revealed only in Christ. In his manifesto in the footsteps of Kierkegaard, he was to write that there is only one revelation but many religions. In the one revelation God addressed the human. In the many religions humanity sought to attain God (Barth 1968: 10, 311, 312). Buber's thought was alleged to be able to relieve the theologically induced depression of Barth's transcendentalism because of the supposed intimacy Buber established between the divine and the human in his conception of the I–Thou relationship. However, his attack on Jung and Jung's response served to expose the superficiality of this intimacy. No doubt such intimacy could be poetically hinted at in works where the metaphysical implications of the poetry did not need to be spelled out. But when the implications of the I–Thou relationship are confronted with Jung's radical sense of interiority, it becomes obvious that the poetry cannot carry its promise. For the dialogue with Jung witnesses to the true nature of Buber's God, who is no less wholly other than Barth's or Kierkegaard's. As such this God could still conceal his origins in the psyche and congeal the energies which an immediate relation to the source of libido creative of the sense of divinity would liberate. From Jung's viewpoint such theological removal or uprootedness from the energies which fund life can only constitute a blueprint for depression, a strange outcome for divinities and their avatars who promise an abundance of life.

What both Buber and Jung need is an ontology and epistemology which would delineate the intimacy in terms of being and knowing, which both claim and which Jung does in fact exploit in his understanding of the mandala, of the relation of the microcosm to the macrocosm, of the universal substrate operative in his thought on synchronicity and especially in his understanding of the presence of the ultimate to consciousness in the ground of humanity as the same "Ground of all empirical being." All of these sides of Jung's mind point to the immediate participation of all that is in its creative ground and to the ability of consciousness to live more or less residually out of this ground as the culmination of it development. All of these conceptions are credible and intelligible only if they rest on a pantheistic position of the mind's native inherence in an energy in its depths seeking its realization in its consciousness, in a religious idiom, the God within seeking incarnation in an ever fuller humanity. Buber's language points to such immanence but in the dialogue with Jung reveals that it is a facade for the affirmation of a wholly transcendent God. Though Jung's formulations lack a philosophical precision and he describes himself as a philosopher *manqué*, the movement of his mind is increasingly toward a universalism derivative of a developing conscious relation to the common ground generative of mind, its myths, its religions and its Gods. If humanity is to survive monotheism in its various faces, only such a universal sentiment with the power of an emerging myth will bring such survival about.

Chapter 5

Jung, White and the end of the pilgrimage

I have now seen quite a number of people die in the time of great transition. reaching as it were the end of the pilgrimage in sight of the Gates, where the way bifurcates to the land of Hereafter and to the future of mankind and its spiritual adventure.

(Jung 1960b: 604)

The Buber–Jung dialogue exposed the incompatibility of Buber's disjointed or supernatural transcendentalism with Jung's understanding of psychic containment. From Jung's viewpoint the interchange with Buber was never impolite. Yet the exchange did expose Buber's understanding of the I–Thou relationship to be simply a variant, expressed in poetic terms, of a very traditional monotheistic transcendentalism threatened by Jung's appropriation of the foundational gnostic insight that the experiential basis of the relation to the divine and to the depths of the human were, in fact the same relationship. Jung's exposure of Buber's inspired transcendentalism was the basis of Jung's linking Buber's thought with similar conceptions of the transcendent in mainstream Protestant circles as two forms of religious patriarchy. Though always mutually respectful, the exchange was throughout somewhat conflictual.

Such was not the case in Jung's dealing with another form of uprooted religious consciousness which in the end proved equally and tragically incompatible with the wider implications of his own psychology. This second dialogue may well have led to the development of Jung's more mature and wider ranging understanding of the life of the psyche. Among these implications would be the psychological and spiritual inadequacy of a God image in whom their was no evil, reflected in a Christ figure severed from his brother, Satan. Of even greater import is Jung's overriding conception of personal and collective history as the sole theatre in which eternally unresolved antinomies in divinity seek their resolution in humanity. Carl Jung and Fr. Victor White, O.P., an English Dominican priest and theologian teaching for much of the period of their conversation at Blackfriars, Oxford, carried on an earnest conversation for fifteen years from September, 1945, till White's death in May, 1960. Yet in spite of repeated affirmations of good will on both sides, which an examination of the correspondence leaves no reason to doubt, death ended the dialogue on a note of final disagreement between friends again reconciled on the far side of intense dispute. The nature of God's relation to the human, and especially to the human psyche, lay at the heart of the initial enthusiastic meeting of the two minds, continued to enliven their discussion throughout, and finally was the reason for their ultimate impasse. Nor has its distance in time lessened interest in the debate (Lammers 1994; Dourley 2007; Weldon 2007), scholarly fascination evidenced in the recent critical publication of all available letters between the two (Lammers et al. 2007).

Even though the discussion was conducted with a far greater mutual sympathy than the Jung–Buber dialogue, it revealed in White yet another form of theological consciousness which, after fifteen years of intense and sustained effort, could not accept the consequences of the intimate connection Jung's psychology established between the divine and the human. An examination of the progression of the Jung–White correspondence reveals many of the theological implications endemic to Jung's mature psychology which the dialogue itself no doubt helped to form. These implications lie at the core of what makes Jung's psychology then and now paradoxically attractive and yet ultimately threatening to a variety of traditional theologies across the boundaries of the world's religions. They are attracted to the sense of the divine the numinous carries with it throughout Jung's description of the psyche. They are threatened by the intimacy between the divine and the human such numinosity suggests, an intimacy powerfully suggestive of the origin of the sense of the divine in the depths of the human itself.

Before addressing the details of this conversation, the theological positions that Victor White took as a twentieth century follower of Thomas Aquinas with the latter's indebtedness to Aristotle should be placed in historical context. By the 1870s the Catholic Church had faced nearly a century of turmoil in its response to the French Revolution in 1789, and to the urgency toward democracy and nationalism the revolution had unleashed in Europe and its colonies. Throughout the nineteenth century the Papal States had diminished in the face of these forces. After much travail earlier in the century Pius IX (1846–1878) granted a republican (democratic) constitution to Rome only to see the premier of the constitutional government assassinated and himself forced into exile in 1848. But not only was Rome in conflict with the world of politics and its clamor for new freedoms and national identities, but also it was threatened by the contemporary philosophical development, especially of German romanticism and idealism. These traditions established a relationship between the divine and the human too close for orthodox Roman comfort. As a result Pius IX after his return from exile (1850) reacted with a sharp turn to the right. He issued the Syllabus of Errors (1864) against the contemporary, cultural embrace of the ongoing spirit of the French Revolution manifest in various forms of social freedoms. In 1870 he had himself declared infallible at the first Vatican Council. Following this reactive and repressive atmosphere, Leo XIII had Thomas Aquinas installed as the preferred theologian for the Roman Church universal in 1879. The repression of the Catholic mind continued into the twentieth century with the attack on Modernism. This attack had two major targets. The first was the contemporary development of biblical studies aimed at biblicists like Alfred Loisy, whose abrasive thought is summed up in his statement to the effect that the early Christian community expected the return of Christ and the Church came instead. The second target, closer to Jungian concerns, were philosophical/theological issues surrounding the human origin of the religious impulse and the symbolic nature of primordial religious experience aimed at thinkers like George Tyrrel, S.J. (Dourley 2007: 276–279). The following condemned proposition could well stand as an accurate summation of Jungian psychology on matters religious. "Thus the religious sense which, through a *vital immanence*, erupts from the lurking places of the subconscious is the germ of all religion and the explanation as well of all that has appeared in religion's past or will appear in religion's future" (Denzinger 1965a: 677). Again the inquisition is helpful in giving to the heretics a clarity of expression they all too often lacked in themselves.

This trend, rejective of so much of the vitality informing modern religious and philosophical thought, continued into the early 1950s, five years after the opening of the Jung–White dialogue, with attacks on contemporary forms of immanental thought and on efforts to synthesize evolution with Christian belief (Denzinger 1965b: 772–780). In this atmosphere to which it contributed so much, the modern Thomism White so valiantly struggled with and taught at Oxford came into being. It was effectively a philosophy inspired by ecclesial, political and theological needs. It was not in any organic continuity with the development of the European philosophical mind. In fact it was revived in explicit rejection of it. Nor did it leave any legacy to the philosophical world in its wake. It was forced on the Catholic mind and vanished when the force did. A modern historian of Christianity puts it succinctly, "Both Ultramontanism [the concentration of Catholic ecclesial power in Rome] and Neo-Thomism were well considered efforts on the part of the Church to stem the tide of modernity and 'liberalism' in the spheres of politics, ecclesiology, *and* thought" (Livingston 1997: 328).

In choosing Thomism for its late nineteenth century purposes, the Church chose well. It was a variant of medieval schizoid supernaturalism that met current ecclesial requirements. It posed two orders of being, one supernatural, the other natural. Humanity was divested of any immediate experience of the supernatural from which divinity entered the fallen natural order through a series of unsolicited interventions or revelations culminating in the advent of Christ and his continuity in the Church. The dissociated supernatural order filled all the needs for an objective God who presided over the earthly human and Catholic community with universal aspirations embodied in the papacy with its episcopal and sacerdotal extension throughout the world. As Jung points out, such religious perspectives divest the soul of any natural grace. Grace could be imported only from without (Jung 1969g: 482). Efforts to link such importation with the psyche would constitute "'psychologism' [or a] morbid 'mysticism'" (Jung 1969g: 482). On the contrary, for Aquinas an objective God revealed himself from beyond, and presided over a church through which his grace flowed gratuitously to a fallen nature. This fallen nature was in itself wholly unaware of the supernatural order, with the possible exception of the intellectually gifted who could rationally prove the existence and certain of the traits of God then to be supplemented by a surpassing revelation from the supernatural world received through the reception of the equally supernaturally infused theological virtues of faith, hope and charity. Needless to add, the magisterial papacy was to control the interpretation of such revelation.

These would be the theological presuppositions that White would carry into his dialogue with Jung. But White was not a typical Thomist of the period. Even before he began his dialogue with Jung, White was not wholly at home with the Thomism of his day. He had written a thesis on Platonic elements in Thomas' theology, an interesting topic on a theologian renowned for his synthesis of Christianity and Aristotle (Cunningham 2007: 311). The thesis centered on Aquinas' exemplarism, a form of causality with affinities to the influence exercised on consciousness by the archetypal conceived as ideas in the divine mind or *Logos*. He criticized the "infantilism" he found in the Roman Church of the 1940s akin to the influence of a "Terrible Mother" on her suffocating children (Cunningham 2007: 311, 312). He grew increasingly less comfortable with the self-confident and shallow convictions of cultural Catholicism manifest in such prominent thinkers as Hilaire Belloc and G.K. Chesterton (Cunningham 2007: 330). Prior to his meeting with Jung he had already had an analysis with John Layard in England related to psychological difficulties he underwent in 1940 (Weldon 2007: 17–19). His subsequent efforts to introduce an affective element into the logical intellectualism of mainstream Thomism were no doubt prompted by his own disdain for its innate dryness (Weldon 2007: 26–34). These efforts met with only partial success in large part due to the fact that the theme of an "affective connaturality" between the divine and the human on which such efforts are based is peripheral to Aquinas' central thought and, where present, is questionably endemic to human nature and so not clearly an innate human capacity as such connaturality would be with Jung.

So when he contacted Jung in 1945, White was hardly unfamiliar with the man he addressed or with the problem and challenge of correlating

Jung's psychology with his Catholic faith and its Thomistic elaboration. Given the Catholic theological climate in which he lived, his initial optimistic attitude could equally well be characterized as both "naïve" and somehow "courageous" without contradiction (Weldon 2007: 221–222). Jung reveals in his first letter to White in 1945 that White had initiated the relationship by sending to Jung certain of his writings on Jung's psychology and its correlation with theology. In this letter and in consequent early letters Jung expressed delight to be in dialogue with a Catholic priest and scholar and relates that on his instigation Catholic scholars such as Hugo Rahner, S.J. had been invited to the Eranos lectures (Jung 1945a: 381, 382, fns. 1, 2). Obviously Jung thought, at this early stage in their dialogue, that his psychology would receive a warmer welcome in Catholic than Protestant circles, where he allows he was still too often, "condemned as a heretic or depreciated as a mystic." He follows this typical remark with the comment that in Protestant circles mysticism and heresy enjoy "the same bad reputation" (Jung 1945a: 382).

Within two weeks, after having read White's material, Jung wrote to White that he is "the only theologian I know of who has really understood something of what the problem of psychology in our present world means. You have seen its enormous implications" (Jung 1945b: 383). These lines indicate that Jung appreciated White's realization that contemporary Catholic spirituality was no longer a vital force and that ecclesial theology contributed to its insipid condition. Jung's psychological remedy which would put the individual into an immediate experience of the divine through the archetypal unconscious was the apparent substance of the "enormous implications" of the question. This question was there from the first. Jung's remedy was one from which White was eventually to step back as incompatible with his conception of a supernatural transcendence. At this early point in the dialogue, however, Jung is almost effusive in his expression of gratitude at having in White, "a theologian, who is conscientious enough to weigh my opinions on the basis of a careful study of my writings!" (Jung 1945b: 383). Obviously Jung saw in White someone who understood his concerns about the state of the modern soul, at least within Catholicism, and with whom he could converse in the related areas of theology and psychology at a depth and with a sympathy not readily available in others.

In the course of their correspondence over the following fifteen years, many of the issues that touch on Jung's understanding of the relation of his psychology to religion and theology came into sharp relief with what appears in hindsight as a fateful progression. This second letter to White already raises issues which became central to the their entire discussion. One of these issues was the metaphysical status of Jung's psychology. "Metaphysical" in this context is an umbrella term Jung used to include both philosophy and statements of religious faith, especially when divorced from an experiential base. The term would extend to the entire content of theology. In this early letter Jung, in a slightly defensive if not evasive tone, explains that an early work, *Symbols of Transformation*, currently *Volume 5* in the *Collected Works*, was initially meant for a professional psychiatric readership by implication largely Freudian. It was in this context that he described God as a complex in this work, but by this, he assures White, he never meant to say that God was only a complex. As he was to do throughout the correspondence he here appeals to his empiricism which never makes statements about the "divine entity" but rests on empirical material gleaned from the expressions of the psyche implicating divinity (Jung 1945b: 384). At this stage in the development of his own thought, Jung might still have been sincerely able to conceive of his empirical observations of the numinous as the basis of his understanding of humanity's experience of the divine and to understand these observations as compatible with a divine "entity" behind them as somehow their author. In his later work on alchemy and on Job, the convenient distinction between the empirically documented subjectivity of numinous experience and an objective God beyond such experience yet perceived in it seems to be at least questionable if not wholly discounted.

Immediately after the above statement meant to assuage White's fear of the reduction of divinity to a complex, Jung writes two consecutive sentences that typify the ambivalence surrounding his repeated assertions that his psychology has no metaphysical or theological implications intrinsic to it. Already in this second letter to White, Jung makes a familiar claim, "It would therefore be unfair to criticize my opinions as if they were a philosophical system." In itself this is fair enough. But in the very next sentence he makes a statement laden with philosophical and theological import. He writes, "My personal view in this matter is that man's vital energy or libido is the divine *pneuma* all right and it was this conviction which it was my secret purpose to bring into the vicinity of my colleagues' understanding" (Jung 1945b: 384). Here Jung is presenting in a single sentence much of the import of his groundbreaking work, occasioning the split with Freud in the interests of the restoration of respect for the power and dignity of religious symbolism. In this work, it was precisely his understanding of archetypal libido as the energy at work creating the human experience of God, among other experiences, that differentiated Jung's psychology from Freud's and denied them forever a total compatibility. In a typical statement he writes in this work, "in God we honor the energy of the archetype" (Jung 1966a: 89).

In the context of this letter Jung obviously intends to assure White that he does not mean to reduce the reality of God to a complex and to enforce the reduction by giving to it philosophical grounding. But then he immediately identifies human "vital energy or libido" with "the divine pneuma" and admits that this was his "secret purpose" to get the point across to his religiously insensitive professional colleagues. One can either affirm or deny that the experience of libido, in certain intense configurations, is the experience of the divine *pneuma*, in this context meaning the spirit of God, but one cannot deny that the claim carries with it a philosophical import with profound theological implications. In fact we have here a bald statement of Jung's position that humanity's experience of archetypal libido with its attendant numinosity is the sole basis of humanity's experience of God. From Jung's viewpoint the basis in archetypal energies of humanity's experience of God is, then, empirically verifiable not only from the experience itself but also from evidence ultimately resting on the unity in variations of symbols which expressed, and so could induce, the experience of a divinely generated human totality. The experience of such totality was, for Jung, the substance of humanity as an image of God. Among such symbols the mandala reigns supreme. *"Individuation is the life in God*, as mandala psychology clearly shows" (Jung 1976d: 719, italics Jung's). At this point in the discussion, it suffices to point out that the connecting of the archetypally based experience of wholeness as the goal of psychic life with the experience of what believers term the "Holy Spirit" certainly entails a metaphysical position and, in the dialogue with White, came to be one of the points that proved unbridgeable.

Before he ends this paragraph Jung introduces a further position which runs throughout his work as it touches on religion and which is again fraught with metaphysical and theological import. This is the question of the nature of dogma itself. In capsule form, Jung's position on religious dogma, Christian or otherwise, is that originally it served to protect and convey the energies of the unconscious expressed primordially in symbol and myth in the creation of the religion itself. When functioning, dogma would thus not be far distant from a living symbol with all its power and ambiguity serving as a reflective preservation and intensification of the symbolic and mythic content on which dogma rested. Dogma would be an effort to elucidate the meaning and power of the symbol without sterilizing its impact. However, Christian dogma had, for Jung, lost its ability to mediate vital meaning because it had come to take itself and the myth it served literally and historically as a body of objective knowledge about a transcendent being and its incursions from beyond into the human scene. This "objective" meaning of dogma currently concealed rather than revealed whatever life dogma might have initially mediated. Jung elsewhere describes such a literal understanding of dogma as simply "sacrosanct unintelligibility" and "preposterous nonsense" for the modern mind (Jung 1969e: 109, 110). He is here opening up the problem with White which informs so much of his psychology of religion when he writes, "The bridge from dogma to the inner experience of the individual has broken down" (Jung 1968e: 178).

As a psychologist, Jung continues, he can document the experience and expressions of the self as the basis of religious experience and so as the substance of functioning dogma but he cannot do this in an expressly religious or theological idiom. This remains the task of the theologian like White. This position would mean that the truth of functioning dogma is the living and life-giving truth of the self whose expressions Jung can document as an empirical psychologist studying "the objective psyche", a synonym for the archetypal unconscious, and White can both preach and theologically expose as a theologian.

> But it is precisely what the theologian has to say, namely, that the dogma is the hitherto most perfect answer to and formulation of the most relevant items in the objective psyche and that God has worked all these things in man's soul.
>
> (Jung 1945b: 384, 385)

As these words imply, psychologist and theologian in dealing with dogma may indeed be dealing with an identical content under differing formalities, but, again, to say that the legitimate function of dogma is to mediate the energies of the deeper psyche, while accurate, is hardly divested of philosophical and theological import.

This early letter also evidences a shared hope that some kind of integration might take place between ecclesial dogma and psychology. Such integration might take its lead from the Catholic tradition of natural theology which used resources, usually a philosophical tradition such as the Platonic or Aristotelian not intrinsic to the revelation, in order to elucidate the revelation or to relate it more meaningfully to the conditions of contemporary culture. Thus Jung writes, "I would surely be among the first to welcome an explicit attempt to integrate the findings of psychology into the ecclesiastical doctrine" (Jung 1945b: 385). Such an integration of doctrine and psychology was ever close to Jung's own foundational apologetic concern to mediate to society a more adequate sense of religion and an accompanying living spirituality. But the enterprise itself leads to the question, raised in earlier chapters, whether ecclesially approved and mediated formulations of dogma can contain the breadth and depth of Jung's vision or whether his psychology appreciates them even as it undermines them toward a broader perspective? In short is the Christian imagination capable of incorporating Jung's and remaining itself if Jung imagines all mythic constellations to be variant expressions of their underlying archetypal origin?

Later in the letter Jung returns to his abiding concern over the societal pathology accompanying the widespread cultural loss of the symbolic sense and so of the living religiosity that, he implies at this stage in the conversation, Christianity could still provide the contemporary Christian. In his fuller thoughts on this issue, Jung felt that much of the validity of Christianity lay in its mythic depiction of divinely grounded absolute opposites made conscious in the Christ–Satan conflict. This preliminary but immensely valuable contribution of the myth was the basis of its need to be superceded by a myth now in the process of formulation which would unite the opposites that Christianity had made conscious but left unresolved in itself. In this context Jung feared that due to the literalism, externalism and historicism that contemporary Christianity continued to embrace, it ran the risk of premature self-discrediting and rejection especially with the educated and spiritually sensitive. There was a real threat that Christianity could be dismissed because of its loss of a sense of the symbolic before its valid function of identifying the self-contradiction in divine and human life and pointing to their joint resolution in human history was appropriated even by its constituency. Jung condenses all of these points when he writes in this early letter:

> *It is of the highest importance* that the educated and "enlightened" public should know religious truth as a thing living in the human soul and not as an abstruse and unreasonable relic of the past. People must be taught to see where they come in, otherwise you never bridge the gulf between the educated mind and the world of dogmatic ideas, which they comprehend nowhere and which moreover offend their reason . . . The appalling lack of understanding threatens the Christian religion with complete oblivion.
>
> (Jung 1945b: 387, italics Jung's)

Though written about Christianity, these remarks would equally apply to any religion which failed to take itself seriously by taking itself literally and historically to the detriment of its symbolic power.

Once again Jung's apology for both religion and Christianity asks: "Could Christianity endorse a Jungian sense of interiority, see itself as a relative expression of the self, understand itself as at least penultimate, currently seeking its own supersession, and remain itself?" As their dialogue developed, White remained unconvinced that it could, and Jung himself came to see that the full implications of his understanding of the psyche and its current and future development could not be confined to the Christian world view or to any religion that could not answer "Yes" to the above question. But in the warmth that attached to their early conversation such questions remained for the future. Jung concludes this letter by referring to his unconscious as an impersonal "it" which strongly endorsed the continuation of the dialogue: "Well – a long letter! Not my style at all. 'It' has made an exception in your case my dear Father, because 'it' has appreciated your conscientious and far-sighted work" (Jung 1945b: 387). White had engaged Jung's unconscious.

Thus it was no surprise that Jung invited White to spend some time with him at Bollingen, Jung's retreat on Lake Zurich, in August 1946, the first summer after the correspondence began. To receive such an invitation from Jung was, in the estimation of those who knew him, a sign of great favor. Apparently the stay went well. In his first letter to Jung after their initial meeting, White recounted a dream in which he was sailing from Norway to England through perilous waters driven by a strong wind with Jung at the helm. In terms of dream interpretation, it is interesting to note that White's sense of security in the dream rested primarily with the wind. Apparently he was propelled now by a spirit in whom he could trust and by a guide driven by the same spirit (Jung 1946a: 448, fn. 1).

In his reply Jung refers to the "risks" White is running and to their solidarity in running them. "We are indeed on an adventurous and dangerous journey!" (Jung 1946a: 448). Nothing is said of the precise nature of the danger. One can only assume they lay in the area of the integration of psychology and theology in the face of the opposition of religious orthodoxy from White's side and orthodox psychology and psychiatry from Jung's.

Later in November of that same year, 1946, Jung suffered a heart embolism. In December, candidly revealing his own natural spirituality, Jung thanked White for the latter's prayers, commended him on his "purity of purpose" and asks White to continue the correspondence (Jung 1946b: 449, 450). In March of the following year, 1947, Jung put the correspondence and the relationship on a first name basis, addressing White in a letter as "Dear Victor", and asking White to address him as "C.G." (Jung 1947a: 452). In April he invited White to stay with him again in Switzerland "in the style of last year". White was en route to the Eranos conference in Ascona where he was to present a paper on Thomas Aquinas (Jung 1947b: 458). Jung's friendship and respect for White, now elevated to the status of a colleague, were obviously deepening. White visited Jung again that summer at Kusnacht (Jung 1947c: 97) and went on to give a well-received lecture in Ascona.

These successes were followed by a year in the United States, a welcome relief from his teaching duties and a chance to travel and lecture widely in the United Sates (Cunningham 2007: 319, 320). During this year their correspondence continued to flow. In December 1947, Jung informs White that reflection on the self and on the specifically divine Christ as a symbol of the self consumed his current effort and writing. He notes that this reflection has driven him to deeper reflection on the second Christian millennium and elements in it like alchemy and mysticism which "threaten to overthrow the Christian aeon altogether" (Jung 1947d: 480, 481). This is the material on the self and Christ as an image of the self that was to appear in Jung's work on gnosticism and alchemy, now *Aion, Volume 9ii* of the *Collected Works*. Though White did not respond at this point in their dialogue, Jung is here introducing that side of his psychology which constitutes a full-blown philosophy of history and would also be offensive to White's conviction of the culmination of religious history in the Christ event. In Jung's thought on history and the history of religion, the Christian revelation, as all revelation, is a matter of collective compensation and so subject to the laws of the psyche (Jung 1966a: 65–71, 230). As such it is one instance of a compensatory process which will continue throughout human history as the source of history seeks an ever greater balanced incarnation in it. In the context of these presuppositions, Christianity, Jung argues consistently, was itself so one-sided, so possessed of an inherent "fatality", that its negation through supersession was implicit in its foundation (Jung 1968c: 43–45). In this letter Jung includes Western mysticism and alchemy as significant contributors to Christianity's historically necessitated surpassing of itself. At this point the implications of Jung's philosophy of history had yet to come between himself and White. On the contrary, before the year 1947 was out, Jung asked White to lend his name to the list of founders of the C.G. Jung Institute of Zurich. White agreed and thus became an early founding member of the institute (Jung 1947e: 481, 482, fn. 7).

In January of the new year, 1948, it is evident from the correspondence that White had tried to interest Rome in the new institute, apparently without much success (Jung 1948a: 490, fn. 1). This letter also makes it clear that Jung and White continued to trade dreams, some of which dealt explicitly with the substance of their conscious conversation. One of White's dreams prior to his meeting Jung strongly implied that the Holy Spirit addressed consciousness from a depth of the unconscious which articles of faith could not touch (White 1945: 108, 109). Jung read the dream to mean that the unconscious through the anima (in this case Jung's wife and a community of nuns in Zurich) was leading White into the depths from which the Spirit manifests to consciousness (Jung 1948a: 490). In this letter Jung gives a version of a dream of his father recorded also in *Memories, Dreams, Reflections* (Jung 1965a: 218, 219). In the pertinent part of the dream as recorded in his "autobiography", Jung is brought by his father into the presence of Uriah and is unable, unlike his father, to touch his forehead to the floor in a submissive bow to the Uriah figure. In his interpretation in his "autobiography" Jung's inability to bow to the floor reflects his inability to follow his father into Uriah's self-betraying submission to an external divine authority (Jung 1965a: 220). However, no mention of Uriah is made in his letter to White. Rather in this edition, Jung focuses on the locale of the dream, a room in which a Mogul Emperor of India, Akbar, engaged in ecumenical discussion with diverse schools of philosophers and theologians. The sacred power is not that of Uriah but simply that of a "supreme presence". And Jung simply awakens from the dream saying that indeed he did try to touch his forehead to the ground (Jung 1948a: 491, 492). The two versions of the dream raise the suspicion that Jung might have been witholding an element of the dream and changing its overall meaning in order to spare White its implications. For in the later version Jung preserved his mind and autonomy by deliberately refusing to touch his head to the ground in subservience to a human betrayed by his God or earthly representative. At the conclusion of his analysis of the dream in its later version, Jung sums up its meaning as referring to "the idea of the creature that surpasses its creator by a small but decisive factor" (Jung 1965a: 220). This would put the import of the dream far beyond the boundaries of White's theology and certainly White's consciousness in 1947 when White sent him his own dream of fidelity to his own in depth nature as the source of his truth and that of religious dogma.

The relationship continued to flourish throughout 1948. In May, Jung writes to White with enthusiasm over a lecture on gnosticism White had given to the Analytical Psychology Club of New York. Jung confesses the lecture drove him to questions of whether or not he had faith. He takes the position here as elsewhere that he is not the possessor of a faith he could "produce" but that rather he is the holder of a "respect" for a variety of religions that somehow is produced in him as a given, an obvious reference to his experience of the unconscious which cultivates a fascination for the archetypal power in the many traditions it creates in history. In the conclusion Jung expresses hope that he will again see White at Bollingen that summer, their third summer meeting in a row (Jung 1948b: 501–503).

Toward the end of 1948 Jung wrote a strange letter to White, which foreshadowed future difficulties. White had stayed with Jung in Switzerland for a week in September, the 6th to the 14th, after his return from the United States. On September 24, Jung wrote a letter to White shortly after the latter's departure. In it he thanks White for a defense White had made of Jung in an article appearing in *Commonweal* (Lammers et al. 2007: 127, fns. 60–63). Then Jung turns to a discussion of his research in the area of religion and psychology and asked for White's cooperation and a clarification about the theological meaning of the *anima Christi*, the soul of Christ (Jung 1948c: 506). All of this is very cordial and related to their common concerns. But between September and the following December Jung perceived that something was coming between them. Perhaps, as in his relation with Freud, he could feel that there were troubled times ahead. In a letter dated 16 December 1948, Jung writes, "I may be all wrong, but I confess to have a feeling as if when you were in America a door had been shut, softly but tightly" (Jung 1948d: 514). The letter in fact is something of a feeler asking as gently as possible for a response from White disclosing where he was in the relationship and pointing out that he has not heard from White since his departure from Switzerland that September. One must conclude that if Jung felt the door had been closed between them while White was in the United States, he must have perceived it when White was with him that September, 1948.

When Jung writes to White again in January 1949, his letter is warm and notes that White had in fact replied to Jung in response to Jung's request in the September letter for information on the *"anima Christi"*. Jung had simply forgotten about the letter even though he describes it here as "most helpful and comprehensive". But Jung's January letter itself points to something operative at a deeper psychological level between them, since Jung refers to synchronistic events in White's life on 16 December, the day that Jung wrote to him asking about his apparent remove (Jung 1949a: 516, 517, fn. 1). White must have told Jung of these events in his answering letter, now lost.

Jung's January letter implies that what may have been disturbing White was the relationship between his priesthood and his working as an analyst. This may be surmised from Jung's assuring him, "The combination of priest and medicine man is not so impossible as you seem to think. They are based upon a common archetype which will assert its right provided your inner development will continue as hitherto" (Jung 1949a: 517). The letter goes on to refer to White's confessed feelings of isolation in England which White must have revealed to Jung in a lost letter. Again one may surmise that his isolation may have been in large part induced by his efforts to bring the two roles of priest and analyst together in himself in an environment wholly unaware of the difficulty and necessity to do so at least for White at that moment. The risks involved in the integration of Jung's psychology and orthodox theology referred to in earlier correspondence were becoming all the more keenly felt. At letter's end Jung's encouragement to continue in this struggle takes the form of his suggestion to White to find a true brother in the spirit in his community with whom he could share openly his difficulties (Jung 1949a: 517).

Jung's intimation of future difficulties in his letter of December 1948 did prove prophetic. White had again spent some time with Jung in Switzerland in the summer of 1949, his fourth summer in a row. But by the end of 1949, in a letter written on New Year's Eve, the issue which was to prove insuperable, that of the *privatio boni* (evil) as the privation of good, surfaced for the first time in their correspondence (Jung 1949b: 539–541). It marked the appearance of that bone of contention which both were to pursue till it became mutually obvious that it was an issue neither could overcome despite the mutual recognition of each other's good will. It was the first major intractable difference between them and the basis from which most others developed.

The doctrine of the *privatio boni* was that Catholic theological doctrine which addressed the problem of evil by depicting evil as the privation of good, and so attributing to evil a kind of non-being understood as a distortion or absence of the good which ought to be present. The doctrine, given a favorable reading, is based on an essentialism which would locate the ultimate being and goodness of the existent in its essential inherence in divinity. As such the doctrine traces to Plato, Augustine and Aquinas. In essentialist logic, therefore, removal from, or willfully turning against, this essential groundedness in God constitutes evil, a distortion of the being and good of the existent, a diminution which could thus be termed nothingness or non-being. In Jung's own logic of individuation one could make the case that removal from or a wilful denial of the self's importunities to work a more compendious or supraordinate personality constituted a diminishment of the personality analogous to an option for non-being. White may have appealed to such an understanding when he contended in the following debate that evil as a privation of good is endemic to Jung's psychology itself. Needless to say, when the doctrine is read literally or out of the above context to mean that evil does not exist it is difficult to maintain in the face of daily evidence. Though seemingly remote from the world of psychology the issue came to reveal to both Jung and White how different were their conceptions of God and of the nature of God's presence to nature and particularly to the life and nature of the psyche. More, Jung may have been predisposed to deny the doctrine of evil as a privation of the good because he had worked with a client who apparently knew of the doctrine and used it as "a welcome sedative to his uneasy conscience" and an excuse for a questionable moral life (Jung 1969k: 304, 305).

The issue first appears in their correspondence in the context of White's critical review in *Dominican Studies* II: 4 October 1949, of certain of Jung's works which were included in the *Eranos Jarbücher*, 1947 and 1948, and were later to be published in *Aion, Volume 9ii*, of the *Collected Works* (Jung 1949b: 539, fn. 2). White's criticism had been harsh. It referred to Jung's "quasi-Manichean dualism" in his understanding of the relation of good to evil and to Jung's "somewhat confused and confusing pages . . . another infelicitous excursion of a great scientist outside his orbit . . . and a brief and unhappy encounter with scholastic thought" (Lammers et al. 2007: 140, fn. 26). There are, indeed, foundational elements in Jung's work which would consider any encounter with scholastic thought as unhappy for the modern because of the unconsciousness which attached to the medieval theological mind especially in its Thomistic form. Long before his conversation with White, Jung had already expressed his dismay that the Aristotelian mind had so taken over the West. In a letter dated 8 June 1942, he identifies Paracelsus as an exponent of a spiritual movement which "sought to reverse this turning away from our psychic origins as a result of Scholasticism and Aristotelianism" (Jung 1942: 317). However, given the harshness of White's criticism on this occasion, Jung's tone in responding is mild. He refers to White's criticism as a "*correctio fatuorum*", "a correction of fools" but goes on in this letter to touch on nearly all of his major objections to the conception of "*privatio boni*" (Jung 1949b: 539).

Apparently White's critique had pushed Jung in his theological researches. Under White's criticism Jung claims in this letter to have traced the idea that all evil originates with the human (thus attributing all good to God) to Basil the Great (330–379) (Jung 1949b: 540). Jung's point here is complex. It involves his archetypal theory which would place all significant opposites in an undifferentiated state in the collective unconscious or gnostic pleroma. Theologically this would mean that God as the source of nature and human nature is good and evil and that the human psyche reflects the reality of God in this respect. Effectively Jung is arguing that all that is manifest in creation is an expression of its divine ground which would mean that it reflects the originary source of good and evil in God. To attribute all good to God and all evil to the human is to engage in a dualism which denies the reality of evil in God and leaves the human with a negative inflation, i.e., convinced that humanity alone authors archetypal evil.

Jung argues in the letter that it is Christianity itself which has eternalized the reality of the devil, hell and eternal damnation and so made these evils very real, not simply a privation or diminution of the good. He insists that evil has a more than human origin arguing symbolically that the Serpent was in the garden prior to or at least alongside the human. On these grounds he denies that he is dualistic or Manichean. On the contrary he argues, with considerable justification, that Christianity is dualistic with the eternal division it drives between good and evil in its doctrine of the irredeemable nature of the demonic and of the eternal status of the damned. Against this Christian dualism Jung appeals to the "unity of the self", denied in its Christian variant through the absence of the dark principle in its God, in its Redeemer and in its eschatological eternal separation of the good from the damned (Jung 1949b: 540, 541). Jung restates this argument responding to White by name in his work on gnosticism, *Aion*. Here he appeals to his understanding of the self as uniting rather than eternalizing opposites to prove that "my leanings are therefore toward the very opposite of dualism" (Jung 1968c: 61, fn. 74). Jung writes the preface to *Aion* in May 1950, within five months of this letter to White in late 1949. Thus it is more than idle speculation to assume that the discussion with White helped sharpen the problematic at the heart of Jung's appropriation of gnosticism and of his thought on good and evil as opposites in humanity because of their presence in that which precedes and gives rise to human conscious-ness, for the gnostic, the pleroma and for the Christian, God. The same problem is present in Jung's appropriation of Boehme, who would also contend that opposites including good and evil grounded in the divine life stamp every creature and human consciousness.

The realization of the self in individual and history would thus work toward a conscious and historical differentiation and reunification of the opposites that exist as wholly undifferentiated in the unconscious. Such self-realization is a state of consciousness which goes beyond Christian dualism manifest, for instance, in the absolute breach it established between the being of God and of humanity and between good and evil as conflictual absolute opposites personified in Christ and Satan. Jung appreciates the Christian myth as differentiating the opposites of good and evil so dramatically and unequivocally in the personal imagery of Christ and Satan. But the self works to unite all opposites, once differentiated in consciousness. In its furthest reaches this position of Jung's as it applies to the problem of good and evil would mean some form of the unification of good and evil, whose best symbolic description in a Christian idiom would mean the unity of Christ and Satan. It was not a move that White could make as subsequent events revealed.

In this first letter addressed to the issue of the *privatio boni* Jung also refers to its social implications. This concern comes increasingly to the fore in his later letters to White where the political overtones are explicit. Here he argues that there is great urgency for modern consciousness to come to terms with the reality of evil or shadow, collectively and individually. What Jung means by this is that the contemporary mind must become aware of the human potential for evil originating in the depths of the human soul as it inheres in its ambivalent creator and so must refuse to go on giving evil extra-psychic origins or objectification. Failure to withdraw the projection of absolute evil would guarantee its continued projection onto conflicting or contradicting communities or individuals and so fund the continued effort to destroy them in the name of the eradication of evil. Jung writes and underlines: *"The future of mankind very much depends upon the recognition of the shadow*. Evil is – psychologically speaking – terribly real. It is a terrible mistake to diminish its power and reality even merely metaphysically"* (Jung 1949b: 541, italics Jung's). In the face of modern recurrences of "ethnic cleansing", genocidal intent if not reality, and ethnic warfare these lines continue to be profoundly relevant.

Though in this text Jung tends to dismiss the doctrine of evil as the privation of good as "merely metaphysical", it should be noted that there is a certain acknowledged metaphysic of his own operative in his dialogue with White, and beyond this dialogue in the broader implications of his psychology itself. He makes this explicit in a rather unusual passage for Jung, at least for that side of Jung that denied a metaphysical import to his own thought, when he writes, "I firmly believe however that psyche is *ousia*" (Jung 1949b: 540). Here he uses the Greek word that usually translates "substance" or "essence" and in Platonic forms of thought can refer to the ambiguous but eternal truth, real but concealed, of the existential being. What Jung means in this passage is that he attributes what must rightfully be called ontological status to the psyche and to the archetypes as the epistemological ground of humanity's residual sense of good and evil. In effect he is arguing that the presence in human consciousness of the opposites of good and evil bears witness to their presence in the creative precedent to consciousness. In simpler theological language this position would affirm the presence of the essences of good and of evil in God as the creative source of consciousness. In fact Jung is again explicit at letter's end that the grounding of essential good and evil in God as the ground of reality and consciousness is the only way to avoid Manichean dualism. He writes, "Thus you avoid a Manichean dualism without *petitiones principii* and other subterfuge. I guess I am a heretic" (Jung 1949b: 541). These lines then place essential evil as well as good in the reality of God.

In March 1950, White writes to Jung that the discussion on evil as a privation of good had reached a "deadlock". In this same letter he sends on a dream of himself and Jung at Bollingen. The dream centers on the differences of their perspective and ends with an anima figure on White's knee (White 1950: 149–151). In his answering letter, among other points the dream makes Jung suggests that the anima on his knee should indeed attract White's attention. He then returns to his understanding of the psyche as an essence or, more precisely, as the vessel of the essences. He continues that White's metaphysic "posits" while Jung's "doubts". And adds, "i.e., it [White's position] weighs mere names for insufficiently known *ousiae*". Here Jung uses the Greek term in its plural form and obviously means by these "essences" what he means by the archetypes which can never be known in themselves but only in the impact of their symbolic expression on consciousness and then never exhaustively. As such they can be approached only as powers whose cognitive appropriation is never so clear that it could preclude doubt and never so exhaustive as to affirm a final form. Doubt then becomes an element endemic to archetypal experience, as it is to all forms of a lively essentialism, whose fecundity perpetually refuses full expression in the narrow confines of consciousness. On the basis of this difference Jung thinks that White's approach turns the unconscious from an unmediated but always ambiguous experience of "the world of the unknown" into "a system of abstract conceptions". In short White lived in the head and its shallow clarity severed from the life of the essential. Yet in spite of the developing distance between the two men Jung extends to White his hospitality should he come to Switzerland in the near future (Jung 1950a: 152) and White did spend further time with Jung in Switzerland in August 1950 (Weldon 2007: 119, fn. 134).

The next major chasm between Jung and White opened over the Catholic dogma of the Assumption proclaimed on 15 August 1950. Though this event did not bear directly upon the issue of evil and its wider implications it did serve dramatically to illustrate the gulf between the interpretative principles that each man brought to his understanding of religious experience, its symbolism and their dogmatic expression. The first letter after the declaration begins with reference to an article White had written on the Assumption and forwarded to Jung (Lammers et al. 2007: 157, fn. 48). In the article White had distinguished between the particular, referring to the historical event of Mary's physical Assumption into heaven, and the universal, referring to its more universal archetypal meanings. Jung was much more impressed with White's category of the universal meaning of the Assumption, as an expression of archetypal reality, and wholly discounted any historical, literal or "particular" meaning (Jung 1950b: 566, 567).

For Jung the archetypal meaning of the declaration was its only meaning and the only one capable of engaging the psyche of the modern. To interpret it literally as an event in the past in which a physical body would be assumed into heaven would be for Jung to divest the doctrine of its spiritual meaning and reduce it to the level of a freakish historical incident irrelevant to the spiritual life of the present.

> If the miracle of the Assumption is not a living and present spiritual event, but consists of a physical phenomenon that is reported or only believed to have happened some 2000 years ago, then it has nothing to do with the spirit, or just as little as any parapsychological stunt of today.
>
> (Jung 1950b: 567)

These telling lines reveal Jung's hermeneutic to be based on the principle that the meaning of mythical events and their dogmatic preservation is to be lodged in the symbolic content of the affirmation. When it is not, the attendant literalism and historicism destroy or seriously maim the spiritual significance and so the very power of the symbol. This is more than implicit when Jung refers to the relativity of parthenogenetic mythology of which the Christian myth is one variant. "Why should one insist upon the historical reality of this particular case of a virgin birth and deny it to all the other mythological traditions?" (Jung 1950b: 567).

This remark illustrates an important hermeneutical implication of Jung's archetypal theory, namely, that any archetypal expression needs many manifestations in consciousness to approximate without ever emptying the full range of expression latent in the archetype. Why then isolate one such manifestation as literal, historical and unique and deny this status to its other variants? The reduction of an archetypal theme to a unique Virgin birth or Assumption by understanding them as historical and literal serves only to sever them from their archetypal variants and to strip them of spiritual meaning. Jung could have been more accommodating on this issue by contending that the variant of any mythologem will always be particular in its manifestation as one concretion of a universal latency in the archetypal psyche. In this manner do the universal and particular come to coincide in Jungian theory. Yet here Jung seems so taken aback by White's literalism that he does not make this point explicitly. Rather in this letter as elsewhere in his work, the only reason that Jung can attribute to the imposition of a literal, historical and unique interpretation upon a symbolic statement is the need to accommodate a gross mindset not capable of understanding symbolic discourse and so not capable of experiencing the spiritual energies that symbols bear unless they are reduced to literal statements and so stripped of their spiritual meaning and transformative power. Writes Jung,

I can only explain this peculiar tour de force as an attempt to prove the existence of the spirit to a coarse and primitive mind unable to grasp the psychic reality of an idea, a mind needing miracles as evidence of a spiritual presence.

(Jung 1950b: 567)

Not only are myths and symbols to be understood as expressions of the psyche, which function then to lead those they address into the psychic energies they carry, but also their eruption into consciousness can be understood in terms of compensation which throws considerable light on the time of their appearance in history. The same hermeneutical logic depicts the declaration of the Assumption by the papacy in 1950 as the culmination of a two thousand year old compensatory activity of "the living archetype forcing its way into consciousness" (Jung 1950b: 568). What the archetype was forcing into consciousness was the recovery of the divinity of the feminine in Christian symbolism of the Godhead. As Jung put it in this letter, Mary "has attained her place in the vicinity of the Deity" (Jung 1950b: 568). Jung adds that Christianity's recovery of its missing Goddess is the most significant religious event since the Reformation whose consequent unbalanced emphasis on the Word and consciousness the new dogma so thoroughly compensates. He writes:

If the A. means anything, it means a spiritual fact which can be formulated as the integration of the female principle into the Christian conception of the Godhead. This is certainly the most important religious development for 400 years.

(Jung 1950b: 567)

In an explicit rejection of White's effort to combine a personal and historical with an archetypal and symbolic dimension in the dogma, Jung wholly subsumes the literal meaning into the symbolic in order to show the spiritual meaning of the symbol of the Assumption in the context of its compensatory appearance in 1950 as defined by the Roman Church. This means that for Jung the "historical" actors, such as Jesus or Mary, his mother, in living myths have their individuality entirely subsumed into the myth that acts itself out through their lives so that all that remains for the beholder is their archetypal reality mythically portrayed. In a sense their lives are "historical" but it is only the myth that their lives occasion in history that is of spiritual import and lasting value. These principles would apply even to myths which have some claim to an "historical" origin such as Christianity and the other two monotheisms. Jung makes this point more explicitly in this letter to White than he does in many places through his work when he writes:

> When insisting on historicity you risk not only the most awkward and unanswerable questions, but you also help everybody to turn his eyes away from the essential idea to the realistic crudity of a merely physical phenomenon, as it is only physical phenomenon that happen in a distinct place at a distinct time, whereas the spirit is eternal and everywhere.
>
> (Jung 1950b: 568)

In reference to the Assumption, this would mean that the divinity of Mary and the feminine aspect of the divine are hardly confined to one historical woman but are universal traits of femininity and divinity. In 1950 the Trinity divested of the feminine from the outset stood in dire need of such compensation.

The Assumption letter was written in November 1950, but the theological difficulties lingered. In May 1952 Jung wrote a *Foreword* for White's work, *God and the Unconscious* (White 1960a; Jung 1969k). In it Jung is gracious and grateful to White for his theological collaboration on their common problem, the correlation of his empirical psychology with its implications for religion. Since White brings up the issue in the book, in the *Foreword* Jung clings to his position on the *privatio boni* issue, arguing that he grounds himself on the simple empirical fact of the reality of evil as the opposite of good and reaffirms that he remains unable to see any archetypal basis for the affirmation that evil is somehow a diminution of good (Jung 1969k: 304–306). In the *Foreword* he observes that current European society is peopled by "barbarians", by "medieval Christians", by a few who are as conscious as they could be and, again, by a few who are a few millennia ahead of their time (Jung 1969k: 308). Jung does not locate White on this spectrum but the middle two categories might well be appropriate.

Jung goes on to state that those who are locked in medieval categories should be allowed their medievalism and then brands as medieval the failure to recognize "metaphysical figures" as psychic realities (Jung 1969k: 309). By "metaphysical figures", in this context, Jung would include figures of divinity living in supernatural worlds or their representatives and incarnations in this one and is here deftly pointing to their psychogenetic origin. To supernaturalist positions, such as White's, the idea of the psychic origin of the deities was residually offensive. To Jung the alternative appeared medieval. Throughout the Spring of 1952, the issue of the *privatio boni* entered a number of letters as their positions hardened and clarified through the interchange (Lammers et al. 2007: 181–184, 186–188, 188–189, 198–200, 200–204). Against the backdrop of this intensifying debate the two men met in a watershed moment at Bollingen, 17–27 July 1952. Apparently no progress was made in overcoming their difficulties. The editors of the letters look upon this meeting as something of a turning point in the relationship. It led to a deepening "estrangement" in the following years only to dissolve shortly before White's death (Jung 1952b: 74, fn. 7).

The estrangement climaxed over the publication and content of Jung's work, *Answer to Job*. In a letter in early 1952, Jung mentions that he had sent a copy of the newly published German edition of *Answer to Job* to White (Jung 1952c: 51). In his response to Jung on 5 April, White has words of praise for the book which, as will be seen, are strangely at odds with his evaluation of it and of Jung's motives in publishing it a mere three years later with the appearance of the English edition. In 1952, however, White was able to describe the work as "the most exciting and moving book I have read in years: and somehow it arouses tremendous bonds of sympathy between us, and lights up all sorts of dark places both in the Scriptures and in my own psyche" (White 1952: 181). Prior to the final impasse over the publication of *Answer to Job* the discussion continued. The next year White thanks Jung and his wife for a period spent with them in the summer of 1953 at Bollingen (White 1953a: 215). But within two months, in a gripping confession to Jung, it becomes apparent that the truth of Jung's psychology is getting to White and causing an anguish that threatens to drive him out of the Dominican Order, the priesthood and his teaching role. He obviously could not square the experience of the psyche, especially through his dreams, with his theology and Catholic conviction. After citing the inadequacy of the Christ symbol as an adequate symbol of the self, a position central to Jung's psychology (Jung 1968c: 42–44), he lists the devastating personal consequences:

> I have come to realize how many of my friends and "analysants" I have positively helped to get out of the Church! Yet I am paid, I owe my bread and butter, to the alms and gifts of good Christians, who support me in my belief that I am a good Christian priest, labouring to bring all I can into the one Ark of Salvation. Their God isn't my God any more; my very clerical clothes have become a lie.
>
> (White 1953b: 216)

White goes on in this letter to admit the difficulties of starting a new life at 51, but feels he must leave his present situation to save his soul. His personal anguish could hardly be more intense. This letter preceded and provoked two of the most significant letters Jung wrote to White throughout their correspondence, those of 24 November, 1953 and 10 April, 1954. Together these letters comprise something of a compendium of Jung's thought, now obviously maturing through his dialogue with White, on the relation of religion to psyche.

Much of the first letter is a response to White's agony over Jung's implication that Christ is no longer a valid symbol of the self. Jung's intent is to assure White that the symbol of Christ is a still valuable symbol of the self even though it stands in need of a compensatory expansion to include what it currently lacks. He begins this long letter by telling White to forget dogma and to listen to what psychology has to say to his problem. From the psychological viewpoint he then proceeds to argue, "*Christ as a symbol is far from being invalid*" (Jung 1953a: 133, italics Jung's). Yet the conditions Jung attaches to its continued validity are at least challenging to orthodox positions. For he says immediately that the symbols of Christ and of Satan are equally legitimate sides of the self. Both have their origin in the unconscious which, when experienced, Jung equates with the experience of God the creator. "From the psychological standpoint the experience of God the creator is the perception of an overpowering impulse issuing from the sphere of the unconscious" (Jung 1953a: 134). Jung's psycho-theology of the creator flows immediately and organically into his psycho-theology of incarnation. For the creator, here called "Yaweh", is really neither good nor evil but wholly unconscious awaiting the disclosure of his nature through human reflection, and, in particular, human judgment which cannot avoid making conscious the opposites in the unconscious creator. "Thus Yaweh has either aspect because he is essentially the creator (primus motor) and because he is yet unreflected in his whole nature" (Jung 1953a: 134).

In relation to a more orthodox paradigm, it is difficult to escape the blatant implication of this statement that the creation of human consciousness is necessitated by deity's need to know itself in and through human reflection differentiating the opposites inherent in divinity itself. Indeed, for Jung, such differentiation and its synthesis is the base meaning of the history of consciousness and is the substance of the evolution of religious consciousness. Jung proceeds then to isolate and appreciate the specific meaning and contribution of the Christian myth to the process of divinity's becoming conscious in human consciousness. Christianity's immense contribution lies in its absolute severance or differentiation of the opposites of good and evil in the creator externalized in the symbols of the absolute opposition between Christ and Satan. "Thus the very first thing Christ must do is sever himself from his shadow and call it the devil (sorry, but the Gnostics of Iranaeus already knew it)" (Jung 1953a: 134–135).

This severance is for Jung an immense gain in consciousness for it is a powerful statement of the absolute opposition between good and evil made fully conscious, an opposition which was less acutely perceived prior to Christianity. This is what is meant in his statement, "It is a historical fact that the real devil only came into existence with Christ" (Jung 1953a: 134). Thus the conscious differentiation of the absolute contradiction between good and evil is Christianity's great contribution to the evolution of Western religious consciousness and the most valid reason for the retention of the symbol of Christ. As he here elaborates this point, Jung argues that consciousness and a sense of the good must be maintained, indeed given some priority, in humanity's current conscious task and burden following the differentiation of good and evil. This burden is eventually to unite the divine opposites that Christianity and reason have sundered and to unite them in human historical consciousness. This new moral obligation entails the assimilation of the divine shadow itself. Needless to say this can only be done if the light of consciousness, here described as a "candle", and the will not to be engulfed by the divine shadow are maintained. Jung writes:

> The next step is the problem of the shadow: in dealing with darkness, you must cling to the Good, otherwise the devil devours you. You need every bit of your goodness in dealing with Evil and just there. To keep the light alive in the darkness, that's the point, and only there your candle makes sense.
>
> (Jung 1953a: 135)

Thus Jung here and throughout his senior work validates the Christian myth as a statement both of the absolute opposition of Good and Evil in creator and creation and of the need to retain a firm commitment to consciousness and the good in the step which follows this differentiation, the assimilation in history of the divine darkness with the divine good, Christ and Satan in both individual and collectivity.

But the foregoing is not to deny that it is precisely here that Jung does intend a certain invalidation of the Christian symbol in a dialectic whose nuances are very profound but difficult adequately to capture and especially difficult for the Christian imagination to grasp or accept. This dialectic can be seen in one sentence in which he proclaims the Christian symbol as a powerful aid in society's coming to a realization of its shadow even as he admits that some, apparently unnamed contemporaries and certainly himself, may already anticipate the needed supersession of the symbol. This dimension of Jung's psychology must be understood as bearing an eschatology, that is an understanding of the direction or purpose of history, consistent with his understanding of psychological maturation, individual and collective. He writes:

> Our society cannot afford the luxury of cutting itself loose from the *imitatio Christi*, even if it should know that *the conflict with the shadow*, i.e., Christ versus Satan, is only the first step on the way to the far-away goal of the unity of the self in God.
>
> (Jung 1953a: 135, italics Jung's)

The thrust of this visionary passage is far from atypical. Rather it is representative of a foundational theme in Jung's mature psychology. From it one must conclude that he sees in the psychic dynamic, which he calls individuation, a movement toward the "unity of the self" both individually and collectively in which all opposites latent in the unconscious as a universal generator of consciousness, come first into conscious conflictual differentiation and then into conscious unification as the base meaning of atonement. This understanding of the dynamics of the self means that Jung's psychology identifies in the psyche itself that dynamic which gives rise to an eschatological consciousness and impulse understood as the self's drive to unite in consciousness the contradicting opposites which enliven the unconscious and divine life. This psychodynamic then would constitute the basis of humanity's haunting search for that state in which all enmity is dissolved in configurations of a final unity. The jarring note in Jung's thought is that he understands this imagery not only to derive from the dynamic of the psyche itself but also to point to a culmination in a universal maturation which would exclude nothing. For these reasons Jung endorses Origens's doctrine of the recapitulation of all things including the redemption of the demonic or evil. Indeed in his discussion with White, Jung introduces Origen as friendly to his psychology and as inimical to the dualism he sees in White's orthodoxy which had to reject the breadth of Origen's all inclusive "optimism" extended even to the redemption of the devil (Jung 1949b: 541).

As he continues Jung introduces, through the symbolism of the Holy Spirit, his understanding of the transcendent function. For Jung the transcendent function describes that work of the self which first constellates opposites and then works their unification through their suffering in a consciousness which transcends their conflict. The resolution of the opposites is never the work of the old and conflicted consciousness nor of consciousness at all. This is the meaning of Jung's oft repeated phrase, "*tertium non datur*" (the third is not given). The third in this phrase refers to the resolution of archetypally based conflict which is never given to rational solution or conscious effort but is worked by the self through the conflict of opposites which agonize the ego, indeed, lead to its temporary "complete abolition" prior to its rising to a higher or more encompassing consciousness uniting the opposites which bring on its death (Jung 1953a: 135). Jung's reference to the complete abolition of the ego points to the apophatic dimension of his understanding of the psyche. It aligns his psychology with that strain of mysticism which experiences momentary identity with God in a return to a divine nothingness in which ego consciousness undergoes a moment of obliteration in a state beyond any distinction between itself and the divine (Dourley 2004: 49–64).

In Jung's hermeneutic the symbol of the death and resurrection of Christ worked by the Holy Spirit becomes an impressive but hardly the only symbolic description of the major movements in the process of individuation. The symbol of the death of Christ between the opposites of acceptance and rejection points to the futility of the ego to resolve archetypal opposition by its own rational and limited capacity. Only the death of the suffering ego allows the birth of the myth or symbol which unites the opposites which worked the death. The new consciousness surpasses as it includes the conflicting opposites which give it birth through death, a process adequately caught by the specifically Christian symbol of resurrection though this is hardly the only symbol that points to the same process. Indeed from an Hegelian perspective, what Jung here describes is contained in Hegel's understanding of sublation. Resurrection in this context not only describes the new consciousness that arises consequent to the death of the ego into the unconscious and its happy return to consciousness, but also describes what Jung means by incarnation since in resurrection thus understood the self becomes more real or incarnate in the consciousness of the individual who has gone through this cycle. All of this is implied when Jung writes:

> He [the Holy Spirit] is the pneumatic state the creator attains to through the phase of incarnation. He is the experience of every individual that has undergone the complete abolition of his ego through the absolute opposition expressed by the symbol Christ versus Satan.
>
> (Jung 1953a: 135)

In this context Jung centers his remarks on the absolute opposition of Christ and Satan. There are many other forms of such opposition probably as numerous as the archetypally based suffering in every individual's life. Nevertheless this sentence contains Jung's entire psycho-theology since it identifies the psychic reality of creation, the meaning of incarnation, the meaning of redemptive suffering, the meaning of resurrection, the meaning of the Holy Spirit, and the psychic basis for the movement of humanity toward the eschatological realization of the "Oneness of the Holy Spirit", understood as "the restitution of the original oneness of the unconscious on the level of consciousness" (Jung 1953a: 135). The meaning of these religious themes shared in variation by a number of religions is grounded in the more profound movements of the psyche as their origin and referent.

Jung goes on to restate the paradox at the heart of his psychology and of his analysis of contemporaneity. On the one hand the symbol of Christ must be reaffirmed and its values clung to in the face of the "coming darkness", though this darkness itself is destined to be integrated in a manner which will transform both Christianity and its adversary. "The *adventus diaboli* does not invalidate the Christian symbol of the self, on the contrary: it complements it. It is a mysterious transmutation of both" (Jung 1953a: 136). In this letter, Jung does not clearly identify what the "coming darkness" might be. In certain passages one might assume it marks the advent of political collectivities whose archetypal possession would subsume the consciousness of their members and with it any moral responsibility toward each other. Nor does he do much here or elsewhere to describe more precisely how the union of Satan and Christ are to be worked and what forms their embrace could take. Perhaps it is unfair to press him on the specific content of a still emerging myth. He contributed significantly to its delineation in describing the present spiritual climate as crying out for it. In a general sense he does identify the integration of the shadow as the means by which it will come about and reaffirms that such an unlikely unity of good and evil along with other divinely grounded opposites will constitute a total unification of divine potentialities with human consciousness in history. In the mean time Jung recommends working to hinder the invalidation of the Christian symbol either through a premature rejection of its meaning by society or by those who now see beyond it to its supersession in a more inclusive myth. In this context the Church and its values are to be maintained "until it is understood what the assimilation of the shadow means" (Jung 1953a: 136).

It is on these grounds that Jung exhorts White to stay in the Church even if it means staying behind one's vision and, at the same time, not to be disturbed if his analysands leave the Church and if he continues to receive no support from it. The meaning of the Christian symbol, as a statement of the conflict of divine or absolute opposites destined to find a currently evasive historical resolution, is still valid for the contemporary (Jung 1953a: 137). Jung shows considerable humility in the face of the problem which his own psychology sets when he argues that White would be remiss if he were to abandon a symbol system out of the vision of that surpassing and future consciousness which as yet neither he nor White could adequately describe nor had personally "made real" (Jung 1953a: 137). This for Jung would not be an honest way to contribute to the emergence of the new consciousness, the age of the Spirit. On these grounds Jung urges White to stay in the Church as an enlightened interpreter both of the meaning of the Christ symbol and as one who sees the need for its supersession. Jung allows that even he in looking ahead must not destroy "the things that are" (Jung 1953a: 137).

> Thus making the statement that Christ is not a complete symbol of the self, I cannot make it complete by abolishing it. I must keep it therefore in order to build up the symbol of the perfect contradiction in God by adding this darkness to the *lumen de lumine*.
>
> (Jung 1953a: 137–138)

As noted, Jung leaves White and his reader with few details on how this is to come about beyond his extensive appreciation and criticism of the Christ symbol and the shadow it would have to embrace to become a symbol of wholeness.

The dialectical tension between an affirmation and a supersession of the symbol of Christ lies at the heart of Jung's concluding remarks in this seminal letter where he makes it clear that the completion of the Christian myth would indeed involve the eventual "invalidation of Christ". But this invalidation can be worked only by that same Spirit which constellated the symbol initially. In this context Jung compares himself to Joachim di Fiore, who anticipated in the twelfth century the coming of the age of the Spirit or Paraclete in the near future. Some independent argument could indeed be mounted that the thirteenth century was such a time. For Jung here depicts himself as a modern Joachim di Fiore proclaiming to his times that the Paraclete of the future will indeed bring about the "invalidation of Christ" by working a symbol and consciousness of the self which alleviates the one-sidedness of the Christian symbol through a much wider embrace of what is truly holy. But this is a work of the future even if demanded by the present. In the mean time one must suffer toward the new consciousness by under-going rather than fleeing the constriction and splits of Christian conscious-ness. "Christ is still the valid symbol. Only God himself can 'invalidate' him through the Paraclete" (Jung 1953a: 138). Jung leaves it clear that the psychic process of invalidation had begun in his time but remains, except in most general terms, ambiguous about its details.

White's response to this long letter was favorable. He wrote later in November 1953 of his gratitude for the letter and for Jung's suggestion that a futuristic ideal was no justification to flee present conflict (White 1953c: 223, 224). Apparently White mulled over the very rich letter throughout the winter. He wrote on 3 March 1954 that he agreed with most of it but could not see how it could be squared with "Catholic doctrine" (White 1954a: 228). In particular he had difficulties with Jung's conception of Christ's shadow. White's difficulties in this matter were due to his commitment to a very traditional Christology depicting the Christ figure as free of all shadow and so of any significant deficiency. The editors of the Jung letters indicate that the deficiency of greatest concern to White was the threat that Jung's Christology posed to the Christ figure's omniscience (Jung 1954b: 163, fn. 1). In this the editors are correct since Catholic tradition did assume that Christ was omniscient (White 1954a: 228, fn. 8). But White was also concerned about the much wider implications of Christ's shadow. In the footsteps of Christ he feared that both the individual Christian and institutional Christianity projected its shadow on other individuals and communities. Its constricted consciousness turned it into a "police state" currently obsessed by its major enemies, sex and communism. Furthermore White could no longer believe Catholicism's claim to be the sole source of salvation (White 1954a: 229). Once again he wonders if he can stay in his current position in all honesty even in the face of finding a job in a world beyond the Church for which he would be ill equipped (White 1954a: 230, 232).

Though the theological imagination supporting White's conception of a shadowless and omniscient Christ figure betrays a literal and infantile imagination, Jung tried to do with it what he could in his reply on 10 April, 1954. Jung labors to relate the meaning of Christ's omniscience to Christ's peculiar contact with the collective unconscious depicted in this letter as well as in his alchemical work and in his thinking on synchronicity as the ground of everything. Thus the Christ figure would depict an individual in whom the unity of the microcosmic and macrocosmic, the individual with the unconscious, would extend to all. "It is an astonishing fact, indeed, that the collective unconscious seems to be in contact with nearly everything" (Jung 1954b: 164). Christ as an archetype of the connectedness of the individual with the totality would be "far more divine than human, universal than individual" (Jung 1954b: 165). The reality of his universal connectedness becomes the basis, then, of the Christ figure's omniscience.

Whatever the merits of this explanation Jung takes up the same position in relation to Christ that he took in interpreting the Assumption. The figure of the Christ of the gospels is really a mythologem, in effect, a personification of the archetype of the self. Efforts to reduce this figure to an identifiable historical person have no support from the scriptures as historical documents because little biographical detail shows through their archetypal dress. More, to want to reduce the Christ figure to an historical personage is to divest that figure of its archetypal nature and so of its lasting and true power as a redeemer figure. Again Jung is affirming that what the religious mind calls redemption or salvation can only be worked by the power of the self expressed in the symbol and the energies it bears, not by a conscious turning to "historical" individuals or literal accounts of their exploits. For Jung this means that Christ is divine as a symbol of the divinity of the self, an historical variant of a universal truth and this is as it should be. Here Jung is close to the conclusion reached by generations of biblical scholars searching for the "historical Christ". He cannot be found behind the myth that soon enveloped him and an authentic religious sensitivity should not be engaged in such hero worship.

Jung goes on to restate the necessity of the split between absolute good and evil, the separation of Christ from his shadow, addressed in his previous letter to White. Here he turns again to the mystery and challenge consequent to this split at the heart of the Christian myth when he asks the question his psychology demands. "But how can absolute evil be connected and identified with absolute good?" (Jung 1954b: 166). In answering this question in this letter he elucidates his understanding of the psycho-symbolic meaning of Christ's death in ways that surpass his treatment of this theme in most of the *Collected Works* with the exception of his *Answer to Job*.

He begins his answer to the question he himself asks by referring to the transcendent function as that power of the self which bridges the unbridgeable by providing a unifying symbol whose power can work the needed synthesis between absolute opposites. In this letter Jung understands the symbol of the "cross" as just such a uniting symbol. Jung sees the Christ figure's union with the cross as a symbol of the union of a consciousness severed from nature and so from the depths of life with "the tree of life" and so with the whole-making power of the archetypal mother and her elemental powers compensating the Christ figure's "extreme spiritualiza-tion". In the process depicted by this symbolism the Christ figure dies to a pathological spiritual one-sidedness into a truly nourishing "nature", namely, the life and energy of the unconscious working toward a wholeness which negates through death and consequent resurrection the Christ figure's unbalanced spirituality removed from the totality nature would afford (Jung 1954b: 166, 167). The implication is that the recovery of the more fully natural is an ongoing agony for a disordered imbalance to the spiritual. Jung makes the same point elsewhere when he points to the need to crucify the overly spiritual Christ. "The Christ image fully corresponds to this situation: Christ is the perfect man who is crucified. One could hardly think of a truer picture of the goal of ethical endeavor" (Jung 1968c: 69). There may be a sardonic note in this statement. Implied is that ethical endeavor and even the attainment of moral perfection need to be crucified and in life usually are.

In any event the extended implication is that contemporary Christian consciousness itself is now to be crucified toward a resurrected conscious-ness of wider embrace. As he goes on in the letter Jung repeats the position of his previous letter and describes the need to take a strong conscious option for the Good even if such option is to undergo a crucifixion toward the birth of a now emerging myth which would embrace all that the Christ figure could not including Satan. Jung describes how this conscious option for the good is ultimately inadequate and cannot be held. "You must not get stuck with it, otherwise you grow out of life and die slowly" (Jung 1954b: 167). But this does not mean that one simply capitulates to evil. Rather in terms of cross-imagery it would mean that the death of a con-flicted and restricted consciousness becomes the occasion of the renewal of life through its descent into the compensating energies of the unconscious as a prelude to resurrection into a more balanced consciousness vested with a more extensive empathy, especially for those vast domains of the actual not held as sacred by the Christian myth.

In a line of argument characteristic of his psychology which rejects a more orthodox literalism by internalizing its import, Jung notes that Christian imagery identifies this "renewal" in a macabre fascination with post-temporal life. The problem is that "the solution takes place after death" (Jung 1954b: 167). But his alchemical work suggests to the contrary that the adept does not step through the "window into eternity", that is, into the next world as the locus of fulfillment but that such completion occurs, at least in approximation, in the here and now of finite life (Jung 1970: 471, 476). Again in his work on the Mass, Jung reworks the rite to suggest it enacts the full process of the death of the ego (Christ) into the unconscious and the death or at least suffering of the self (God) as it forsakes its eternal prerogatives for realization in the here and now where alone it becomes incarnate and self-conscious (Jung 1969c: 263).

This latter implication is perhaps the most important one contained in this letter. Jung makes it explicit here that the process he describes through the imagery of the death and resurrection of Christ is one in which individuals through the processes of unity with the unconscious worked by the self come into a conscious approximations of their personal divinity and in doing so contribute individually to the fulfillment of history. "This is a formidable secret and difficult to understand, because it means that man will be essentially God and God man" (Jung 1954b: 167).

Jung tries to delineate the wider collective meaning of this position by suggesting that the move into the age of Aquarius may resolve the contradictions symbolized by the image of Pisces and so will be an age of synthesis fostering a wider and so socially safer appropriation of the native divinity of humanity. Such a consciousness would be fully aware of the split in God, made manifest in such imagery as the split between Christ and Satan, the specific revelation of the age of Pisces. Such consciousness would also be aware of humanity's personal and historical responsibility to heal this and all archetypal splitting in itself (Jung 1954b: 167). This realization entails a new morality whose imperative is to work the unity of divine opposite in individual and historical consciousness. This vision leads Jung to suggest that such a consciousness in those in "visible positions" would have immense political implications. Communal leaders vested with such a spirit would forgo building community through the demonization of those united under different forms of archetypal cohesion and perceived as such as a hated collective shadow (Jung 1954b: 168). Intimations of this vision may already be present in, at least, campaign rhetoric in certain democracies though the vision may be hard to implement when power is attained in the face of set political faith positions.

At this point the letter takes on a more personal note and addresses some of the problems that White had shared with Jung regarding his vocation. Jung acknowledges that certain evils do exist in the Church, "Pharisaism, law consciousness, power drive, sex obsession, and the wrong kind of formalism", all of which greatly disturbed White (Jung 1954b: 168, 172). But Jung encourages him to remain faithful to his truth and to his introverted character. "A true and honest introverted thinking is a grace and possesses for a least a time divine authority, particularly if it is modest, simple and straight" (Jung 1954b: 168). Jung continues that loyalty to his truth had isolated White from the ecclesial collective, just as it had isolated Jung from the collective in which he lived. But rather than reject a religious institution and its congealed dogma, Jung advises White that the true assimilation of doctrine by the individual in any depth actually changes it. Superficial and literal acceptance of doctrine in the name of faith is for "corpses" whose faith affirmations are like a "gramophone record". However, a deeper appropriation of religious truth changes and enlivens it. "If, on the other hand, you truly assimilate the doctrine, you will alter it creatively by your individual understanding and thus give life to it" (Jung 1954b: 169).

As the letter continues, Jung moves to even more personal advice. He refers to a psychological practice, that of geomancy, the two had apparently practiced during one of White's visits to Bollingen to discern the processes at work in his becoming a monk. Jung describes the yield as drastic. But while suggesting to White that he may be in "the wrong place", he holds out to him the understanding that there may be a deeper meaning to his circumstances and that White might be one of those whom the Church attracts and hopes unconsciously "will be strong enough to carry its meaning and not its words into the future." He adds, "The man who allows the institution to swallow him is not a good servant" (Jung 1954b: 169, 170). He goes on to encourage White to remain in the Church in spite of his current suffering in order to raise its consciousness through his influence on those around him. "Doubt and insecurity are indispensable components of a complete life" (Jung 1954b: 171).

He further advises him to accept whatever dogmatic means tests White may then have been facing. Here Jung could be referring to the Oath Against Modernism, an arch conservative and reactionary oath Catholic academics then took against unacceptable forms of modern mostly theological thought. Moreover, as a Dominican in the Catholicism of the first half of the twentieth century, White would be forced to teach a form of twentieth century neo-Thomism which would be simply unaware or wary of the role of the unconscious in religious experience. Jung felt that White's conscious association with the unconscious would in itself be a transformative power in his environment of religious and theological unconsciousness. "Certain things transmit themselves by air when they are really needed" (Jung 1954b: 171). He concludes this section of the letter with the suggestion, "I should advocate an analytical attitude, which is permissible as well as honest, viz., take the Church as your ailing employer and your colleagues as the unconscious inmates of a hospital" (Jung 1954b: 172). White was to stand alone in an unconscious Church and religious community. In his response to this letter White informs Jung that it had been helpful and that he has decided to stay in his order and the priesthood (White 1954b: 243). The waters were temporarily calmed.

The following year, 1955, saw the break in the relationship which lasted into the year prior to White's death. White had become the leading candidate for the position of Regent of Studies at the Dominican studium at Oxford. The position was denied to him either through opposition from conservatives within the Order or probably by a conservative Holy Office in Rome opposed to liberal thought in all its forms (Cunningham 2007: 322–326). Instead he was asked to go to the Dominican house in Oakland, California, for five months. He writes of this turn of events to Jung: "I am still very much in the dark both about why I have been moved, and what I am supposed to do when I get there" (White 1954c: 247). Apparently he soon became busily engaged in lecturing on the relation of religion to psychology and psychiatry. However, in a letter early in January 1955, White anticipates the storm brewing over *Answer to Job*. "I am frankly rather relieved that 'Answer to Job' has not yet appeared in USA! It would queer my pitch rather badly among these mostly very naïve, but very well meaning Catholics" (White 1955a: 254). Jung could hardly have been more prescient in his response: "I know you will have some difficulties when my 'Answer to Job' becomes public. I am sorry" (Jung 1955a: 213). Yet in the same letter he twice expresses happy anticipation at seeing White again in April in Switzerland. White was to lecture at the institute that spring.

Just how right Jung was in his anticipation of White's discomfort with his *Answer to Job* is born out in White's next letter to him. On 17 March 1955, while returning from the United States on the *Queen Mary*, White wrote to Jung expressing his grave reservations about the wisdom of publishing the English version of *Answer to Job*, which he was to review harshly in the March issue of *Blackfriars* (White 1955b: 259, 349–356). In this review White goes beyond the boundaries of academic criticism to personal attacks on Jung, attacks he was to delete when he was to republish the review in a later work (White 1955b: 259, fn. 23). Even at this early date White confesses, "Even so there are passages I would now wish to have kept to myself" (White 1955a: 259). In this letter White affirms that when Jung gave him the manuscript of his work on Job, Jung assured him that he would not publish it. There is no such evidence of any such assurance on Jung's part anywhere (White 1955b: 259, fn. 24). His position is now a far cry from his initial enthusiasm on reading a version of the work three years earlier. He writes in his letter of 17 March:

> I just do not understand what is to be gained by the publication of such an outburst [*Answer to Job*]. I can only see harm coming out of it, not least to my own efforts to make analytical psychology acceptable to, and respected by, the Catholics and other Christians who need it so badly.
>
> (White 1955b: 259)

One is left to wonder why White thought that Catholics and Christians then stood in such great need of Jung's psychology. One suspects that White shared Jung's insight that the insipid state of collective Catholic and Christian spirituality could not offer what its constituency needed out of resources endemic to it, at least not in the same way a direct dialogue with the unconscious could. But White had to hide from himself, or at least not bring fully to his own consciousness, that Jung's psychology so greatly needed, in his opinion, by the contemporary Christian could not be contained within the confines of Christian orthodoxy. In spite of his own professed agony over the issue, he had yet to realize that Jungian psychology into Christianity simply does not reduce. To become perfectly clear on this issue White would have to face the deepest question in his differences with Jung. The question was whether Christianity could mediate to its followers a spirituality deriving from an unmediated dialogue with the unconscious and what it then and still urged and remain true to itself and to its foundational mythical and dogmatic affirmations and practice. Rather would Catholic Christianity not have to admit, as White never could, that the recovery of its health lay in the recovery of what it had excluded as heresy in the historical processes of its own self-making and truncation? And if it refused or was unable so to recover its lost, or never wholly attained wholeness, would not such failure provoke a situation, as it did in White himself, forcing those who grew up within it to grow out of it or beyond it in the name of their spiritual maturity and even sanity? The publication of his work on Job would make these questions and Jung's answer to them inescapably clear even to a sympathetic though theologically traditional conversant such as White.

Jung replied that he would not apologize for publishing the work even though it might cause some disturbance in theological circles (Jung 1955b: 239). In fact Jung's initial response demonstrates the political relevance of his psychology. For he begins his defense by affirming that he had to surface the theme of divine self-contradiction as it impacted on history to counter the current conflicts propelling humanity toward "impending world catastrophe" (Jung 1955b: 239). This initial response and defense clearly shows Jung's concern for the contemporary political situation of the Cold War where political absolutes in conflict could terminate humanity itself. This response also shows that Jung felt his psychology could contribute to the resolution of the clash of powerful political opposites by making each relative to a future synthesis enriched by their unification. At the very least the demonstration that religious and political faith shared the same origin and posed the same threat to the survival of humanity is obvious.

At a more personal level he twice accuses White of misrepresenting his motives in White's offensive review. He writes, "Your criticism of my motive concerning Job is certainly unjust and you know it" (Jung 1955b: 241). He sympathizes with White's plight caught personally and theologically with the problem of a divinity conflicted in itself whose conflicted nature White could neither affirm theologically nor avoid psychologically. From Jung's point of view, White's only way out of his suffering lay in fidelity to the demands of his self wherever that might take him. For Jung, the work on Job remained but "a straightforward application of my psychological principles to certain central problems of our religion" (Jung 1955b: 241). Jung denies, as White had suggested in his March letter, that the work was a matter of spleen and concludes by asking White to look at his own temper (Jung 1955b: 242).

In remarks that come, for the first time in their dialogue, perilously close to an attack on White's person, Jung points out that his social independence gives him an intellectual freedom which White, as a member of a Catholic religious order, did not have. Here Jung, in considerable tension with his earlier exhortations to White to remain in the order, includes White among those afflicted with the puerility of the motherbound living in a pattern of physical and intellectual dependency on the Church. Their true opinions must be guarded as the price they pay for "being fed by an institution for services rendered" (Jung 1955b: 242). These latter remarks, though scathing in terms of Jung's understanding of the negative psychology attached to dependency patterns of any kind, may hint that Jung, even at this point in their relationship, felt that White might have remained privately appreciative of his work on Job but could not voice his appreciation because of his position in the Church and his dependence on it. To do so would be to risk his "social existence" (Jung 1955b: 242). The state of growing alienation may be indicated in the conclusion of the letter. Jung states that he will be at Bollingen when White arrives to lecture at the Jung Institute that spring and extends an invitation to stay with him at his house in Kusnacht, and not at his private retreat in Bollingen where previously he had always stayed (Jung 1955b: 243).

Such a stay was never to happen. While White was lecturing at the institute that spring, Jung wrote in a brief letter on 6 May, 1955 that his wife was recovering from an operation and adds somewhat cryptically that since he continued to be the "cause of much discomfort " to White, he would leave it up to White as to whether they met. In the letter Jung says he is not interested in a "conventional" call and that "a straightforward talk may be painful and not desirable" (Jung 1955c: 251). But White seemed undeterred in his pursuit of the many issues he had with Jung. On 10 May, 1955, White forwarded to Jung a formal agenda of five extended points around which their meeting would turn. They read like an inquisitor's indictment but do clearly illustrate how unacceptable to White's theology Jung's position was, even though some of the foundational points in Jung's psychology are, at best, tenuously grasped by White even at this late date (White 1955c: 267–272). The meeting was never to materialize. At the time Jung was caring for his wife Emma, who was to die from cancer later in that year. Their only meeting was at a convalescent home where Emma was a patient. In a letter of 21 May, 1955, White writes after that meeting that he had lacked a certain tact, indeed, had been ruthless in pursuing his intellectual difficulties while Jung was himself so stressed with his wife's illness (White 1955d: 272). He indicates that he must now work on his problems by himself. And yet the tone of an enduring friendship deeper than their disagreement is well captured in White's lines:

> perhaps . . . I may tell you how deeply I feel with you personally in this wrestle with the Divine Mysteries and with Brother Death. I must leave the outcome trustingly to them and to your own fearless honesty and

humility . . . For myself, it seems that our ways must, at least to some extent, part. I shall never forget and, please God I shall never lose, what I owe to your work & your friendship.

(White 1955d: 272, 273)

In some tension with these words White reveals the volatility of his state when he concludes the letter with words somewhat confirming his confessed ruthlessness: "The horrible impression has come upon me in Zurich (I hope it is wrong) that my dear C.G. has around him only sycophants & flatterers: or people requiring audiences or transferences which no mortal can carry" (White 1955d: 273).

From May 1955 till late October 1959, within a year of White's death, Jung wrote no further to White, though White occasionally wrote to him (Jung 1955c: 251, fn. 1). They were to meet once more, in June 1958. White refers to the meeting in a letter in which he thanks Jung for giving so generously of his time (White 1958: 277). No mention is made on this occasion of the religious issues that had divided the two after then thirteen years of discussion.

On 17 April, 1959 White was seriously injured in a motorcycle accident. In July, Mother Michael of the Blessed Trinity, the Prioress of a contemplative Carmelite Order in Presteigne, wrote to Jung assuring him that White did not wholly disapprove of Jung's psychology (Weldon 2007: 210). White had been associated with her community for some time. Jung wrote back to the Prioress in September glad that White did not "fully disapprove of my work" (Jung 1959a: 516). The prioress relayed these reconciliatory remarks to White and he wrote to Jung in October. In this letter he fully affirms that he could never wholly disapprove of Jung's work. In fact his approval of it had earned him Rome's disapproval and put his future in doubt. At the time there were efforts being made to remove ecclesial approval of his then out of print *God and the Unconscious* (White 1959: 281, fn. 6). Jung reveals in his reply that in the light of White's public negativity he was puzzled as to where White really stood. "Concerning my doubts about your general attitude I must mention in self-defense that you expressed yourself publicly in such a negative way about my work that I really did not know what your real attitude would be" (Jung 1959c: 518). Even at this late date Jung apparently was uncertain where White stood personally.

On 18 March, 1960, White wrote to Jung informing him that he had had an operation for a malignant growth in the intestines. It was in fact cancer. In this letter White claims he cannot identify the negativity Jung referred to in his last letter. Apparently White had forgotten about the review of *Answer to Job* in 1955 whose offending sections he had to remove from his *Soul and Psyche* just then coming out. Again he once more expresses gratitude to Jung for all Jung has given him (White 1960b: 283). In a truly astonishing letter,

Jung, apparently unaware of the gravity of White's physical condition, continued the debate with him on the now residual issues. In January 1959, White had written a review of Jung's *Psychology and Religion, Volume 11*, of the *Collected Works* for the *Journal of Analytical Psychology* in which he had argued that Jung's understanding of archetypal reality provided an excuse to attribute one's personal difficulties to the gods and "put the blame on them" often at the cost of ignoring elementary, that is, personal, psychology altogether (Jung 1960a: 545, fn. 3). Jung's reply was that White was accusing him in effect of "appealing to the archetypes first and omitting the shadow". The brunt of Jung's response is to the effect that indeed the personal shadow must be faced but that the shadow is more than personal and cannot be adequately understood and addressed unless its archetypal ground is also addressed (Jung 1960a: 544–546).

Even in this final exchange over matters of substance, and engaging the problem of evil one final time, Jung refused to reduce the shadow to personal shadow. Jung defends his hypothesis of the archetypes and by implication of the archetypal shadow whose denial would involve the individual in a negative inflation attributing all evil to oneself and all good to God. In this letter Jung argues that such strategy results in despair or resignation over purely personal failure and circumstances. This is where exclusively personalistic psychologies devoid of the sense of the archetypal end and Jung here extends this fate to Freud and his psychology. The basic thrust of the letter is that White has failed to achieve an archetypal viewpoint and so is condemned to a limited personalistic view. It was rather an aggressive letter to write to a correspondent afflicted with terminal cancer, even though Jung admits in the letter it was prompted by the aggressiveness in White's review of his work (Jung 1960a: 546). Jung did explain to the same Mother Prioress after White's death that he did not yet know at the time of the writing of "the seriousness of the condition" (Jung 1960b: 604). Prior to White's death he would have gone to England, claimed Jung, to "reassure him of my feeling", had it not been for his advanced age of 85 (Jung 1960c: 552). In a letter to a mutual friend about his late critical letter, he confesses that "I had sinned against my better insight" but that even that late letter was in the spirit of asking for forgiveness and to offer him some "relief" in his situation (Jung 1960d: 563). Jung himself was to write to White on 30 April, weeks before he died, advising him not to be worried about his last critical letter of 25 March. In this letter he makes a final statement of his good will toward White. "I want to assure you of my loyal friendship. I shall not forget all the useful things I have learned through our many talks and through your forbearance with me" (Jung 1960e: 555).

White replied to Jung's letter of 25 March with a letter dated 6 May, 1960, sent with an accompanying letter dated 8 May in response to Jung's last letter of 30 April. (White 1960c: 289, fns. 32, 33). In the first letter White refers to the misunderstandings which continue between them, culminating in the publication of *Answer to Job*. Again he repeats his unsustainable conviction that Jung had agreed not to publish the work. He admits that the shadow has an archetypal aspect but that it always has to be faced at the personal level. Though the differences remain, White sounds the profoundly reconciliatory note of the letter in its opening lines. He longs for another impossible face-to-face dialogue "as in times gone by". And he brings the tragedy of their parting to an emotional peak as he continues: "And such are our several conditions that it seems unlikely that we shall be able to meet and talk again in this world" (White 1960c: 289). In his second letter White's last words to Jung remain: "May I add that I pray with all my heart for your well-being, whatever that may be in the eyes of God. Ever yours cordially and affectionately, Victor White" (White 1960d: 292). Their mutual friendship and loyalty intact to the end, White died on 22 May, 1960.

Prior to White's death Jung revealed in a letter to the Prioress that he had considered "in vain" that White might be the candidate to carry on his "*opus magnum*", his psychology itself (Jung 1960f: 536). In the wake of White's death, in a letter written to Catherine Kusler-Ginsberg, who with her lay community cared for White in his final days, Jung acknowledges how he felt in himself a tragic inability to get to White's mind. "I was at the end of my resources and had to leave him *nolens volens* to the decree of his fate. I saw that his arguments were valid for him and allowed of no other development." Later in the letter Jung implies that the historical background which had formed White's mind made it impossible for Jung to "pierce through to his understanding". In a deeper, almost sinister note, he hints that the gravity of the questions that were raised between them proved for White, as for others gifted with a tortured spiritual sensitivity, to be "a matter of life and death". Jung suggests that it will take many centuries to make acceptable the insights he could not successfully convey to White which might have changed the outcome of his life:

> As I have so earnestly shared in his life and inner development, his death has become another tragic experience to me. To us limits are set which we cannot overstep, not in our time. Perhaps what has evolved in the course of the centuries will not cease to be active for just as long a span. It may take many hundreds of years for certain insights to mature.
>
> (Jung 1960d: 563)

Here Jung suggests that the acceptance of the perspective, and especially the perspective on religion, his psychology fostered is centuries away from widespread acceptance.

In an earlier letter written to the Prioress, Jung spells out in terms that cannot be misunderstood just what was at stake in his dialogue with White and by extension what may be at stake in wider society over the issues they raised at a personal level. Jung writes that he has seen others who have died in times of radical change and who in some sense seem to slip into death rather than engage in the adventure and challenge of a different spiritual future.

> I have now seen quite a number of people die in the time of a great transition, reaching as it were the end of the pilgrimage in sight of the Gates, where the way bifurcates to the land of Hereafter and to the future of mankind and its spiritual adventure.
>
> (Jung 1960b: 604)

To accept Jung's psychology would have cost White his faith. To reject it and with it humanity's future spirituality, cost him his life. Nor is this reading an isolated one. It has been supported by others (Weldon 2007: 233). Moreover, these passages link White's questions to humanity's. They infer that Jung felt contemporary humanity was on the brink of a radically new spiritual possibility to which his psychology was a significant contributor even though its fuller acceptance would be a matter for the centuries. It was this spiritual adventure which death, aided by his theology, denied to White.

On White's limitations, especially around the question of evil, Jung in the late 1950s was to write in a harsher vein:

> What Victor White writes about the assimilation of the shadow is not to be taken seriously. Being a Catholic priest he is bound hand and foot to the doctrine of his Church and has to defend every syllogism.
>
> (Jung 1976d: 710)

What is crucial to understand is what Jung meant by "shadow" in this citation and so what it was that White could not assimilate. Tracing the major lines of development in their conversation, the shadow that White could not assimilate are foundational points in Jung's psychology summed up in his late *Answer to Job*. Murray Stein reads this work accurately when he notes that while it may be an answer to Job it is Jung's definitive answer to White himself provoked by their dialogue (Stein 2007: x). It was an answer incompatible with White's theology and by extension, with any theology based on the supernatural/natural split and the one-sided divinity such split endorses in the still reigning theisms.

What then in Jung's *Answer to Job* proved an unassimilable shadow to White's theology? In this work Jung makes it clear that humanity's relation to the divine is the ego's relation to the archetypal unconscious. Whether a self-sufficient God or divine entity exists beyond the psyche or not this God's sole means of revelation to the human is through the psyche. That no such entity does exist beyond the psyche is both suggested if not demanded by Jung's theology of incarnation and philosophy of history in this late work. The unconscious impelled by the self is forced to create consciousness in order to know itself and its antinomial life through human consciousness. Only in historical consciousness can the divine self-contradiction be perceived and resolved. Suffering toward its resolution is the base meaning of history's movement, its eschatology and teleology, and this resolution would involve the embrace of good and evil, as well as all archetypally grounded polarities, in a consciousness transcending each opposite in itself.

In religious language God and humanity are involved from the outset in processes of mutual redemption. In religious-psychological language the goal of the process becomes a utopian state in which the unconscious would be exhaustively expressed in consciousness, the biblical equivalent of "God all in all" (1 Corinthinas 15: 28). Though this is a state which can never be achieved but only approximated in finitude it is a state toward which the psyche naturally drives. Its allure is beyond human realization or evasion. Effectively it can be approximated only through the dangerous process of responsibly ushering the divine urgencies of archetypal energy into personal and collective consciousness, a process of educating God through human history. In this context Christianity as a necessarily one-sided compensation toward the spiritual contains within itself the seeds of its own surpassing. In Jung's mind the compensation Christianity now itself needs is to be found within its own canon in the imagery of the sun woman of the Book of Revelation giving birth to her son and so reuniting the human with the totality of nature from which Christianity had, for an epoch, to remove it (Jung 1969d: 438–444, 453, 458, 459). Because it unites divinity and humanity in a religious and historical evolution of religious consciousness, Jung's late religious and philosophical world view eliminates all forms of supernaturalism that would imagine a self-sufficient God existing over against creation and addressing if from without. Such a creation would then be reduced to a divine afterthought since such a God could have no stake in the outcome of the historical drama. The latent iconoclasm of such a stance is hostile to any religious or political claim to possesses the ultimate revelation exhaustive of the source of revelation in the unconscious though in effect all monotheisms do. The relativism of Jung's position renders such claims less lethal and opens them to a promising mutual compassion for all religious expressions of their origin in the archetypal unconscious.

All these positions central to Jung's mature work are hostile to White's theological and philosophical stance as they were to Buber's and as they remain to all forms of monotheistic orthodoxy. The foregoing is the substance of the shadow that White could not assimilate and which the monotheistic mind still cannot. Today in the face of the ever more obvious connection of violence with religion, the quest grows ever more intense for salvation from religions rather than through them. The Jungian response would be a more sustained and widespread attention to the powers previously associated with a divine beyond to a more immediate experience of the divine within as the source of all divinity and as the font of a now emerging and surpassing myth. Such a myth would foster greatly expanded compassion between archetypally bonded communities as partial expression of a power that births and transcends them all. Whether such a turn will occur remains a question but an analysis of the devastation left in the footsteps of the Gods as they escape psychic containment lies well within the corpus Jung has left humanity. To such an analysis the following chapter turns.

Chapter 6

The mystical fool and why the killing must go on

The paradox

The incompatibility of Jung's psychology with any form of traditional monotheism or simple theism has far reaching political implications. A frequently heard criticism of Jungian psychology attacks its allegedly solipsistic individualism. Such criticism fails to distinguish an unrelated individualism from the process of maturation Jung describes as "individuation". This latter process is hostile to an isolated individualism because it rests on the experience and agency of the ground of the individual psyche as the source of consciousness universally. Intercourse with such an agency breeds in and of itself a universal sentiment and a compassion as encompassing as the universality of its ground. This same ground is also the source of archetypal patterns of social, political and religious bonding needed by every society as the basis of its social cohesion. However, this very bonding needed as a community's support can also be its coffin. Latently such cohesion can induce in its members an unconscious adhesion to its values whose intensity is frequently directly proportionate to its aversion for differently bonded communities. More, Jungian psychology understands the unconscious to seek historical archetypal realization in individual and archetypally bonded communities in such a manner that no realization of individual or communal archetypal expression can ever exhaust the source of such expression. The final kingdom can never come.

Consequently this aspect of Jung's social psychology is profoundly iconoclastic. Rather than being apolitical or divested of social concern, Jung's understanding of the psyche is, in fact, subtly but powerfully anarchic because it is thoroughly subversive of all claims by any collectivity or individual to the possession of a political, religious, ethnic or cultural absolute truth within the confines of history. The corrosive nature of the archetypal psyche toward all such absolute claims is based on the inability of any archetypal expression to exhaust its source. As the previous chapters suggest, these elements of Jungian psychology are evident in Jung's rejection of both Buber's and White's theological positions. Both would claim that their particular Gods were absolutes in themselves. They demanded an absolute adherence on the part of the communities they privileged in history whose mission was then to submit the world to their absolute.

As will be seen, Jungian psychology extends religious faith to political faith and denies an absolute truth to both. Where this denial goes unheeded Jung can then indict both unqualified religious and political faith with collective unconsciousness and so as a threat to a wider humanity. Nowhere is this concern for the social implications of archetypal power so evident as in Jung's first response to White on White's admonishing him for publishing *Answer to Job*. Jung answers that he felt compelled to publish the work to offset "the drift towards the impending world catastrophe" (Jung 1955b: 261). Jung's point was that unless humanity became aware of the archetypal origin and power, in this case, in the conflicting political faiths of the Cold War, those faiths themselves could destroy it.

It is in this sense that Jung argues that humanity is now morally compelled to attend to the psychic origin of its religious and political beliefs and to look to this same origin for the possibility of transcending the current conflicting constellations of religious and political faith. He writes, "Everything now depends on man" (Jung 1969d: 459). He goes on immediately to explain that the resolution of divinely based conflicts, personally, religiously and politically, now becomes the basis of a new morality and so the substance of humanity's "new responsibility" (Jung 1969d: 461).

This ethical responsibility has to face the paradox at the heart of the human psyche as the origin of social organization. The inescapable need of each society to rest on an absolute archetypal affirmation beyond the possibility of historical realization points to a profound problem in humanity itself and in Jung's understanding of the working of the political psyche. The psychological impossibility of any civilization and its supportive archetypal foundation, whether explicitly religious or not, to give exhaustive expression to its creator, the archetypal unconscious, coupled with the implicit claims of every civilization that, in fact, they do, points to a dark, possibly insoluble paradox, at the heart of the human plight clearly identified by Jung's social psychology. All civilizations, past and present, owe their existence and endurance to archetypal bonding expressed in their religions or functional equivalents currently often particularly well disguised in so called "secularism". Secularism may well indeed promote values which transcend those promoted by institutional religions but the promotion of such values itself takes on a religious zeal and can be as devastating as religion itself in its proselytizing and political activity especially when militarily supported. Whether explicitly religious or in secular form, archetypal bonding works a double effect. It at once legitimizes the society's claimed cultural supremacy and usual missionary zeal among and toward other societies, but, in so doing, such bonding inevitably carries with it a latent hatred of differently bonded societies. The hatred need not become actual but it is undeniably present as possibility in the archetypal foundations of communities thus bonded and all are.

The ambivalence of archetypal bonding rests on Jung's clear conviction that such bonding lowers the consciousness of those bonded in direct proportion to its bonding intensity. The greater the commitment such bonding works the lesser the individual consciousness of the bonded. With the lowering of collective consciousness comes an attendant and inevitable lowering of the moral responsibility of the group and so of the individuals in the group. The psychodynamic Jung here describes leads to the following grim psychosocial law. Effective social cohesion is based on archetypal energies which breed an immoral or at least amoral unconsciousness in direct proportion to the strength of the social cohesion they provide. This cohesion is the ultimate basis of the potential fear and hatred that then necessarily exists between archetypally bonded communities. Jung writes of such group possession, "This ghastly power is mostly explained as fear of the neighboring nation, which is supposed to be possessed by a malevolent fiend" (Jung 1969b: 48). The societies victimized by such societal faith are left with little ultimate choice in their interface with the other than the options to convert or kill. This was the case with the ideological warfare of the twentieth century. Sometimes the option becomes to convert and kill, as in the European attack on first peoples in the invasion of the Americas and elsewhere following their discovery.

The foregoing is a general sketch of the paradox at the core of Jung's social psychology. Let us now turn to the specific elements that contribute to the paradox. Jung identifies at least four intersecting or synergistic elements that together identify the role of the archetypal in the creation of cohesive civilizations and cultures and so contribute to the potential hatred and destruction that attaches to them.

Jung's appropriation of Levy-Bruhl

The first two elements in Jung's social psychology are heavily indebted to Levy-Bruhl's sociology and ethnography. From them Jung appropriated the ideas of the *participation mystique* and the *representations collectives*. Bruhl and the ethnological community were eventually to disown the conception of the *participation mystique* much to Jung's dismay (Jung 1969g: 504; 1969l: 265, fn. 12; 1970: 250, fn. 662). In spite of his reluctance to abandon the formulation entirely, Jung's reception of the idea and the psychology behind it is ambivalent and ultimately deeply critical, hedged about with caution and warnings of its questionable morality. On the one hand, Jung will occasionally express an almost wistful regret that contemporary Western consciousness has lost the possibility of the experience the *participation mystique* describes. The lost experience is that of the continuity, if not identity, of the individual with the surrounding world of nature and of human community worked in consciousness by the dynamic "All-oneness" of the underlying unconscious (Jung 1971a: 255). In this side of its meaning, the phrase insinuates an immersion of ego in its unconscious source associated with a theophany, the total transparency of one's environment to its matrix, familiar to nature mystics and to romantics and also to be found in most variations of microcosmic/macrocosmic experience. It is also the basis of Jung's appropriation of the alchemical *unus mundus*, one world, in which the ego, in intimate resonance with the universal unconscious, can perceive itself and its surroundings from the perspective of their common inherence in a universal generative ground (Jung 1970: 534).

Jung both appreciates and criticizes the sense of community as communion such an experience generates. In terms of this discussion, Jung identifies the primary characteristic of the *participation mystique* to be the creation of that tight cohesiveness and corresponding lack of a sense of individuality characteristic of "archaic" societies (Jung 1969l: 265; 1971b: 10). At the same time Jung sees the *participation mystique* operative in a wide range of human activities and relationships. It is at work in Rousseau's later and more sophisticated, though romantic, understanding of universal relatedness (Jung 1971c: 82). As such it may have entered into French Enlightenment theory of the collective will. Such unconsciousness can work a deeper bond between analyst and client in processes of transference (Jung 1966c: 182, 183, fn. 27). It is operative in any form of projection in which an archetypal reality is identified with an object which can then be related to the divine as, for instance, mana or vilified as the hostile other, now a denier and so threat to one's own sacred truth (Jung 1964f: 64, 65; 1969o: 65).

Jung's ambiguity about the *participation mystique* lies in his appreciation of the power of such experience to unite the individual, with community and nature even as he deplores the "*state of identity in mutual unconsciousness*" such a state so easily breeds between individuals and between individuals and the total environment (Jung 1964g: 37; 1966a: 327; 1966d: 206, italics Jung's). The *participation mystique* can foster both the most intense sense of mystical communion with all that is, as well as the "mass intoxication" or "psychic epidemics" of collective regression to "mob psychology" (Jung 1968d: 125–127). The ambivalence of the phenomenon forces Jung to wonder, in the end, if critical consciousness and morality are compatible with it especially as it recurs in "the civilized mind" (Jung 1969g: 504, fn. 28). In the end Jung's evaluation of the *participation mystique* reflects the valid tension in the psyche between an autonomous individual and the relation of such autonomy to a connectedness with the totality and expanded compassion now lost in Western consciousness. Isolation in a rational but shallow individuality is fragmenting and at the heart of much of the modern malaise. The loss of individuality to the collective is at the heart of personal insanity and collective war. The reality of the *participation mystique* will not subside because it is a psychic and so human inevitability. How it is dealt with remains a major challenge to the human individual and community.

Closer to our time, Jung extends the operation of the *participation mystique* to the post-Enlightenment Western consciousness individually and collectively. In certain ways these communities are much more highly developed consciously and technologically. However, their one-sided imprisonment in reason renders them dangerously vulnerable to seizure by archetypal energies still operative in the collective unconscious whose existence and power these communities ignore, vilify or suppress. As a consequence of such denial these societies are consistently victimized by the lethal ideological possession of archetypal forces. For when collective or personal reason chooses to distance or, worse, to sever itself from reason's archetypal roots, it does not mean that archetypal powers cede their suasion to such consciously induced ignorance. Rather such ignorance provides the precondition for the ideological captivity of the mind by the very archetypal world whose reality it denies often from the window of its ideological cell in the imprisonment variously imposed by the archetypal in the wake of the reduction of the human to the rational. Such uprootedness of the mind and its consequent infection by archetypally induced political and religious faith has turned the twentieth century and the earlier part of our own into the epoch of genocide. The holy soil of the father or motherland, the home of the ancestral spirits, the one true religion, political system or movement remained for Jung but thinly disguised forms of the *participation mystique* in contemporary dress (Jung 1966e: 82). Jung is profoundly sensitive and to some extent appreciative of the power of such attraction but in the end his psychology starkly exposes its dangerous shadow. His critique effectively identifies contemporary political, religious, nationalist and ethnic bonding and their various combinations as little more than remnants of tribalism with the ever present danger of tribal warfare. In matters religious and theological it may be difficult to accept Jung's insinuation that ecclesiology, the nature of the churches, and missiology, their expansion, share so much in common with the dynamics of a more primordial mob psychology.

Jung and the *representations collectives*

As he develops Levy-Bruhl's related idea of the *representations collectives*, Jung's thought becomes more recognizably pertinent to contemporary society. He identifies these "*representations*" as symbols working social cohesion as expressions of archetypal energies. These unifying symbols can devolve into the psychic equivalent of a magical salvation offered to rationalist societies under the form of "religions and political ideologies" (Jung 1966a: 156). Because they carry archetypal power unrecognized by the communities they seize Jung lays squarely at the feet of such symbols, "the psychic epidemics of our time before which the witch-hunts of six-teenth century pale by comparison" (Jung 1966a: 156). Again there is the same ambiguity in Jung's appreciation of these bonding symbols and their mythology which are in fact the ground of all ideology. Admittedly they can be "therapeutic" when the consciousness of the individual can identify and integrate their archetypal power (Jung 1966a: 442). Their potential healing power is no doubt due to the fact that they arise to consciousness from that dimension of the unconscious common to "mankind in general" and so could bear with them the emotive sense of relating the individual to a wider and eventually to the total human community (Jung 1971d: 417–418). What then distinguishes the therapeutic from the pathological impact of the "*representations collectives*"? Pathologically they can induce the loss of conscious autonomy and so moral responsibility when they possess individual or community. Therapeutically, when assimilated consciously, they stabilize and enrich consciousness by reconnecting it with the ground of consciousness itself from which they emerge. In the former situation the mind is destroyed or maimed by the faith, religious or political, they symbolize. In the latter case the mind is reconnected with its roots and so is supported and broadened by the living power they mediate. It is one thing to be a willing but unconscious participant in the Nuremberg rally under the suasion of the swastika and another to admit the need for symbols to give a deeper meaning and order to personal and collective life. Saluting the flag or addressing one's God would then be done in the context of a deeper reflection on what archetypal values these powers carry and would not so easily be divested of a critical analysis of their impact. In the end possession or sustenance by the *representations collectives* is always tenuous. The difference would lie in the strength of a consciousness able to recognize the ambivalence of the powers with which it is dealing and so engage in a measured response to them rather than be swept away by them.

Thus embedded in the psychic fabric of humanity, the *representations collectives* appear in the distant past in more primordial form and in the present as much more finely honed images of societal absolutes held by contemporary cultures and civilizations. There are no such cultures without them and in these communities these powers function as a collective super-ego dictating collective mores (Jung 1966f: 120). More, they carry with them an emotional power making them irresistible to individuals and societies whose lives they can permanently possess and transform for better or worse. The quality of the transformation they work is wholly to be measured by the degree to which the ego assimilates them in the restoration of its connection with the unconscious over against the degree to which ego is lost to their overwhelming power in usually destructive ecstasies of com-munal faith, patriotism and dubious forms of socio-political commitment and aggression (Jung 1969m: 121, 122). It becomes increasingly obvious that Jung's appropriation of Levy-Bruhl would envisage the ideal participation in wider culture and civilization to consist of individuals critically aware of the origin, power and values of the energies and imagery that unite them in distinguishing their communities from others. Such consciousness would forbid an easy collective obeisance to authoritative calls for the surrender of moral acuity to alleged collective needs through the political manipulation of the mythology and symbols bonding one's own collectivity. In the contemporary situation summons to war would fall on ever more critical ears even though such critical consciousness obviously remains a distant ideal in the light of the continuing appeal of the bellicose.

Reflecting further on the nature of the *representations collectives* for Jung, in the insane they are the voice of God sometimes commanding irrational destruction, sometimes a hyper-ethical mission (Jung 1954c: 116). Elsewhere Jung remarks they create as wide a range of phenomena as the dominant themes in the religions themselves, personal religious figures such as messiahs, and prophets, good poetry and mysticism as well as the lowly slogan (Jung 1966g: 145, 146; 1967b: 347; 1969m: 121, 122). In the deeper sense Jung gives to them they connect the individual throughout the moments of human history with the underlying and ever present unconscious and its vitalities, as these provide the bases of societies (Jung 1966f: 120). They can do this in the form of reconnecting the individual with ancestral forces, which themselves can be understood as the power of the divine. At a certain primordial level, the personal recedes fully into a transpersonal origin and the ancestors become the Gods. Religiously they are the basis of the living substance of whatever truth is transmitted through esoteric teaching (Jung 1968j: 5). While Jung is speaking, in this context, of the transmission among primordial peoples of spiritual powers he elsewhere implies that Christian dogma, and by extension all dogma, once carried the possessive energies of the *representations collectives* (Jung 1976f: 240; 1976g: 253). Recovered, these energies in the symbols support a vital spirituality. Made literal, these energies are denied and their current symbolic expression is either unintelligible or lethal to the spirit.

Where they fail consciously and so responsibly to reconnect or reroot individual and society with the unconscious, the mind is cut adrift from its stabilizing deeper roots and becomes vulnerable to the above mentioned "psychic epidemics" (Jung 1968d: 127; 1968k: 278). Then collective and political liturgies take over entire communities in the celebration of death and destruction. Jung's repeated references to psychic epidemics address the full paradox of the *representations collectives*. Without them the individual is cut off from the adaptation these symbols can afford as grounding the individual in the unconscious, usually through a community and its founding mythology, symbols and rituals. But with them and under their spell the individual can easily be led into an unconscious tribal conformity and divested of responsible moral judgment.

While the impact of the *representations collectives* create historical epochs with their successive revelations (Jung 1964h: 549) and are, for Jung, among the deepest healing resources when consciously assimilated yet, like the *participation mystique* that they express and foster, they can reduce societies to the level of an unconscious beast. Writes Jung in a passage first published in 1934 whence the title of this work derives:

> There is no lunacy people under the domination of an archetype will not fall a prey to. If thirty years ago anyone had dared to predict that our psychological development was tending towards a revival of the mediaeval persecutions of the Jews, that Europe would again tremble before the Roman fasces and the tramp of legions, that people would once more give the Roman salute, as two thousand years ago, and that instead of the Christian Cross an archaic swastika would lure onward millions of warriors ready for death – why that man would have been hooted at as a mystical fool. And today? Surprising as it may seem, all this absurdity is a horrible reality . . . The man of the past who lived in a world of archaic "representations collectives" has risen again into very visible and painfully real life, and this not only in a few unbalanced individuals but in many millions of people.
>
> (Jung 1968l: 48)

This citation precedes the holocaust but its prophetic import does not. As yet few analyses have addressed the psychogenic and closely related religious bases of that event. What might Jung write about the current reappearance of archaic humanity possessed by conflicting *representations collectives* under whose power national or tribal leaders can call each other and their opposing empires "evil" or "satanic" and go not only unchallenged but also cheered on by the masses. More recently the same tribal convictions are evidenced in the missions to impose "human rights" under the banner of democracy and globalized laissez-faire capitalism at gunpoint on peoples with different but equally religiously based conceptions of public polity. Again the need for "mystical fools" and their prophetic insight would seem to be as great or even greater at this moment than when Jung penned these lines in the mid-1930s.

Jung's ambivalence toward the *representations collectives* as the agent of archetypal bonding is even more dramatically evident when he attributes to their power the origins of such morally opposite movements as Hitler's regime in the twentieth century and the witch hunts in fifteenth and sixteenth century Germany as well as the rise and spread of Christianity in the second and third centuries and Islam in the seventh (Jung 1966a: 156; 1976a: 607). These texts dramatically witness Jung's conviction that the birth of these new religions springs from the archetypal energies and imagery that create them and enable their easy almost contagious initial spread. At the same time, though morally of contradictory nature, the rise and spread of Christianity and Islam in contrast to medieval witch hunts and twentieth century German fascism proceed from a common source, the archetypal unconscious. All are charged with the identical archetypal impulse and energy which can work for or against the communities they create and possess. The implication for a contemporary social and political consciousness would support an iconoclastic caution around solicitations of any collectivity to an uncritical alignment with any mass movement, secular, religious or in combinations of both. An outstanding current example of the collective possession Jung warns about is the coalition of Jesus with American capitalism and militarism in its still current wars in the Middle East. A Jungian critique would undermine in principle the increasingly obvious renewal of the Crusades in the Middle East because it would divest both secular and religious leaders of their power to exploit an ever ready constituency in the interests of limited collective goals and not infrequently hidden agendas involving power, money and oil hidden under a religious idealism or political ideology. The untruth if not lies exposed in these endeavors would not have to await the damage done by them for correction. Such exposure might well be capable of aborting them in the womb.

In their capacity to deprive their victims of conscious discrimination and moral autonomy a connection exists between Jung's understanding of Levy-Bruhl's *representation collective* and his use of Pierre Janet's *abaissement du niveau mental*. Both describe states of loss or deliberate surrender of conscious control to unconscious forces (Jung 1971d: 451). Thus the practice of active imagination may deliberately lower the threshold of consciousness with the purpose of a more immediate or continued dialogue with unconscious forces in the interests of their greater conscious assimilation, for example, in the reactivation of a remembered dream. Unfortunately such loss can also be worked involuntarily by the power of archetypal attraction itself (Jung 1969n: 436). When this occurs the total personality, possessed by one dimension of archetypal energy, can easily regress to the status of a limiting and so demeaning single-mindedness (Jung 1968d: 120). Unfortunately the same psychology can apply to competing cultures themselves in conflicting claims to their status as somehow final, superior or chosen.

In linking the *representation collective* to the *abaissement du niveau mental* the profile of archetypally informed cultural and political faith as a diminishment of the individual's freedom and sympathy and so as a danger to a wider world community becomes much clearer. Where humanity has lost sight of the psychic origins of faith and its power to work constricted conformity in individual and society, and here Jung usually has the Enlightenment's faith in rationalism and its current inheritors in mind, religion has transformed into secular ideologies and archetypally inspired slaughter continues now under the auspices of reason itself unconsciously victimized, even in its self-deification, by collective archetypal possession.

Jung and the "isms"

Jung's critique of the archetypal cohesiveness afforded culture and civilization at the cost of individual consciousness and morality continues with his attack on the "isms". The "isms" are but a further precision on the archetypal powers and symbols that bond society. Jung describes such collective unconsciousness in terms of "the demons and gods of primitives or the 'isms' so fanatically believed in by modern man" (Jung 1969f: 175). The "isms", too, can "paralyze and blindfold" their societal victims (Jung 1976a: 607). They constitute a "magic word", effectively a new religion (Jung 1969f: 206), which drags those adrift in a wholly conscious world into immersion in mass collective unconsciousness. "Our fearsome gods have only changed their names: they now rhyme with –*ism*" (Jung 1964i: 234).

Not infrequently, notes Jung, religious leaders themselves extol such loss of consciousness as a commendable faith commitment to what is from his perspective a parochial revelation seeking universal and exclusive acceptance. In so doing these spiritual leaders maim the very "spiritual development" of their pastoral victims through immersion in the religious collective (Jung 1969f: 219). At this point religious and political faith intersect. Modern political "isms" are but "a variant of the denominational religions" (Jung 1968m: 61, 62). Yet no one, for Jung, is exempt from the influence of a "supraordinate idea" in one's individual psyche (Jung 1968m: 62). It is to this personal "ism", the inner capacity and near necessity to commit to archetypal suasion, that the contemporary political and cultural "isms" appeal. The chaos in the wake of such collective conflicting faiths breeds a kind of "terrorism" in their interface, even as such communities destroy individual development and personal moral responsibility in doing so (Jung 1968i: 349). Jung would here align himself with thinkers like Paul Tillich in identifying a dimension of faith in the very constitution of human consciousness. Tillich would agree with Jung's position that no one can lay aside faith without assuming another one. On the impossibility of a faithless life, Tillich reflects Jung when he writes, "Our ultimate concern can destroy us as it can heal us. But we can never be without it" (Tillich 1957: 16). The paradox at the heart of Jung's thought on these matters can now be restated. Humanity cannot be without faith, whether in explicitly religious or more disguised secular, political and cultural form, even as it becomes increasingly aware that specific faiths in their particular collective concretions now pose a serious threat to humanity's common future.

The collective shadow

Jung's understanding of the collective shadow adds a fourth and final dimension to what has been said about archetypal bonding. For with archetypally bonded communities any differently bonded society becomes its shadow, a threat to the "truth" of its bonding power, and a residual and living insult to the absolute claims of its God, culture and values. The tighter the archetypal bond, the stronger the shadow it casts on the other. When the communal bond is so deep that those bonded by it can proclaim themselves in possession of an ultimate truth, religious or political, the differently bonded are easily demonized. The dynamic of the collective shadow strongly suggests that the projection of the shadow in the demonization of the other is either a founding necessity or an inevitable consequence in the making of a believing community. What is even more terrifying about Jung's reflection on the collective shadow is his location of "absolute evil" in the collective unconscious and so, effectively, in God or, more precisely, in those archetypal agencies which universally give rise to the experience of the divine and to the communities, religious or political, gathered in the name of the divine (Jung 1968n: 10). Communities bonded in archetypally induced faith are in possession of and possessed by a saving truth, religious or secular, which confers a privileged position on them as the chosen with the right and duty to spread the good news. When it is realized that the archetypally conferred primacy and goodness of any and every group proceeds from the same unconscious source in which Jung locates absolute evil, differently bonded communities necessarily become evil and quickly attain the status of the demonic. The bonding archetype splits. Out of the split comes a fatal projection. Our absolute goodness demands their absolute evil. If absolute evil is, in fact, an archetypal power, it is ever present as a possibility and more likely to be activated by individual or community in possession of the absolute good. Our goodness can be criticized by the prophets faithful to the bonding but never abandoned. Historically no punishing God or critical prophet has ever switched tribes. In processes of the projection of the collective shadow demonization becomes the first step to dehumanization and then to elimination. This is sadly true historically and presently. Those against whom war is waged must first be demonized before they can be destroyed.

The truth shall set you free; the doubt freer

In the light of such analysis, the contemporary disciplines of psychology, the social sciences, the humanities, and religious studies are currently challenged to search for modes of communal affirmation that could move beyond the possibility of the demonization of the different. This collective effort will entail a deeper examination of archetypal hatred as the shadow side of archetypal faith, currently the ever more obvious still reigning agency in the making of competing civilizations and the growing body count in their interface. Anything less will be ultimately evasive and in denial. For the fact remains that to date no significant civilization has achieved self-affirmation without the cohesion provided by the hatred of the evil other. More will be said on Samuel P. Huntington's theories in Chapter 7. On the issue of collective hatred he writes, "Over the centuries, however, differences among [religiously based] civilization have generated the most prolonged and the most violent conflicts" (Huntington 1993: 25). Jungians have contributed a great deal to the problem of the personal shadow. This contribution remains valuable. Humanity's survival may now depend on extending this interest to the resolution of the collective shadow. This means that the murderous shadow of collective faith as bonding cultures and civilizations would have to be faced without flinching.

In this joint effort one ploy needs to be ruled out immediately. That ploy is the option for a solution based exclusively on the powers of consciousness. Humanity may eventually be eliminated in a final *auto da fe* (act of faith) by archetypally generated competing faith based civilizations but humanity cannot free itself from this threat through solely intellectual or willful resources. "*Reason alone no longer suffices*" (Jung 1964c: 298, italics Jung's). The denial of the unconscious basis of collective unconsciousness is the first and surest step toward the next holocaust. Jung's strategy would be different. Rather than a reliance on exclusively conscious strategies, his psychology works to persuade humanity of the power of the unconscious in matters not only personal but also societal as the first step in acknowledging humanity's fearsome role in ushering the unconscious into historical consciousness without destroying history in the process. Since Jung wrote his late *Answer to Job*, humanity has been challenged to accept consciously its role as the redeemer of divinity at the insistence and with the concurrence of divinity itself. In psychological language this challenge means the endless ushering of the illimitable energies of the unconscious into the flow of historical consciousness toward that point, always beyond attainment or evasion, where consciousness would reflect the totality of its unconscious ground.

In this process an attitude of residual and saving doubt that any archetypal manifestation can be exhaustive of its sponsoring archetype should accompany every archetypal concretion in individual and society. Such conscious reserve would then serve as a major resource freeing cultures from the devastation within and beyond themselves of archetypally induced collective unconsciousness. Archetypally grounded doubt is the doubt that Jung affirms when he writes in reference to his debate with Martin Buber, "I 'abhor' the belief that I or anybody else could be in possession of an absolute truth" (Jung 1957b: 378). In his alchemical writings he confesses that he is grateful that his life has been enriched by "the gift of doubt" which does not violate the "virginity" of what lies beyond certitude (Jung 1968a: 8). As seen in Chapter 5, it is to this doubt that Jung refers in a letter to Victor White, in response to the latter's vocational insecurities,

"Doubt and insecurity are indispensable components of a complete life" (Jung 1954b: 171).

These remarks are not peripheral to but are, on the contrary, consistent with the substance of archetypal theory because archetypal theory would deny to any and every archetypal expression the possibility that it would or could exhaust the wealth of its source. Jung is explicit on this point when he describes the unconscious in terms that evoke an infinite fecundity. The unconscious is "of indefinite extent with no assignable limits" (Jung 1969c: 258). The degree of realization of this fecundity in any individual and, by extension in history, is always surpassed by a remaining potential yet to be realized. In fact this always unrealized potential is for Jung the only psychological and so real meaning of transcendence. Transcendence then becomes the eternal difference between an intrapsychic and timeless plentitude demanding realization in the finite and historical and the degree of its current realization there. This dialectic is the psychic substance of the meaning, the joy and the tragedy of human life, personal and collective.

In this sense doubt and psychic transcendence coincide and the redemptive quality of both emerge. Archetypal doubt is aware that all archetypal expression including the great civilizations and their supportive religious and cultural values share a common origin in the unconscious whose creativity outstrips its expression in any and all of them. On these grounds alone claims by any of them to being history's culmination becomes absurd since such claims pit themselves against the human psyche. More, a keen sense of their common origin should endow each cultural expression with a relativity that would enable each to see the differently bonded not as threats but as variants of a common matrix in the ongoing historical play between consciousness and the unconscious seeking to express the totality of its resources in conscious humanity and its history. The idea that any concrete expression would complete the process would be dismissed not only as dangerous but as immoral. The need to kill or convert would cede to a sense of awe at the art and genius of the unconscious expressing in other notes and keys the substance, and, in many cases, an expansive furtherance of one's own tradition.

The doubt that makes archetypal bonding relative and so safe for the world is one of Jung's major contribution to a strategy for survival because it identifies the source of the sense of the absolute and the doubt that should humanize it in its historical concretions as two aspects of the same psychological process. In its ability to unite a sense of the absolute with a living doubt, Jung's psychology is one of the few modes of modern thought to combine the sacramental and the iconoclastic, and so appreciate the foundations of the sacred affirmed by a more traditional modernism and the corrosion of the foundational by the post-modern period. Jung's sacramentalism, deeper than that offered by the traditional West, rests on the proclivity of the unconscious to generate archetypal and so numinous experience in the creation of the divinities and their communities or, indeed, in all that is held sacred. The psyche itself is the ultimate sacrament since it carries in itself the potential and necessity for the experience of the Gods and so of the human as holy. His iconoclasm is based on the equally foundational psychic fact that the wealth of the unconscious cannot rest with any of its expressions. However, his integration of the sacramental and the iconoclastic as the basis of the sacred nature of all cultures and of the doubt that renders their innate sacredness relative and so safe is not the only resource he offers the contemporary world. There are others to which we now turn.

Very occasionally Jung will speak of therapies or therapists as "intercepting" incipient mass movements and so offsetting their potential devastation. In these passages he seems to envision individuals or therapies able to discern the archetypal nature of incipient social psychoses or pathologies and aid in the legitimate integration or compensation that may lie behind their urgency in whatever truth their archetypal allure might bear (Jung 1964i: 229, 236, 237). No doubt in these rare passages Jung was speaking of himself and his analytic psychology as contributing to the early interception or, at least identification, of that archetypal possession that funds psychic epidemics such as National Socialism. It is not a theme that he develops widely in his work, possibly because such a process of interception would demand too much from any therapist. For one must assume that any therapist would be deeply involved in the very political and social milieu about to be overcome by archetypal forces as Jung himself may have been in the period immediately before National Socialism revealed its true face. To ask a therapist to be immersed in and yet somehow to transcend such social forces in the interests of their more gracious personal and societal integration is to make an immense demand. Yet it cannot be denied that Jung does point to this possibility as a dimension of his own psychology in those who would relate to collective consciousness through their own immediate dialogue with the unconscious and so attain a certain purchase on what the unconscious was then urging into consciousness. Such a purchase on its always present thrust toward the new would be a great asset in ushering the current demands of the unconscious into an enriched personal and collective life and avoiding the pitfalls of the urgency of the new becoming a form of collective possession.

As briefly discussed in Chapter 1 an equally great demand is made when Jung proposes as the ultimate resistance to mass epidemics the organization of one's personal psyche worked by the self in cooperation with the ego. The cultivation of the self in the individual would hopefully match the organization of an archetypally possessed society. Writes Jung on this proposal, "*Resistance to the organized mass can be effected only by the man who is as well organized in his individuality as the mass itself*" (Jung 1964c: 278, italics Jung's). But how many individuals in Nazi Germany were as well organized as the Gestapo or how many today are sufficiently organized to see through the New World Order and its proposed globalization of a Western economic particularity? In this proposal Jung would seem to suggest that the next war, holocaust, or ethnic cleansing can best be avoided through the birth of the self in a critical mass of conscious individuals acting as a psychic prophylactic against unconscious archetypal fecundation and its consequent mass faith. This assumption is reinforced when Jung more than once affirms that only the grace of inner transformation or personal "spiritual renewal" would stand as the ultimate resource against the emergence of the murderous proclivity of mass psychoses making the Nazi period appear as a mere "curtain-raiser" (Jung 1964j: 216, 217; 1964i: 243). In a letter to Bernard Lang, amplifying the remarks cited above, he is explicit in locating personal political freedom and effective resistance to mass movements in those individuals who feel themselves to be "'anchored in God'" (Jung 1957c: 371). Again in this formulation Jung contends that the sustaining experience of the self and of God are effectively the same experience and the only ultimate resource against a social environment collectively possessed by an archetypal power.

Jung will describe this turn inward to the support of the self or of the divine as the culmination of the religious development of the West. Such inwardness is the current term of "a millennial process" (Jung 1969d: 402). This kind of reliance on the inner life amounts to the conscious recall of the Gods and all absolutes to their psychic origins, a movement to be discussed at greater length in Chapter 8. As inner powers the conscious individual can converse with them in a psychic containment that is safer and promises more for the human future. Why is this so? It is so because as long as humanity continues to perceive the absolutes, in the form of the Gods or political programs, to be imposed upon the individual and not as originating within the individual, that individual and the supporting community are relatively helpless in the face of such divinities, religious or secular. When these powers are realized to be externalizations of powers native to the depths of human interiority commerce with them becomes safer though more painful. One then has to deal with the inner dogmatist, fascist, communist, democrat, capitalist, socialist, nationalist, racist as potentially overwhelming shadow and shadow is always one's own potential. The same process must apply to the bevy of divinities that escape psychic containment and continue to deal arbitrarily with the human from their position of eternal self-sufficiency beyond the processes of history itself. Their return to source would modify if not eliminate their tyranny from beyond history and the conflict between their communities within history. If humanity does not kill over differences in bodily effluents why does it do so over such equally natural psychic effluents as the divinities and their incarnations in religious or secular form? The rising consciousness of their origin within the human should make it more difficult to take human life on their behalf.

Jung's myth as an ultimate resource

In the end and in conclusion, the greatest resource that Jung has to offer in the overcoming of archetypally based hatred between conflicting collectivities is the deeper dimension of his own myth, that is, those dimensions that are specific to his myth and distinguish it from others. Jung's psychology is a myth in conscious continuity with largely peripheral precedents in Western culture. In pointing to these oft excluded sides of the Western soul, Jung's psychology contributes to and fosters their current resurgence. In continuity with certain streams of Western mysticism, alchemy and nearly every form of Platonic and neo-Platonic philosophy, especially in the forms it has assumed in and since the Renaissance, the core of Jung's myth would have it that the unconscious creates consciousness to become conscious in it. This means that each bearer of human consciousness shares a solidarity of origin with every human and that the universal, yet always unique, moral responsibility of the individual is the ushering of this origin into a life enhancing consciousness within one's allotted share of time.

Each of Jung's master images of the self; the mandala, the anthropos, the reality of synchronicity, alchemy and its crowning symbol, the *unus mundus*, point to the natural inherence of each individual's consciousness in the source of all consciousness in the depths of the human as the foundational possibility of an ever widening universal compassion. The life of the individual derives its greatest meaning in allowing itself to become the servant of the self in the emergence of a more "compendious personality" whose sympathy would move to an embrace as extensive as the universal ground from which it emerges (Jung 1969c: 258). This perpetually emerging consciousness would always be in some tension with the more constrictive collectivities into which it is born. In this sense the emergence of self in individual and society is always potentially subversive to the status quo. And yet the deepest instinct of the self is always to supersede extant states of consciousness toward a more conscious and related human community.

Humanity's universal vocation thus understood is fraught with danger, and now, possibly with the danger that the process would be prematurely ended. The danger is based on the fact that human solidarity and its oneness is only in the unconscious. As the archetypal unconscious creates consciousness and then seeks ever greater ingression in it, it splits the conscious world into many compelling if not overwhelming manifestations whose social incarnations divide humanity into warring factions, religiously, ethnically, politically and in so many other ways. It remains humanity's task, then, to give to conscious differentiation of the archetypal world in the many communities it creates a mutual respect and admiration fully cognizant that each such expression is of a commonly possessed human profundity and should be not only tolerated but also celebrated by other expressions. Unless a sense of the common deeply human origin of cultural archetypal differences becomes the centerpiece of a myth superseding currently competitive myths and the cultures they empower, the clash of civilizations will be interminable and likely tragic. The only real question about the future would become who will win and how to win in the ensuing international mayhem.

Jung's myth has more to offer humanity than such collective despair. One image among many that reveals its power in response to current need is that of the alchemical *unus mundus*. This consciousness comes as the crowning moment of an arduous and never ending ascetic process. However ephemeral or residual the experience may be, the consciousness the symbol describes is one that perceives the world from the vantage point of the "eternal Ground of all empirical being" (Jung 1970: 574). Effectively the image describes the perception of the other from the perspective of the common ground of individual and other. This vision is nothing less than a theophany making personal or collective hate impossible in the consciousness that humanity and nature share a common origin beyond archetypal differentiation which should prevail in historical differentiation. In fact the consciousness of the *unus mundus* enables the embrace of the other as other, both individual and collective, through the experience of their inhesion in and emergence from a common source. Otherness as alienation or threat is overcome and an embrace of the different as different becomes possible.

To give such consciousness real significance in the face of real politic and power appears romantic and vulnerable to ready dismissal. It should be remembered that Jung saw the emergence of such vastly extended sympathy as that state to which the psyche moves in history by its own nature and dynamic. Though so apparently fragile, Jung's social psychology is in a position to make a substantial contribution to strategies for the survival of the species and to confront alternative solutions with many questions. For instance it could ask:

> If such a universal compassion is not generated in historical consciousness by the source of consciousness itself are not all other solutions to archetypal differentiation purely conscious? If so, are conscious solutions of no more hope for the future than they have been in the past. Such solutions deal with symptoms not the illness itself. They cannot touch the ground preceding conflicting historical differentiations and so remain unable to foster a myth that would lessen or heal the antipathy such differentiation brings with it in any real depth?

Rationally contrived solutions may lower the body count for a time but never touch the enmity behind the count. In fact such efforts in the forms of treaties, cease fires, economic packages, redrawing of borders and so forth seem but to delay rather than undermine the next archetypal disaster. Nor does the learning curve seem to rise. The twentieth century began with the

First World War through an assassination in the same culturally turbulent area where the century ended with ethnic cleansing.

Jung himself was to die in the tensions of the archetypal divide and its competing "isms" known as the Cold War. Though the political divide may have been as dangerous to human survival then as it is now, Jung did not die in despair. His confidence that the quality of mind he sought to describe in the image of the alchemical "one world" might itself attain the globalization it sought is evident in his lines, "The afternoon of humanity, in a distant future, may yet evolve a different ideal. In time even conquest will cease to be the dream" (Jung 1969g: 493). The social implications of Jung's myth may yet have an important role to play in humanity's reaching that distant afternoon.

Chapter 7

C.G. Jung, S.P. Huntington and the search for civilization

Huntington on the primacy of religion in bonding civilizations

Chapter 6 sought to surface Jung's thought on the role of archetypal energies in the formation of cultures and the apparent inevitability of the projection of negative shadow onto differently bonded cultures as the basis of civilizational conflict between them. It surfaced what might be called a Jungian law governing the bonding of civilizations, namely, the greater the archetypal cohesion uniting a given community the less conscious and so morally responsible are its members. More, the contention that archetypal energies are the bonding power working all cultural and civilizational cohesion and differentiation identifies these forces as, at bottom, religious forces or their secular equivalents providing their societies with the sense of ultimacy and substance needed for their collective identity. In this respect Jung shares much in common with Paul Tillich when the latter writes, "culture is the form of religion, religion is the substance of culture" (Tillich 1963: 158). With Tillich this substance could be explicitly religious as in the Middle Ages or secular in its modern variation. His point and Jung's is that whatever dominant unites a culture functions as its religion in whatever guise such unifying power may assume. Jung's thought on this issue does not move to the possibility of a society, culture or civilization not united by some archetypal power. Rather it forces the question of the possibility of communal bonding that would not need to demonize or demean the other as an essential element in its own self-understanding as community. Is there a possibility of an archetypal grounding of a culture divested of the urge to convert or kill other such configurations? The concluding remarks in this chapter will address this question.

With the purpose of expanding reflection on this issue, it is appropriate here to note that Jungian psychology would also understand that where expressions of archetypal import are made they are usually made in variation as the natural consequence of the depth from which they emerge and the fecundity of such depths. This phenomenon can be seen, for instance, in fairy tales. As they move from culture to culture they take on altered detail whose variation clarifies the underlying archetypal import of the tale. The same is true of the variants of monotheistic Gods as well as those of mythological and religious figures like Christ and Dionysius as variants of the ongoing cyclical drama of life, death and resurrection. As humanity progresses in its self-consciousness one would expect variants in the various breakthroughs that contribute significantly to its advance. Any single expression of such a novel depth would hardly be expected to exhaust the meaning that is there. Such newness could easily become eccentric or idiosyncratic if variants were not in evidence. Jung himself needed to find parallels to his personal experiences of the archetypal powers in the history of consciousness if his own experience was to be credited as more than personal deviation. He found them in gnosis, alchemy, the grail legend and mysticism to name but a few. In this respect it would be surprising if a mind so deep and broad as Jung's on the nature of religion and its role in creating differing cultures and civilizations were not to find a certain affinity with other prominent positions around the same issue. No significant resonance with other voices of his time would relegate Jung's thought to the intellectual and cultural periphery as eccentric and isolated.

In this context the expected different but real reverberation of Jung's social and political psychology is, indeed, to be heard to some significant extent in the thought of Samuel P. Huntington. Huntington served as the Albert J. Weatherhead III Professor at Harvard University and chairman of the Harvard Academy for International and Area Studies. At the time, already a controversial figure, he published an article in the journal, *Foreign Affairs*, which made him look like an uncanny prophet in the wake of the events of 11 September 2001 (Huntington 1993). The title of his seminal article was "The Clash of Civilizations?", since elaborated into a full length book, *The Clash of Civilizations and the Remaking of World Order* (Huntington 1996/2003). Huntington thus coined the now familiar phrase, "the clash of civilizations", referring to current and possible future conflict between civilizations throughout the world. Huntington's greatest affinity with Jung lies in his identification of religion as the most significant factor in the creation of civilizations and so of the conflict that exists between civilizations. The affinity continues in his identification of religion based cultures as providing the individuals they unite with their collective identity, but with questionable levels of individual consciousness and responsibility. Finally Huntington's work relates closely to Jung's analysis of modern cultural conflict as collective archetypal possession, frequently taking on a political face but not different in origin from the earlier more obviously religious conflict between the religions themselves. In these senses Jung's social psychology would lend a certain support to Huntington's contention that the future of warfare will be religious warfare between religiously based cultures. On the brighter side both Jung and Huntington seek what the earlier Huntington terms human "commonalities" as the basis of an emerging Civilization which would alleviate the conflictual interface of existing civilizations and their supporting religions in the interests of a safer and richer human sympathy.

This chapter will present Huntington's thought on the relation of religion to culture and cultural conflict, consider analogous positions foundational to Jung's social psychology, and contend that Jung's response to the problem, though tenuous in its remove from collective consciousness and acceptance, is ultimately more effective and hopeful than Huntington's.

Religion as the basis of hatred and the clash of civilizations

Huntington is explicit in his conviction that religion is "the principal defining characteristic of civilization" (Huntington 1996/2003: 253) and so the ultimate source of the enmity that exists between them (Huntington 1996/2003: 28–29, 129–130). So closely does he link civilizations to their religious foundations that he predicts that as political ideology cedes as the basis of civilizational unity, future wars will be between civilizations themselves and thus effectively will be religious wars (Huntington 1993: 29; 1996/2003: 253, 254). In its function of creating distinct civilizations, religion creates a collective mentality of difference, easily fostering a sense of division, a sense of us against them, of our good against their evil (Huntington 1996/2003: 266). In broadest terms Huntington identifies the greatest religious and civilizational cleavage as that between "the West and the Rest" (Huntington 1993: 48; 1996/2003: 183), though he is also deeply, if not primarily concerned, with the cleavage between Islam and Christianity as Islam's long-time other: "Islam had bloody borders" (Huntington 1993: 35).

In the context of Christian–Islamic conflict Huntington, the geopolitician, moves with considerable acuity into the realm of the religionist. Such attention to the role of religion in personal and collective life by members of disciplines not devoted to the study of religion is to be welcomed. Such attention provides a critical position difficult to attain for those who study religion from within a current or previous commitment to a religion as do most theologians and religionists. Huntington attributes the enmity between Christianity and Islam to their being monotheistic faiths incapable of accepting other Gods and each with claims to possession of the one true faith informing their universal missionary zeal (Huntington 1996/2003: 210–211, 263–265). This critique could be easily extended to all forms of monotheism, religious and secular. The combination of having an exhaustive purchase on religious truth can hardly avoid the conflict that has grown up between rival claimants. Though Huntington explicitly refers to Islam's "bloody borders", he is far from limiting such bloody borders to Islam. His critique would logically extend to all forms of monotheism, religious or secular, which can be assigned geographical identities in relation to each other.

In Huntington's view religions' grip on humanity as the basis of inter-civilizational warfare is so unrelenting it leads him to agree with the novelist Michael Didbin's statement, "There can be no true friends without true enemies. Unless we hate what we are not, we cannot love what we are" (Huntington 1996/2003: 20). On this point both Didbin and Huntington are remarkably close to Jung's conception of the collective shadow. In its religious or absolute form this level of shadow is the ground of the projection of demonic evil on the other. Again in specific relation to civil-izational and religious identity and the enmity it generates Huntington simply states "It is human to hate" (Huntington 1996/2003: 130). Put simply collective identity requires the hated other. He labels as "secular myopia" the ongoing denial by academics and geopoliticians that religion is "the most profound difference that can exist between people" (Huntington 1996/2003: 254). He traces the history of war from the Treaty of Westphalia (1648), which among other advances resolved religious conflicts dating from the Reformation and its wars, through wars between princes, then nations, then political ideologies to their contemporary culmination in wars between religiously bonded civilizations (Huntington 1993: 22, 23). The civilizations he identifies are: Western (Jewish and Christian), Confucian, Japanese, Islamic, Hindu, Slavic-Orthodox, Latin American and African (Huntington 1993: 25). As differentiations between civilizations intensify they engender a "hate dynamic" which "demonizes" the opponent as a precondition to their elimination (Huntington 1996/2003: 266, 271–272). This dynamic became all too obvious in both Gulf wars where the leader had first to be demon-ized before his country could be invaded and the leader eventually mur-dered. Indeed, Huntington attributes to such demonization as a prelude to war or repression a near Hegelian necessity given the religious bonding funding the collective unconsciousness that fuels their inevitability.

Wars between civilizations Huntington terms "fault line wars". These wars occur when different civilizations exist on opposites sides of the fault line, that is, of a common border or when differing civilizations share common geography in a nation or state made up of them (Huntington 1993: 29–35; 1996/2003: 252–258). His most compelling example of the latter remains the recent war and ongoing tension in the Balkans following the dissolution of the Yugoslavian state. The communist state had largely repressed civilizational and religious differences within its borders through a unifying ideology effectively functioning as a secular religion able to prevent the bloodshed which resulted when it was dissolved. Once this unifying force was removed the fault lines between the three major religions in the area, Roman Catholicism, Eastern Orthodoxy and Islam, became apparent in the resultant bloodshed and heightened body count along the fault lines of these disparate communities within what had been a single nation (Huntington 1996/2003: 271, 272). Ironically the dissolution of a "secular" ideology became the prelude to religious warfare and extensive loss of life. Huntington could just as easily have pointed to the situation in Iraq where tyranny held together opposing religious factions with a comparatively low body count. The removal of the tyrant unleashed a blood bath between these forces rivaling the bloodshed spent in the tyrant's overthrow by forces themselves bonded by the archetypal energies informing democracy, capitalism and Christianity. The triumphant coalition of the unconscious became arguably as "evil" as the tyranny it overthrew.

At this point it might be said that it is difficult to refute the factual basis upon which Huntington rests his case for the evolution of war into current clashes between religiously based civilizations. But Huntington lacks an analysis of religion itself or at least of the powers that create religious commitment either in specifically religious forms or in their modern secular and political variants. A Jungian response to Huntington's factual base would ask a question that evades Huntington: "What is it about religion that enables it to unify civilizations even as it pits them against each other? From whence does religion draw its unifying and destructive power?" This question does not invalidate Huntington's analysis as far as it goes in its indictment of the role of religion in civilizational conflict. Rather it pushes it further into a reflection on the nature and function of religion itself as providing the bonding power of civilizations even as it instigates the hatred, always potential and frequently actual, which exists between them. In the end Huntington can point to the truth of the religious basis of intercivilizational conflict but draws back from an analysis of religion itself and its proven ability to sponsor conflict between the communities it possesses.

Religious identity, the *Revanche de Dieu* and civilizational affirmation

Huntington joins others in noting that the early twentieth century projection by "intellectual elites" that religion would cede to modernization and secularization has been dashed by the "return of God" (Huntington 1996/2003: 28, 29, 95). For Huntington it has not been a happy return. Again his analysis of the return is insightful. He argues that an earlier phase of modernization saw non-Western civilizations turning to the West for the acquisition of the knowledge, skill and sometimes values to work the modernization of their own civilizations. By modernization Huntington usually means a productive technology supporting a lively economy, education, literacy, urban living, rule of reason and law, and all that makes modernization as initiated in the West attractive beyond the West.

At this point Huntington introduces his conception of "indigenization". In his context indigenization points to the fact that non-Western civilizations no longer need to go to the West to accrue the skills that make modernization possible. Now they can do it at home out of resources they have appropriated from the West, resources presently residual in their culture and transmissible from generation to generation (Huntington 1996/ 2003: 93). Indigenization, thus understood, then extends to the reviviscence of the historical religious tradition as the basis of an autonomous civilizational identity. It does so in a number of ways. At a preliminary level religion parries the societal disorientation attendant to modernization, such as the move from rural to urban centers, by providing the uprooted with the sense of communal identity needed in times of transition. At a much more consequential level religion fosters indigenization in providing the spiritual foundation for non-Western societies who want to modernize but not Westernize. In this constituency, already substantial and growing in Huntington's view, religion serves as the buttress providing the modernizing civilization with the religious resources to modernize without losing its cultural soul to what it perceives as the decadent West in lethal processes of "Westoxification". "We will be modern but we won't be you" (Huntington 1996/2003: 101).

This function of religion in non-Western civilizations brings about interesting forms of consciousness. It fosters fundamentalism not only among the masses but also within the educated elites who capture sophisticated economies, technologies and societal arrangements rivaling if not surpassing those of the West (Huntington 1993: 26; 1996/2003: 112, 113). Such religious consciousness makes possible the integration of those sides of modernization which are universally attractive while fostering the affirmation of non-Western and now frequently anti-Western endemic religions and their values viewed by their holders as vastly superior to the West. For instance, Huntington makes the point that, in civilizations whose religious values put society ahead of the individual, the Western liberal emphasis on the individual and "human rights" can be and is perceived as "human rights imperialism" (Huntington 1993: 41; 1996/2003: 195). He also makes the telling point that when Western democracy is imported into non-Western civilizations, especially when done at gunpoint, the free vote can and has turned against candidates sympathetic to the West. The irony here is that, unless manipulated from beyond, an infant democracy in non-Western countries can overthrow itself in a return to previous often harsher forms of theocracy (Huntington 1996/2003: 94).

This burgeoning aspiration on the part of non-Western civilizations to recover their religions in a strategy to modernize but not Westernize grounds the opposition to the now operative and destructive Western missionary and imperial approach to non-Western cultures (Huntington 1996/2003: 184). Huntington contends that the defeat of Communist socialism by Western liberal democracy has convinced the West of its vocation to universalize its triumph (Huntington 1996/2003: 225). This is an arrogant and disastrous assumption when acted out. It provokes direct confrontation with non-

Western cultures and their religious values. For Huntington such missionary universalism culminates in a Western imperialism which is blatantly "false", "immoral" and "dangerous" (Huntington 1996/2003: 310). To counter such imperialism his first response is to invoke the *"abstention rule"* (Huntington 1996: 316, italics Huntington's). This rule would forbid the West and, indeed, any core state within any particular civilization, military intervention in other civilizations. Rather it encourages dominant or core kin nations of those in conflict to seek resolution through dialogue with each other and with the national communities directly involved in the conflict. Huntington call this second rule the "joint mediation rule" (Huntington 1996/2003: 316). For example, should war break out between the more Western Christian allegiances of the Western Ukraine and the Orthodox allegiance of the Eastern Ukraine, London and Washington could talk directly with Moscow and both of these core states with the local Ukrainian participants in the conflict in the interest of its resolution. Washington, London and Moscow would not intervene militarily in a civilization other than their own.

As his most meaningful, and ultimately only, alternative to imperial and missionary imposition of one civilization on other civilizations, Huntington appeals to the West to recognize the unique quality of its civilization and to fortify it through strengthening the ties between its members, North America, Britain and Western Europe (Huntington 1996/2003: 311). The constituent members of Western civilization will "hang together or hang separately" (Huntington 1996/2003: 321). In this position Huntington does not deny the contributions that other civilizations have made to the West including those of Islam. All the monotheisms are coming currently to be understood as the Abrahamic religions and all have contributed to the cultural values and polity Huntington describes as "Western". He simply insists that in its current form, Western civilization is distinguishable as an entity in itself just as the great religions grounding the distinct civilizations are distinguishable among themselves. It is correct to speak of Islam or Judaism "in the West" but it cannot be denied that the phrase itself refers to a "West" in which they are.

Huntington's appreciation of Western civilization and its unique values leads him to a nuanced position. On the one hand Western civilization should not attempt its globalization, an effort wrongheaded in itself, and which the West may currently or soon lose the capacity to realize and enforce. On the other hand the West should not bow to a multiculturalism that would dilute and possibly lose its liberal values, democracy and order founded on the natural law, all derivative of its Christian European heritage (Huntington 1996/2003: 318). He raises considerable doubt as to whether or not these values can truly be maintained in a multicultural context. If they are to be so maintained, it would seem that the assimilated traditions making up a multicultural society would have to acknowledge the primacy and preservation of the values which make the West, in

Huntington's mind, "unique". The possibility of the assimilation of other cultures into the presiding Western culture Huntington views as problematic at best and corrosive at worst. The problem he raises remains legitimate for any nation attempting to foster a multiculturalism while maintaining its traditional values such as democracy, and the rule of law related to the natural law and its endorsement of reason and equality, both derivative, in Huntington's view, from the Western Christian tradition.

In a more recent work, *Who Are We? The Challenges to America's National Identity* (Huntington 2004), Huntington's positions become clearer and his appreciation of Western uniqueness somewhat less attractive. In this work he contends that the core of the American tradition rests on a Creed whose origins can be traced to the Anglo Protestant and Puritan dissent of the earlier settlers. Their biblical and highly individual faith was later to intersect with Enlightenment values to produce the current democratic and liberal core of the American ethos (Huntington 2004: 59–69). In Huntington's view American culture, thus understood, is currently threatened by all forms of mutliculturalism and movements such as bilingualism and increasing dual citizenship. One particular target here is the rapid spread of an Hispanic subculture throughout parts of the United States (Huntington 2004: 221–256). In the end he faces current America, and by extension the West, with three choices. It can become cosmopolitan or multicultural and risk losing itself. It can become imperial and try to globalize itself. Or it can reaffirm the ultimately religious values of its founders, and become effectively an Anglo-Protestant nation behind a secular facade (Huntington 2004: 363–366). Strangely Huntington sees the current American religious revival, largely a function of the political right, in continuity with what he calls the American Creed or its founding values. Of the three options he proffers, this questionable third is his obvious preference (Huntington 2004: 340–357). This preference would make of the United States a religion based culture with the same proclivity to enmity that exists between all other religion based cultures imbued with the same geopolitical need for preservation and expanded areas of influence. As such the United States would become but another instance of Huntington's earlier analysis, a religion based culture in conflict (but, for Huntington, non-military conflict) with competing civilizations.

In these analyses Huntington again highlights the ambivalence of religion even when he endorses the religious foundations of the American state. In his last work he again locates religion as the source of inter-civilizational strife. It supports both the self-affirmation of civilizations hostile to the West even as it lies at the heart of the Western and American renewal of faith in themselves (Huntington 2004: 357). The scenario resonates with the tensions in the film, *High Noon,* and forces the question of whether or not the forces of mutually projected civilizational good and evil between the West and the rest are headed for a final civilizational shoot-out.

Huntington's final function of religion in relation to civilizational conflict may offer a more hopeful response to these tensions though it must be admitted that this more hopeful dimension of this thought advanced in the conclusion of his first two works cited in this chapter falls out of sight as he moves in his last work to his preferred maintenance of the purity of the unique and implicitly superior Western Christian civilization.

Religions as the bases of a surpassing Civilization

In the final but brief sections of two of his earlier works on religious and civilizational conflict (Huntington 1993: 49; 1996/2003: 318–321), Huntington addresses the possibility of identifying commonalities held by the differing religions and civilizations and making of them the substance of "higher levels of Civilization", a word he capitalizes and uses in the singular to distinguish it from currently clashing civilizations. "If humans are ever to develop a universal civilization, it will emerge gradually through the exploration and expansion of these commonalities" (Huntington 1996/2003: 320). The consciousness informing such a universal civilization could be termed "secular" but it would incorporate the values that extant civilizations and their religions hold in common with admittedly still significant differences in hierarchical emphases. Again it must be frankly admitted that these differences border on the irreconcilable. Huntington does not flinch in the face of an inquiry into the problem initiated by the Singapore government. This inquiry concluded that in the West the highest value lies in the individual and takes precedence over extended social groups such as family, and wider society. In the East this hierarchy is reversed and relation to the wider society such as nation and family take a moral precedent though the report is careful to note that the individual must also be developed to contribute to the demands of a technological society (Huntington 1996/2003: 318–320).

In the final analysis the only deeper hope in Huntington's work lies in the emergence of these commonalities as the basis of a more universal empathy developing through the now conflicted civilizations and yet surpassing them in their individuality. Writes Huntington, "peoples in all civilizations should search for and attempt to expand the values, institutions and practices they have in common with peoples of other civilizations" (Huntington 1996/2003: 320). In this context he quotes the former Canadian prime minister and statesman, Lester Pearson, from a 1955 work, *Democracy in World Politics*. Pearson argues in this work that differing civilizations will have to appreciate their cultural differences if they are to avoid "catastrophe" (Huntington 1996/2003: 321). In his search for such commonalities Huntington does not suggest a "common denominator" God such as the Enlightenment sought to counter the desolation of Europe in the wake of the post-Reformation religious wars. Rather than such a God stripped bare of all but traits universally acceptable to reason, Huntington seems to suggest an evolution of civilizations in which the religions currently supporting the moral, social and cosmological perspectives of their diverse civilizations would naturally evolve to a higher more mutually inclusive consciousness and embrace. He lists the various religions supporting their various cultures and sees even in their diversity points of common values through not all share the same hierarchical esteem. Sadly the search for such commonalities toward the making of a superior Civilization seems in his more recent works to have died at the hands of a parochial, superior and somewhat idolatrous adulation of a "unique" Western civilization superior to the others and to be strongly defended in geopolitical maneuvering.

The earlier hopeful notes in Huntington's conclusion could be amplified and deepened in various ways to lend them greater force. Huntington, by and large, seeks the commonalities between civilizations in the realm of religious and philosophical values and morality as they determine and differentiate the consciousness of the civilizations they unite. Yet these religions and quasi-religions usually wrap their morality, personal and social, in a cosmic myth that offers their adherents not only a religious, moral and cultural identity but also an identity within the universe as the basis of their differentiation from other civilizational identities. Huntington has much to offer in arguing that civilizations and their conflicts derive from the religions that support them. But he is much less profound in his suggestion that a future universal civilization will result from an exclusively conscious analysis of points of possible commonality and lack thereof between civilizations. What Huntington's search for commonalities demands is more than a point by point purely rational list of agreed upon religious and moral values across civilizations promoting a universal Civilization. What Huntington's search for a universal Civilization needs is an emerging myth. Such an altered perspective would bow to but transcend the myths that currently differentiate the civilizations. It might well form around the vision that the evolution of civilizations is toward that universal Civilization he sketches in his concluding remarks and that this evolution is grounded in human nature itself. Such mythic consciousness moving toward global proportions would ensure the future and its spiritual wealth in ways that the religions bonding current civilizations cannot because of their relative insularity, parochialism, and dangerous competing claims to universal and exclusive validity. Huntington does refer in passing to the fact that religion in creating civilizations meets humanity's deeper "psychological, emotional and social needs" (Huntington 1996/2003: 99, 267). It does so by providing civilizations with the myths they need to give meaning to their collective lives. In his search for commonalities he implies that these communal religious myths now seek their own supersession toward a sensitivity of more universal embrace in a manner reminiscent of an Hegelian view of history shorn of its Christian parochialism. Nevertheless Huntington's geopolitical insights, as valuable as they are, stand in need of a supporting myth that would move toward such a global religious sentiment by locating its possibility and necessity in humanity itself.

The social aspect of Carl Jung's psychology supports Huntington's search for the commonalities and the transcending Civilization to which the religions might yet contribute. More, Jung could offer to Huntington's search the power that only a myth can provide and that Huntington's analysis needs. With Jung the myth would be that of a currently developing consciousness, in living touch with the psychic source of all religions and their cultures, coming to permeate each existent civilization from the same human depths that initially created them and their differences. Conscious resonance with their common origin in the interests of the survival and enhancement of the species would thus proffer to the religions and their civilizations the possibility of a mutual embrace across their valuable differences. This vastly extended embrace through their differences would arise from the same human matrix that has authored them all and now seeks a unity transcending each but to which each would contribute.

The Jungian psyche as the primordial commonality

What follows describes the resources Jung's psychology could bring to bear in a response to Huntington's quest for the commonalities constitutive of a surpassing Civilization. Initially Jung would distance himself from Huntington's analysis of the historical evolution of war to its culmination in the current clash between religiously based civilizations. Rather Jung would ground all significant social bonding on various forms of archetypal cohesion as the basis of communal faith, whether secular, religious or combinations of both. Chapter 6 argued that all religious, national and ideological faiths are based on archetypal bonding. Hence Jung would be less likely to differentiate between national, ideological, religious and civilizational wars. Effectively, in his extended sense of religion, he would argue that all wars are and have been religious since they are fought between archetypal forces. His only distinction would be between wars fought on explicitly religious grounds such as most of the Thirty Years War (1618–1648) following the Reformation and wars fought on less explicitly religious but nonetheless archetypal grounds as religion morphed into political ideology often informed by ethnicity and sometimes by an explicit religious component in modern times. The conflicts such warring societies enact represent the conflicts between the archetypal powers bonding the conflicted communities. These archetypally based conflicts rest on archetypal absolutes and Jung will name them. Fascism rests on the archetypal power of the benign but powerful father (Jung 1964a: 190). Communism is grounded on the archetypal fall from and return to the unqualified unity of humanity through the millenarian recovery of paradise lost (Jung 1964b: 536, 537). Democracy exalts the atomic individual ego or "the Goddess reason" freed from religious constraint and limited in the societies over which she presides only by an enlightened self-interest. In the explicitly religious sphere such archetypally based conflicts can be variations of a single dominant archetype evident in the projection of the Self in the creation of the three monotheistic Gods, Yaweh, God the Father and Allah, with the consequent conflict between their devotees. Until the aforementioned are recognized as three variants of the same myth peace among their communities will remain beyond reach. Among devotees of a particular religion conflict can follow from the split between the iconoclastic and sacramental dimensions of the religion-creating psyche. These powers lie at the bottom of the oft bloody cleft between Reformed and Roman Christianity. Even as he goes beyond Huntington in his understanding of all war as archetypal conflict, Jung would add to Huntington's search for commonalities by grounding them in the archetypal dimension of the psyche itself. The archetypal psyche would thus be clearly identified as the common human source of specific religions, the civilizations they inform and the conflict between them. The problem of attaining Huntington's Civilization is the problem of the emergence of harmony between the concretions that archetypal energies have assumed as the bonding powers of current civilizations.

For Jung the archetypal psyche does not only create the Gods presiding over the various religions. The process of their creation is also the process of the creation of faith in them and so of the civilizations they inform. This is so because the archetypal psyche creates the Gods through its capacity to generate the sense of the numinous as the universal basis of religious experience which will always be found in the origins of specific religions (Jung 1969b: 7, 8). This experience creates the religions in a variety of ways. The experience is individual in the cases of the "historical" founders of religion, who may with difficulty be separated from the myth that immediately envelops them, such as the Buddha, the Jewish patriarchs, Jesus, Paul and Mohammed. Their experience generates their following, their scriptures as the mythical figures they become for their followers, and the civilizations their followers create. Where a religion is impersonal or transpersonal and does not rely on such notable and "historical" individuals, religion also provides access to the numinous as in the Taoist or Hindu traditions or legitimizes the social order with a numinous validation as with the Confucian tradition where an "historical" founder, in fact, existed but not as a mythical figure. In a Jungian perspective, then, the archetypal psyche is the common source of that numinosity which at once creates the Gods and the faith of their communities in them. Jung and Huntington are to this point in total agreement that such faith then serves as the basic bond of each civilization, differentiates it from the others and provides the potential if not necessity for enmity between them. However, Jung would go beyond

Huntington's analysis by providing Huntington with the identification of the common ground of this bonding in a psyche shared by all of humanity.

Having identified the common source of religion and civilization, Jung is then faced with the identical problem that Huntington and current humanity face. For the commonality Jung identifies in the psyche and the commonalities Huntington perceives and seeks in history lie in and are expressions of the archetypal unconscious and its infinite fecundity. Once this universal potential "of indefinite extent with no assignable limits" (Jung 1969c: 258) concretizes in the historical generation of the Gods and their civilizations their differentiation breeds the inter-civilizational conflict that currently threatens the continuation of the species (Dourley 2008: 111–126). Communities differentiated by their archetypal bonding, with the ever present danger of being rendered unconscious by such bonding, face immense problems in their interface. They can readily find themselves compelled through the archetypal enmity such bonding generates to destroy the common human psyche that created them through their religious foundation, much as kidney stones or cancer move to destroy the body to which they owe their existence (Dourley 1987). This scenario would be realized if competing religion based civilizations were to terminate the human psyche through nuclear conflict and so frustrate the psyche in bringing itself through history into an ever fuller and richer consciousness now understood as the base meaning of incarnation and as the deepest meaning of history itself. At a more immediate level, individual and collective acts of terrorism can ultimately be traced back to the religious and so archetypal conviction of the terrorist which in turn rests on a faith filled allegiance to a civilization in conflict.

The power of archetypal bonding can be given a number of names. Some of the more common are "faith", "patriotism", "ethnicity" and "ideology". All pay tribute to the absolutism and attendant unconsciousness that the archetypes can constellate in the communities they unite through collective possession. When a specifically religious faith intersects with patriotic and ideological faiths the devotion to the absolute in question increases synergistically. A dramatic example of this lethal combination is the marriage of capitalism, democracy and Christian fundamentalism, a coalition of three archetypal horsemen of death currently riding rampant through portions of the Middle East.

Jung on the shadow side of the religions and civilizations

At this point the psychosocial law at the heart of Jung's social psychology developed in Chapter 6 needs to be repeated. The greater the power of the religious and/or secular bonding of a community, the lesser the consciousness of the individual in that community and so the lesser the collective moral capacity and responsibility of that community in relation to counter bonded communities. Huntington joins Jung in his explicit references to the numbing of consciousness such bonding by the absolute works, especially in its religious forms (Huntington 1996/2003: 130, 262–265). Though Huntington keys some of these remarks on Islam, the problem would naturally extend to each of the monotheisms themselves. With each of their three particular Gods claiming universal validity, it is not difficult to understand the bloodshed along the fault lines where their communities meet. As seen earlier in the chapter, Jung's understanding of shadow projection by communities possessed by any one of the one and only Gods can easily move to demonizing those not belonging to the faith community thus possessed. Huntington writes, "It is human to hate" (Huntington 1996/2003: 130). He makes this remark in the context of community bonding requiring a hated other in the process of its own self-definition. Huntington would join Jung in the negative evaluation of contemporary inter-civilizational conflict when national or tribal leaders can call each other and their opposing empires "evil" or "satanic" and go, for the most part, unchallenged by theologians, philosophers of religion and social ethicists to roars of approval by their loyal but unconscious constituencies. Chapter 6 argued that Jung is clearly contending that the archetypally conferred and claimed primacy and goodness of any civilization proceeds from the same archetypal source in which he locates evil and absolute evil. On the basis of the presence of absolute evil and good in the common source of religion and civilization, the dynamics of hatred between civilizations can be better understood as a collective splitting reflecting the split between absolute good and evil in the archetypal unconscious. Our absolute goodness generates their absolute evil. This psychodynamic is evident in Huntington's formulation of "the West against the rest" (Huntington 1996/2003: 183). Jung's formulation goes deeper and strongly suggests that the identification of an evil opposite is necessary to the religious bonding constitutive of the civilizations themselves. The question then becomes what can be done to lessen or remove the current threat that faith based communities pose to the human endeavor itself? This question would lead to the further inquiry. Can a civilization be founded on a religious premise that does not require the projection of evil on sister civilizations?

Too often past and recent history demonstrate that the only option that the split among competing civilizations affords is to convert or kill. Where conversion fails, as it will when faith meets faith, the process of the projection of the collective shadow is activated and demonization becomes the first step in dehumanization as the necessary prelude to attempted elimination evident in ethnic cleansing and real and near genocide in twentieth century history and current events. Huntington's analysis of the clash of civilizations in terms of an us against them is thus fully supported and greatly deepened by Jung's understanding of the psychic dynamics involved. However, Jung's taking the issue to the archetypal level adds a depth to Huntington's analysis which suggests the problem of the clash of civilizations defies a wholly rational or geopolitical resolution. In the end all Huntington has to offer is geopolitical rationality and its scheming among the players involved. In his later works this becomes his sole resource as references to a commonality associated with Civilization disappear and he opts for the implied superiority and maintenance of the Western Anglo Protestant tradition informed by Enlightenment values and located in North America and Western Europe. In contradistinction to a purely rational approach Jung's psychology contends that only the conscious identification of the origins of religion and civilization in realms transcending consciousness, but not the psyche, will suffice to relativize and so humanize the absolutes (our good against their evil) in a growing recognition of the common ground of all such absolutes in the depths of universal humanity. Such recognition could hardly fail to be powerfully irenic. To kill for one's variant of a common experience would become as absurd as contending that one of Grimm's fairy tales was normative to which all other tales should bow.

Jung's eschatology and the one world

There is an all-encompassing cosmology and philosophy of history embedded in Jung's understanding of the psyche (Dourley 2008: 116–118). They rest on the dynamic of the universal and unbounded unconscious becoming increasingly manifest in human consciousness as the telos and direction of history itself. This dynamic is the basis of Jung's cosmology and its eschatology. Eschatology is here taken in its theological context to mean the direction history takes on as it moves toward its fulfillment. As such eschatology is always a form of teleology and the teleology of psyche is one of Jung's greatest achievements. Jung's most dramatic statement of his eschatology and where he used the term explicitly is in his work on Job. In the symbol of the Christ figure's dying in despair on the cross, Jung argues that God and the human are redeemed in the suffering of each other borne by both and that this mutual redemption constitutes the foundational movement of history itself.

> Here his [Christ's] human nature attains divinity; at that moment God experiences what it means to be a mortal man and drinks to the dregs what he made his faithful servant Job suffer. Here is given the answer to Job, and, clearly, this supreme moment is as divine as it is human, as "eschatological" as it is "psychological".
>
> (Jung 1969d: 408)

The eschatology Jung here delineates would understand the conflicted but inexhaustible unconscious to create consciousness in order to become conscious in it. The form this dialectic takes is that of consciousness perceiving the divine self-contradiction and suffering its resolution in history at the insistence of the archetypal unconscious, that is, at the insistence of the divine itself. In this process the human redeems the divine and the divine the human through the ongoing conscious resolution of archetypal opposites in historical humanity. It need hardly be said that Jung is here using a specifically Christian image to describe a process that is universally human. There is no proselytizing on behalf of any specific religion.

The archetypal power at work in the process is that power the religions call "God". These themes are the foundational themes of Jung's late Hegelian work, *Answer to Job*. They are ultimately rooted in Jacob Boehme, who is the common spiritual and intellectual ancestor of both Jung and Hegel. Religions in support of civilizations are, at least for collective consciousness, the most significant expressions of the unconscious. The ongoing tragedy in past and present is that they tend to congeal into conflicting opposites though they share a common source in the unconscious. Religiously put the religions are variant expressions of the one true God, the primordial source of the variant religions which proceed from it. The tragedy in the process is that each variant takes itself as the primordial source of all the variants. On the basis of these master themes in Jung it will only be through the resolution of the religions' conflicted historical interrelationship that the more inclusive Civilization and religious sentiment envisaged by Huntington and Jung will evolve. But the condition of the evolution toward the Civilization that Huntington sought and Jung envisages would rest on religious and political absolutes realizing their common origin in humanity's depth. Such realization would make each of them relative and drive each to seek a superceding unity beyond their current conflicting petrifaction. Given the intransigency with which these absolutes have to be maintained by both political and religious leaders significant self-transcendence of the prisons of faith, religious and secular, remains remote. Religiously such empathy would be heresy. Politically it would be treason. In a democracy it would likely entail the removal from office.

If there is to be a solution to this compelling human problem, the first factor contributing to it is to be found in the very dynamics of Jung's eschatology. For, in key passages, he will describe the unconscious as vested with a boundless fecundity which would defy a final and exhaustive expression in personal or collective consciousness and, by extension, in the consciousness that the whole historical process could yield (Jung 1969c: 258). For Jung that state of rest or completion when God would be all in all might well serve as a heuristic goad toward such a state but would remain a psychic impossibility in the unfolding of historical human consciousness. For such an eschatology implicates not only a common source of all religions and cultures. It further strongly suggests that none of them could claim the kind of ultimacy and finality exhaustive of their common source which each tends, in fact, to claim, an ultimacy that lies at the heart of inter-civilizational conflict. In this manner Jung's eschatology does two things. It acknowledges and respects the archetypal basis of the sense of the absolute or archetypal ultimacy carried by the faith which informs conflicting civilizations, even as it makes such ultimacy relative by forbidding it exhaustive expression in each and any of its religious or cultural manifestations. Critically, such an eschatology would corrode all claims by competing civilizations and their religions to an unqualified ultimacy as arrogant and, in the current world situation, anti-social and so immoral. Here Jung would provide Huntington with substantial psychological support for the latter's attack on the missionary or imperial globalizing of a civilizational or religious particularity especially when carried out militarily. Positively, such an eschatology would encourage those who stand in one particular religion or civilization to look to other such communities, to their symbols and to their values for variations of their own. In so doing, such seekers would unearth the commonalities they share with each other and, where such commonality is not in evidence, still be enriched by aspects of the unconscious revealed in an archetypal perspective other than one's own. Even then the realization that the history of consciousness itself would remain incapable of fully manifesting the wealth of its origin would be a sobering and paramount factor restraining all unilateral claims to an exhaustive possession of a saving truth.

Making relative the omnipresent absolute is but a preliminary contribution Jung's social psychology makes to the alleviation of the clash of civilizations. More importantly not only does his psychology contend, in the theoretical sphere, that the source of the world's religions and civilizations lies in the depth of human subjectivity, but also his psychology works to enable the individual's experiential access to that common source. Personal and unmediated experience of the universal source of the religions and their civilizations within human interiority can only generate an extended compassion or sympathy for the totality on the part of the personality undergoing such experience. This dynamic of the intensification of the individual's sympathy for the totality, through intersection with the source of the totality as the foundation of the individual's being, is the common element in the master images of maturation in Jung's corpus. The mandala, the *anthropos*, the "one world" of the alchemists, the dialectic of macrocosm and microcosm, and the phenomena of synchronicity, all imply that each individual intersects with the source of the totality in that individual's depths. These images further imply that the dynamic of individual and collective or civilizational maturation moves toward the realization in individual consciousness of that universally shared point of intersection of the individual with the whole.

Jung's most forceful depiction of the experience of the point of intersection between individuality and totality lies in his appropriation of Dorn's understanding of alchemical transformation. In this alchemical tradition a radical interior asceticism imaged by the soul's removal from the body, death itself, followed by a more total immersion in the world through the reunion of such a soul with the body culminates in the state Jung and Dorn termed the "*unus mundus*" (the one world). The consciousness described by the phrase is one in which the individual's perception of the world, human and natural, derives from a conscious connectedness with "the eternal Ground of all empirical being" (Jung 1970: 534, 535). In much of the German religious and mystical tradition the term "ground" is effectively a synonym for God and carries the connotation of both cause and substance while denying equation with either. "Ground" implies that God causes the creature but is not removed as cause from the creature caused. "Ground" also implies that the creature is in substantial continuity with its origin but never to the point of an unqualified, permanent identity. In terms of the current discussion the consciousness of the unitary world underlying the empirical multiple would imply the ability to perceive one's religion and civilization from the perspective of the ground of all religions and civilizations. Such a perspective could hardly evade a deepened appreciation of one's own tradition modified by a heightened sensitivity for and embrace of all other traditions as derivative of the same source.

This consciousness adds a note of greater depth and substance to the commonalties that Huntington seeks as the basis of a surpassing Civilization. It points to the depths of human subjectivity as the locus from which these commonalities will (it is hoped) rise to consciousness. Jung's myth not only identifies the source of these commonalities but also argues that the archetypal unconscious as the maker of historical epochs (Jung 1964h: 549) is currently birthing yet another. This epoch would be characterized by a turn to human subjectivity in the search for the human origin of religious and civilizational affirmations which would reveal in their very variations their nuanced commonalities. For instance Western religious extraversion would differentiate from Eastern introversion in the recognition by each of the needed truth of the other. Jung was confident that such an inward turn would produce a consciousness at once appreciative of and yet transcending the extant concretions of the religious impulse, a consciousness that would contribute greatly to both the survival and the enhancement of the species. In fact in the light of his eschatology an epoch resting on a global consciousness of the inner origin of all absolutes, religious or secular, would describe the teleology of history itself. Huntington's geopolitical strategies for the preservation and strengthening of Western civilization will no doubt remain important for the conservation of the considerable contribution that Western civilization continues to make to the world. However, if the level of Huntington's strategies is the only strategic level, it would appear that his strategies and the counter-strategies of the West's opponents hold out but a bleak future of ongoing conflict between contending civilizations unconscious of what possesses them and empowers their mutual enmity.

From a Jungian perspective, only if the source of the commonalities Huntington envisions comes gradually into fuller historical consciousness will humanity ever go beyond the Sisyphean clash of civilizations and of the Gods that found and support them. If the drive to become conscious of such commonality can be linked to the movement of the psyche and so of history itself and, if this drive can be shown to be immediately accessible to the individual, the attendant consciousness would greatly enhance the hopes of realizing a surpassing Civilization. Jung provides the missing link between the individual's unmediated access to the human source of the religious impulse itself with its current increasingly global urgency to become conscious in contemporary humanity in the form of a more universal embrace of the differently archetypally bonded. This linkage is one of the foundational elements and dynamisms of his myth. Jung's psychology could serve and further Huntington's acute analysis of civilizational conflict and his search for a surpassing Civilization by providing it with the depth that only a mythic grounding can provide. Jung's myth would do this by uncovering both the origin of religious or civilizational conflict and the resources for its resolution in the human source of all civilizational differentiation. The widespread experiential recovery of this dimension of humanity would foster the mutual embrace of the different civilizations moving them toward a richer, more encompassing Civilization, because it would so clearly identify the author of the religions, of their civilizations, of their conflicts as well as the resolution of their conflicts to be the human psyche itself.

Chapter 8

Jung and the recall of the Gods

Jung on religion: the coincidence of theory and therapy

The preceding chapters make it clear that Jung's understanding of psyche is incompatible with the supernaturalism explicit or implied in the monotheistic imagination. These chapters also clarify the disastrous social and political consequences attendant upon the escape of these divinities from the containment of the psyche into an independent existence in the skies of theological transcendence. At the same time, when it is realized that the response to these various Gods in projection enabled humanity to understand the movements of the human psyche that created them, the moment of their externalization can be helpful if they can now be recalled to their origin and addressed there. Consequently any and every form of monotheism that would understand divinity to be an entity, personal or transpersonal, possessed of a self-sufficiency even potentially disengaged from nature and the psyche would fall far short of Jung's understanding of the relation of divinity to humanity. The existence of such a remote entity would fail to accommodate Jung's dialectical interplay of divinity and humanity intersecting in history in processes of mutual completion. Further inquiry revealed that the intimacy Jung established between psyche and religious consciousness extends to his social, political and cultural psychology. It does so because religious, political and civilizational faith jointly derive from the same archetypal basis generating faith in all the Gods, religious and secular, as the basis of these civilizations. It follows that the religious and political/cultural Gods, then, are but two variants of a common generative source. Historically, at least in the West, the former preceded the latter but the latter, in the guise of modern secularity, are no less divested of a divinely based exhaustive ultimacy than were the transcendent Gods who preceded modernity. The problem for the contemporary, delineated by the current collusion of geopolitical insight with psychology, is that faith communities bonded by either religious or secular faith continue to contribute to the body count in their geographic and historic interplay.

Jung's basic strategy in response to such communal conflict was to attempt consciously to reroot or reconnect the individual with the God-creating energies of the psyche and so restore to the individual the highest possible freedom from collective unconsciousness and communal faith as the basis of the courage to face and affirm life consciously in one's immediate environment. Living out of the power of one's personal and unique truth would then constitute the greatest contribution the individual could make to the amelioration of the broader society in which the individual lived. Though always the carrier of social consequence, on closer examination, accessing such freedom and courage turns out to be a highly individual enterprise and to centre, in one form or another, on a lengthy, if not indefinite conversation with the unconscious. This conversation is always with a power of universal extent and so is never solipsistic. On the contrary a more universal sentiment arises from the conversation between two partners. One partner is the individual ego in space, time and the particularity of a never to be repeated life. The other is source of that life and all of life and so capable of breeding a deep compassion for what is. For Jung this process attains a certain maximum intensity in analysis understood as an unmediated and usually protracted conversation with the unconscious and its immense energies through the personal revelation of the dream as the bearer of a position other than and transcendent or "supraordinate" to the ego's. Such practice would move to an ongoing incarnation of the self, the author of the dream, in the consciousness of the dreamer. It would engender what Jung calls the "more compendious" personality in whom the unity of consciousness with the unconscious would ideally deepen over the course of a lifetime (Jung 1969c: 258). This is not to say that such conversation would not take place under psychological auspices other than analysis and, indeed, under auspices not explicitly psychological at all such as religious ritual, traditional spiritual direction, conscious collective political action or various forms of creative expression in any of many media, such as the many faces of the arts. It is to say that for Jung the connection with one's individual divinity is worked in a primary and most effective manner through the dream dialogue in the intensifying containment of analysis. For that reason it is of interest to explore the implication that the analytic event between two people is, in and of itself, religious since it rests on material expressive of the same source as that of the world's religions, a source, in Jung's view, currently calling for a myth superceding the current and variant mythical bases of the West.

In the context of the immediate experience of the archetypal brought to a certain conscious height in analysis Jungian theory and therapy unite with each other and both unite with religion. Jung's greatly extended sense of religion rests on the unmediated experience of the numinous. Among other venues the numinous impacts consciousness most powerfully through the symbols and their interaction in the dream as an individual myth contributing to the individual's more total myth revealed over a lifetime. The sustained attention given to the dream symbols is what Jung means by living the symbolic life. Effectively it is the living into one's personal relation to the divine as the energy that sustains one's life and so is in and of itself religious.

In its more impressive incursions into consciousness Jung understands the numinous, in whatever form it may take, to work toward a synthesis made up of psychological characteristics which at first sight would seem to be in considerable tension. For he strongly suggests that the numinosity attaching to the power of the self works ever more intense patterns of personal or individual integration with universal relatedness. Such a synthesis of apparent opposites not only defeats more traditional dualisms between individual and totality. More, Jung understood the lived union of the opposites of individual integration and universal relatedness as the experience underlying humanity's understanding of itself as an "image of God". Such unity is the hallmark of the ego's experience of the self as Jung describes it, "The self then functions as a union of opposites and thus constitutes the most immediate experience of the Divine which it is psychologically possible to imagine" (Jung 1969c: 261). Jung's master images of the self, such as the mandala, the alchemical *unus mundus* and the reality of synchronicity all rest on the experience of the individual's connection with the totality worked through the connection with the self as the ground of individuality. Jung could hardly be more explicit. "If mandala symbolism is the psychological equivalent of the *unus mundus*, then synchronicity is its parapsychological equivalent" (Jung 1970: 464). The power expressed in the symbols of the mandala, and in the experience of the *unus mundus* and synchronicity all imply the individual's connectedness with a universal energy underlying what exists in which what exists naturally participates.

The experience of the numinous lies not only at the heart of Jungian theory. It is the substance of Jungian therapy. Without it no significant transformation takes place. Again Jung is explicit. "But the fact is that the approach to the numinous is the real therapy and inasmuch as you attain to the numinous experiences you are released from the curse of pathology" (Jung 1945c: 377). When the experience of the numinous becomes the basis of both religion universally and "real therapy", the distinction between Jung's theory of religious experience and the practice of his therapy collapses. The doing of classical Jungian therapy as it engages the numinous, especially as carried by dreams observed in sequence over time, becomes itself a religious event. The religious nature of this event stands in contemporary and, perhaps, constant need of clarification so that, at least, the analyst is made fully aware of what is at stake in the analytic process. For it is one in which the analyst and analysand together foster the birth of the self in the analysand's consciousness through the dream dialogue with the self. In effect the analysis becomes a revelation of the individual's unique myth originating, in Jung's view, from the same source that gives rise to all religions, namely, the archetypal dimension of the psyche.

This process is initially a freeing one. The discovery of one's unique archetypal truth enables the individual to distinguish one's personal myth and so oneself from the myths into which one is inevitably born. As stated in Chapter 1, these are the layers of collective mythology such as ethnicity, religion, nationality, social status, etc., which can serve, in varying degrees, as impediments or resources in the emergence of the self. But it is only the emergence of the self in the consciousness of the individual that frees the individual to relate one's inherited mythologies to the uniqueness of one's own. As this truth emerges into consciousness the individual is progressively released from a compulsive and unconscious adhesion to received mythologies toward a more discerning response to them out of the power of the inimitable and sustaining truth of the personal self. This response can range from outright rejection to a heightened appreciation of the symbolic, ritual and more meaningful dimensions of the mythologies one inherits at birth. The point is that wherever the response lies along the scale from rejection to integration of inherited truths, it is a response in living touch with the power of the individual's personal myth. Here the psychological, religious and political dimensions of Jung's myth coalesce. In the end the power of the individual's self is, for Jung, the only power that enables the individual to respond to the collective as an individual. Once more, *"Resistance to the mass can be effected only by the man who is as well organized in his individuality as the mass itself"* (Jung 1964c: 278, italics Jung's). Hence processes of the ingression of the self into the consciousness of the individual are never without social and political consequence. But, as argued in Chapter, 1, being as well organized in one's person as is the mass itself is a daunting challenge and demand. It forms the harshest and most difficult to attain moral imperative at the heart of Jung's myth.

Yet the morality attached to the sense of self means that the individual's growing into one's personal myth in the analytic or any other process is never a solipsistic event. Such growth is a significant social resource because it provides society with individuals endowed with the critical perspective that only living out of their personal myth affords. This side of the religious role of the analytic process is peculiarly pressing in a time of epochal change. As seen in Chapter 5, Jung thought his time and ours was a time of such epochal change. He refers to "the end of the Christian aeon", to "the invalidation of Christ", and describes himself as a modern Joachim di Fiore whose psychology contributes to a new age of the Spirit (Jung 1953a: 138). In this context the analytic endeavor can be revisioned not only on a personal level as an occasion for the surfacing of individual mythologies. The analytic endeavor becomes, through the individuals it touches, a major contributor to the emergence of a more encompassing collective myth or now dawning societal revelation which Jung and his psychology anticipated but understandably could not describe in more than general terms.

The turbulence surrounding the birth of a new societal myth is presently vividly evident at the collective level. The educated and spiritually sensitive turn away in great numbers from religious institutions that continue to take their founding poets, the writers of their Holy Scriptures, literally and then rely on legalism and authority to enforce belief in the unbelievable. Traditional theology thus remains where it was in Jung's day. "It proclaims doctrines which nobody understands, and demands a faith which nobody can manufacture" (Jung 1969e: 192). With the departure of those with a native religious sensitivity and/or developed mind, collective religion is largely abandoned to various forms and degrees of fundamentalism in both West and East. The numerical surge of institutional fundamentalism, religious or political, bears stark witness to those baser human lusts collective religion so often serves, namely, the need for instant certitude collectively reinforced in the face of the anxiety and fear of living with doubt. For instance in the Catholic tradition, with which I am most familiar, the spirit of renewal promised by Vatican II in the 1960s has been broken by more than a quarter century reign of imperial papacies with ideological roots in the thirteenth century. The head of the Inquisition during much of this period has now succeeded his predecessor to the Papacy. Romanism is far from the only religious tradition to have circled the wagons in an instinctive defense against the emergence of a secularity of higher moral instinct informed by a still fragile but growing religious sense of a broader compassion and more inclusive embrace.

For many contemporaries caught in this current situation the religious import of the analytic process could serve as the "*tertium*", the third, not given or not entertained as a possibility by those whose dismay with traditional religion holds out but two bleak options. Many opt either to grind their teeth and stay in their tradition often to their spiritual and human detriment. The other option is simply to walk away from it, perhaps to a religious commitment to various forms of social activism but more often to the sterility of a life without the depth that functional religion can provide. Jung's tertium, the third possibility, would hold out the option of accessing the source of all religions as the basis of one's personal religious life through accessing the collective depths of the personal psyche. The experience of the psyche's profundity and energy could restore the vitalities of religious experience to those who would engage it, its arduous demands, and its quiet rewards, with an immediacy devoid of institutional need or intervention. Such access might bring to some a transformed and heightened appreciation of their former traditions, symbols and rites now freed of their literal misinterpretation and authoritarian imposition. As an example, such experience would be of help to a now sociologically discernible group known as "recovering Catholics", those who are living their religious life from an immediate sense of the divine and accommodating the ecclesial collective to the demands of such personal immediacy. Whether or not such recovery mediated by the natural religious impulse of the psyche takes place within or beyond ecclesial confines or combines both, it would restore a vitality that only the experience of the endemic religious depths of the human can provide in the form of a natural grace.

Or, on the other hand, and in a more gnostic vein, many today may have to go it alone and simply "stand before the Nothing out of which All may grow" (Jung 1964d: 75). In this passage Jung suggests that this alternative may indeed be the face of a present and future religion for the truly "modern" though few might currently be able to bear its demands. On the one hand Jung will point to and endorse the gnostic appreciation of immediate experience at the heart of contemporary spirituality. "The spiritual currents of our time have, in fact, a deep affinity with Gnosticism" (Jung 1964d: 83). On the other hand he regretfully concedes that such spirituality is still far beyond the capacity of mass believers. He writes in a spirit of sober evaluation, "For a longer time and for the great majority of mankind the symbol of a collective religion will suffice" (Jung 1969o: 59). Deeper than either a gnostic or collective religious option and the many variations that lie between them is Jung's contention that recovering and abiding in one's personal revelation, the consciousness of one's "distinctiveness", is the greatest contribution the individual can make to the surpassing myth, the new revelation, now struggling for birth in the religious culture of the West (Jung 1969o: 59). Those vested with the sense of distinctiveness are a challenge to collective consciousness and from such challenge culture moves forward. Consequently the birthing of the modern religious myth makes the exploration of the religious implications of the analytic process, the melding of the theory and practice of religion in a Jungian sense, worthwhile.

Capping the volcano

As outlined in Chapter 1, Jung's understanding of the psyche rests on a conception of containment which tolerates no invasion of the psyche by agencies beyond the psyche. Such containment eliminates all commerce between an allegedly self-sufficient supernatural world of divine beings and the all encompassing natural world of psyche. From the viewpoint of the religionist such containment means that the psyche creates all the divinities and, in so doing, all personal and collective faiths in them. Faith, at least initially in the founder and then among the community, is simply the powerful numinosity attendant to the creation of the Gods either in the form of transcendent entities or their human incarnations. This perception is the basis of Jung's pervasive and expansive pantheism. Everything that is is "God become concrete" (Jung 1969d: 402). For Jung this now dawning consciousness marks the culmination of a millennial evolution of religious maturation one which carries with it a moral imperative. This imperative demands that responsible religion recall the Gods to their psychic origin where dialogue with them would continue on the basis of the individual's conversation with the powers presented in the dreams. Jung's manifesto states "everything of a divine or demonic character outside us must return to the psyche, to the inside of the unknown man, whence it apparently originated" (Jung 1969b: 85). This inner dialogue would be at once socially safer and personally more harrowing. It would be socially safer because it would undermine the conflict between religious communities who claim a universal truth for one or other of their particular still competing transcendent Gods. The dialogue would be more harrowing because it would face the individual with an inner critique more personal, rigorous and defiant of evasion than any religion can muster. Internalizing the conversation with deity would also, in Jung's words, terminate "the systematic blindness" that "God is *outside* man." It would force humanity to confront its Gods and its faiths in them within the confines of the psyche from which they first are born. Attention would turn to "*the God within*" (Jung 1969b: 58, italics Jung's).

Recent Jungian reflection on the internalization of the relation to the divine has illuminated the Jungian options to the inevitable question Jung's work poses, "Is there a God beyond the psyche?" As exposed in Chapter 1, at this point Lionel Corbett's work becomes again pertinent. Corbett points out in strict continuity with Jung that the experience of the numinous is the basis in humanity for the experience of God. This leads to only two options in relating the numinous to the possibility of a God beyond the psyche. Corbett puts it this way: "To reiterate: numinous experience arises from an autonomous level of the psyche that is either the source of, or the medium for, the transmission of religious experience; empirically we cannot say which" (Corbett 1996: 8). If the unconscious is the source of the numinous experience there would be no need to posit a God beyond the psyche. If the unconscious is the medium of the numinous experience then one could posit the reality of God beyond the unconscious yet somehow constricted to address the human through the unconscious. This would lead to the question of why such a God in his creative role would use such an ambivalent medium as the unconscious to make his presence and project known in his redemptive role. This option, when closely examined, imagines a God or divine power along theistic lines. In his disputes with both Buber and White, Jung dismissed such imagination as a regression to medieval theism and incompatible with his conception of psyche. The remaining much more abstemious option affirms that the unconscious is, in fact, the source of the numinous and requires no reality beyond it for the generation of the numinous as the basis of humanity's experience of the divine. The option for the unconscious as the source of the numinous would lead to the responsible and organic conception of a wholly intrapsychic transcendence, one that would affirm that the unconscious infinitely transcends ego consciousness but that nothing transcends the total psyche. Jung's own apparent waffling on this issue might well have a number of causes. Among the more likely are the progressive development of his thought, particularly as spurred on by his dialogue with White's medievalism, and his sometimes less than candid dialogue with theologians disguising the fact that he knew or suspected his developing position was incompatible with their orthodoxies. As seen earlier in this work, he was, however, quite frank in his debates with Victor White and Martin Buber that the disguised or explicit supernaturalism of both thinkers was incompatible with his understanding of the psyche in its religious function.

Corbett is also accurate in his perception that Jung's psychology rests on an Eastern Vedantic notion of a point of residual identity between the divine and the human within the human. He goes on to comment that, though this position is consistent with certain Western mystics like Eckhart, it is in serious conflict with orthodox Jewish and Christian insistence on an objective transcendent God. He notes, "So far Jungian depth psychologists have largely been dualistic in this regard, presumably reflecting the unconscious bias of their Judaeo-Christian heritage" (Corbett 1996: 42). Corbett's is a rather strong indictment of Jungian analysts who cling to a theistic and supernatural conception of divinity as an objective entity beyond the psyche usually understood as its creator and later as the source of further revelations. At a more philosophical level this position rests on a subject/object split between the divine and the human which Jung's mature work rejects in favor of a position that would understand divinity and humanity to share a point in common invalidating the subject/object split. Corbett's critique that the dualism between the human and a wholly other God evident in so much Jungian commentary is hostile to Jung's understanding of the psyche has much to validate it. It is difficult to reconcile such a divinity with Jung's statement, "The naive assumption that the creator of the world is a conscious being must be regarded as a disastrous prejudice which later gave rise to the most incredible dislocations of logic" (Jung 1969d: 383, fn. 13). Rather in the context of his work on Job, Jung would frame the ego in a much more immediate relation with its creator, a power as beastly as good, looking for the reconciliation of its opposites and so its own redeeming consciousness in human consciousness. In terms of the analytic process the reality of incarnation takes place in the Jungian sense that the divine and human move into greater integration in the consciousness of the analysand as the self becomes conscious there through the dreams and the analyst as catalyst. The suffering of analysis in its depth is the suffering of the resolution of whatever side of the divine self-contradiction seeks its relief in the history of the individual in analysis.

Humanity's current participation in the ongoing divine/human drama calls up the image of the volcano that now needs to be capped in the wake of Jung's recall of the Gods to their psychic origin. Jung confronts contemporary humanity with the question of whether it is up to suffering divinely based conflict in the immediate precinct of human interiority, the matrix of all the Gods, without breaking containment and destroying itself in the name of transcendent divinities or their secular equivalents. Failure to meet Jung's challenge would only continue the sad current situation of externalizing the conflict and blowing up, in the name of the demonic, whatever contradicts one's own truncated personal or collective compact or testament with the divine. Thus the recall of the Gods and the internal resolution of their mutual enmity as the precedent of external peace is currently at the heart of the hope of the species that it can survive the Gods and the religion creating proclivity of the psyche in its current productions. It is the fire of this wider hope the analytic process fans through addressing whatever archetypal conflict it faces in the individual circumstances of the analysand. Each individual gain in consciousness contributes to the contemporary emergence of a myth informed by a more universal sensitivity and wider inclusion now sponsored by the unconscious in its role as the maker not only of the Gods but of history. Jung describes this way forward when he writes, "Therefore any advance always begins with individuation, that is to say with the individual conscious of his isolation, cutting a new path through hitherto untrodden territory" (Jung 1969o: 59).

Personal analysis and the emerging myth

A foundational element of Jung's myth is humanity's unmediated experience of divinity and the dynamic this experience presently unleashes. If humanity and divinity naturally share a common point or ground, the thrust of this ground is to manifest its total potential in ever more extensive and so inclusive approximations of human totality. As it drives toward the fullest manifestation of itself in the human, the divine and psychic ground of humanity exercises both an expansive and balancing influence on the humanity in whom it seeks to become conscious. In effect this side of Jung's mythology is addressing the compensatory nature of revelation. Put simply Jung equates revelation with the compensation the unconscious offers to the culture in which the revelation occurs. It does this by redressing the one-sidedness of any cultural constellation but always toward a balanced unity of opposites and so a greatly extended justice and compassion. In effect cultures get the Gods, saviors, and religions they deserve and need. The current quest would be to a God beyond the Gods of theism and to a religious sense which appreciates even as it bids adieu to divinities and their communities making exclusive and exhaustive claims to ultimacy accompanied by a narrowed sense of the naturally sacred.

Bringing these positions to bear on the contemporary situation, Jung introduces a complex historical argument concluding that the Christian God and, by extension, those of the monotheisms provided a much needed compensation to their constituencies in the form of libidinal restraint, a universal love proceeding from the soul and the energies thus freed to create civilization (Jung 1966a: 66–71). These Gods were male and restraining if not repressive. Their restraint made possible the enhanced powers of consciousness contributing to the making of Western civilization. However, the compensation they made in the form of the enhancement of the spiritual currently cries out for its own compensation, that is, for a new revelation at whose service Jung places his psychology. For the monotheisms could not fully sacralize the feminine, the bodily and the demonic nor were they aware of their origins in the religious proclivities of the psyche itself. Indeed as the one-sidedness of their compensation developed the feminine, the bodily and the demonic too often became one in a murderous patriarchal consciousness. The now emerging compensation, the new revelation, would thus address "the fatality inherent in the Christian disposition itself" and do so in accordance with the inevitability of a "psychological law" deter-mining consequent and current history (Jung 1968c: 43). Though Jung identifies Christianity as the premier compensation now needing its own compensation his remarks here would extend to the other monotheisms, whose initial compensatory imbalance toward the spiritual, would inevit-ably fall prey to the same laws of the psyche and evoke their own com-pensatory redress in the course of time (Jung 1968c: 43).

On the precise times and mode of the revelatory forces compensating Christianity, Jung waffles. Sometimes he locates the reversal and expansion of consciousness beyond the patriarchal in the image of the Sun Woman in the Book of Revelation, itself within the Christian canon (Jung 1969d: 439, 458). Consistent with the fuller incarnation the Sun Woman symbolizes, Jung sometimes locates the now emerging compensation of the mono-theistic myth in the gnostic/alchemical tradition, in the medieval Spirit movements, in the mystics of various traditions, and in the devotees of the grail. What these traditions have in common is the sense of the immediacy of the divine often as a maternal power preceding the patriarchal and urging the expansion of natural consciousness to the inclusion of more of her creative wealth. Elsewhere Jung will locate significant moments in the compensation of Christianity in Renaissance neo-Platonism with its extended sense of a residual divine presence to nature and mind. Finally he points to the Enlightenment and to the French revolution (Jung 1968c: 43, 44) with their enthronement of reason as the anti-Christ compensating Christianity through the recovery of reason not without its own problems in the form of a societal rationalism extending to a contempoary culture in search of a depth religion can no longer access or provide (Dourley 1999: 58–65). Take your pick. Such imprecision is hardly the stuff that a more rigorous historical methodology would today tolerate but through it Jung does point to a process that has in fact unfolded historically and continues in today's Western culture.

In spite of his historical ambiguity and the difficulty in dating the appearance of the compensation that a one-sided Christianity in its very imbalance elicited, when Jung gives content to what the new revelation demands and offers he does address social phenomena undeniably visible in contemporary society. For Jung's myth moves from a Trinitarian paradigm of a self-sufficient divinity only contingently involved in the human histori-cal drama to a quaternitarian paradigm (Jung 1969e: 174, 175). In this paradigm divinity and humanity are co-dependents in processes of reciprocal fulfillment in time. Within this context Jung can be very precise on what is lacking in the Spirit of a Trinitarian divinity and needs to be recovered and sacralized by the more inclusive Spirit of the quaternity. The Spirit of the new myth would confer divinity on the feminine as well as the masculine in the movement toward a richer androgynous consciousness. It is this Spirit that informs much of the feminist movement especially as it now matures beyond an initial democratizing patriarchal values through their extension to women. In 1952 Jung is prescient in his reference to "the signs of the times which point to the equality of women" (Jung 1969d: 465). Not many at this early date saw such signs.

The Spirit of the new myth was also operative at an unconscious level in restoring one side of the Goddess to her place in, at least, the Catholic pantheon through the declaration of the Assumption, for Jung, "the most important religious event since the Reformation" (Jung 1969d: 464). But if Jung is read closely he is found to be saying that the son and virgin of Bethlehem are divine, and so "not real human beings at all, but gods" (Jung 1969d: 399). As such they serve as a necessary but somewhat pallid prelude to a fuller incarnation of the divine in " an ordinary woman, not a goddess and not an eternal virgin immaculately conceived" (Jung 1969d: 439). Jung's full analysis of the meaning of the Catholic doctrine culminates in his claim that the conjunction of sun and moon in the woman and child of the Book of Revelation already compensates the less or more than fully human and wholly good Virgin and Son of the synoptic gospels (Jung 1969d: 439, 443, 448, 454). The former do not contain the totality of opposites that the Sun Woman and her child, who unite sun and moon, light and dark, do. What the author of the Book of Revelation took be a reprise of the first incarnation was actually its corrective. Already within the Christian canon a unity of opposites occurs which compensated the one sided and not fully human spirituality of a divine son born of an immacu-late virgin. With this view Jung can then readily connect the full restoration of the feminine in the woman and child of the apocalypse with the divinization of matter, the body and the material universe in a manner reminiscent of Blake's marriage of heaven and hell. This side of the Spirit of the quaternity is at work not only in the resacralization of the feminine but also in the contemporary increased interest in the body, the healing arts, and in the sense of the divine in nature as the depth dimension in even scientific environmental and ecological endeavors.

However, the symbol for the final inclusion of what the Spirit of the Trinity excludes from divinity and yet is so evident in humanity is much more elusive. Such a symbol would entail the Spirit worked synthesis of good and evil, lodging both good and evil in God and demanding that humanity work their resolution in history at the demand of divinity itself (Jung 1969d: 434; 1969e: 174, 175). On how this is to be done and what it might look like, Jung remains vague. In his engagement with White we have seen Jung to say that both good and evil are to be relativized in a perspective beyond good and evil but not at the cost of abandoning the traditional religious virtues which will be needed as this relativization takes place in empirical humanity (Jung 1953a: 136). Jung would concede that at some point we all get stuck (Jung 1953b: 297). It would appear he was stuck on providing greater detail on the emergence of a sense of the sacred in which good and evil, the light and dark sons and powers of the same God, could embrace in history.

One might address this problem and in so doing go beyond Jung by identifying where the problem is most evident in the contemporary world. As dealt with at greater length in Chapter 6, the problem of good and evil is blatantly evident in the mutual projection of evil onto each other by communities possessed by archetypally based suasion dignified by such noble names as "faith", or "patriotism", or "commitment". These euphemisms effectively disguise the loss of personal responsibility to archetypally induced collective unconsciousness. Going beyond good and evil in this context would mean the gracious moderation in individual and collectivity of claims to exhaustive possession of the absolute in any of its forms, religious, political or social. The murderous grip of competing absolutes on their victims' minds would surely be tempered through reflection on their common archetypal origin and on the narrowing influence they too often exert on the communities they bond. Humanizing by relativizing all claims to the unconditional possession of a saving truth would remain compatible with and respectful of Jung's frank acknowledgement that the sense of the absolute, and so of religion, can never be fully removed from human consciousness (Jung 1969b: 6). The only psychological and so real question then becomes how to deal with this fact individually and politically.

Nevertheless, Jung's insight that the unconscious, as infinitely fecund, could never bring itself to exhaustive and so final expression in any finite form, religious or secular (Jung 1969c: 258), would greatly undermine both individual and collective proclivities to project evil onto the other out of a sense of one's own identity with the absolute good or God. Spelling out the broader religious and political implications of Jung's thought in this manner is not to take them out of the analytic container or out of the specifics of a given analysis. Every analysis as it leads to greater conscious approximations of the self not only reveals the individual's myth but contributes to the sense of the individual's continuity with the totality and so breeds a universal sentiment hostile to premature and now dangerous communal or personal claims to an exhaustive possession of a saving truth. The experiential appropriation of one's individual myth corrodes the tyranny of mythologies claiming privileged access to a definitive salvation as all religious and many political mythologies continue to do. In this sense every analysis, every realization in the individual of what Jung calls "individuation" is a political act. The easy equation of God's will with atrocities currently perpetrated in the Middle East stands out as a blatant example of this dynamic at both religious and political levels.

As the inclusive consciousness of the incarnate self would spread, the claim of any ultimate, and especially a religious ultimate, to complete expression of the unconscious would be viewed as psychologically immature and socially unethical. Exclusive monotheisms, political or religious, would be deemed immoral. Humanity could finally come to see the connection between claims to the final revelation and the final solution. The dawning consciousness that all absolutes, and especially the religious, are products of a common generative ground would lead devotees of each to recognize the common ground of all. Archetypally bonded communities could then appreciate each other as variant expression of a shared human profundity. In short the now reigning need to convert or kill would be undermined in principle.

Conclusion: recovering our health from our heresy

Jung's psychology honors the priority of the Goddess or Great Mother in deference to the maternal nature of the deepest unconscious (Jung 1966a). If his psychology were to be given creedal or theological formulation it might read like this. In the beginning was not the Word but the maternal silence. Out of the silence the Goddess created her child, consciousness, that she might become self-conscious in her offspring. Consciousness was aware that the conflicted powers in its purview were disparate expressions of herself. Though from the outset she already dwelt in her child, she had to recall her child to a moment of immersion in herself from which the child returned, not once but many times, better able to unite her opposites in itself and in society (Jung 1969d: 459). This process is redemptive both of the Goddess and of the human who have from the outset been parts of each other in a common life. The Spirit of the Goddess thus always works toward the fullest manifestation of her infinite but conflicted energies in a humanity enriched by their syntheses. A significant aspect of this synthesis must be the symbolic embrace of her more prominent sons, Christ and Satan. The incarnation of the Goddess and her redemption in humanity is the base meaning of individual and collective life and suffering as well as the direction in which all of history moves (Jung 1969e: 179). As such it grounds a new eschatology based on the resolution of divine conflict in humanity, a divinely grounded mandate humanity can neither evade nor hope to complete in time. The mandate cannot be evaded because it is felt immediately in every individual's experience of the self. It can never be completed because the fullness of the unconscious will always outstrip its historical concretions. There will be no situation in history in which God will be all in all just as there can be no human life wholly divested of the drive toward such a consciousness.

The question that arises from the religious formulation of Jung's psychology is this. Can it be accepted by the religious mind currently prevailing in the West or has that mind in each of its significant variations in the process of its self-making excluded as heresy each of the above-mentioned foundational elements of Jung's myth? Western theological reflection on a good God in the wake of the holocaust has become what Jung calls "a universal religious nightmare" (Jung 1969d: 453), a one-sided truncation of the human spirit now in desperate need to recover its heresy if it is to heal its pathology. It remains to be seen whether the great religions, at least in the West, can affirm humanity's natural inhesion in a divinity that asks of humanity its cooperation in enabling the divine to become increasingly conscious through the manifestation and unification of its fullness in the only theatre available for that purpose, human consciousness (Jung 1969d: 461).

Beyond the identifiably religious sphere Jung's myth would seem to be enacted wherever a more extensive embrace of the totally human and the human totality is endorsed and realized, and especially in the extension of a full humanity to those members of the species whose full divinity had been denied or qualified by the still reigning religious and societal collectives. Within the religious sphere the mystical impulse would seem to be the most vital carrier of Jung's myth because of the mystics' unmediated experience of the divine and the mutual need of divine and human this immediacy implies. This is especially true of Jung's favorite mystics, the mystics of the apophatic tradition, who for a moment lost themselves in the maternal nothingness from which all form is born (Dourley 2004). One of them, Marguerite Porete, was to write of her soul, "without such nothingness she cannot be the all" (Porete 1993: 193). A Jungian translation might read, "My embrace of the world will never be more inclusive than the depth of my entrance into the mother of the all." In a period when a theologically terrorized humanity looks for salvation from its saviors to avoid its extinction, Jung's myth points to a moment of dissolution in the mother of the all as the ultimate resource to the lethal squabbles between her children fatally possessed by mere fragments of her always surpassing and redeeming wisdom. This is the wisdom which seeks to become conscious in every analysis, a wisdom moving through the individual into society.

Chapter 9

Rerooting in the mother

The numinosity of the nothing

The numinous

Chapter 8 presented Jung's conviction that significant therapeutic transformation, "real therapy" he called it, always entailed the experience of the
numinous generated by archetypal forces endemic to the psyche itself (Jung
1945c: 377). Further, Jung considered religious experience, the symbols
which frequently bear the experience, and especially mystical experience, to
be archetypally based and so to constitute the height of numinous experience (Jung 1976c: 98). More will be said of Jung's understanding of mystical experience in these final chapters. At this stage in the discussion it need
only be stated that the mystics who drew Jung's sustained attention
experienced an "identity" with the divine through a moment of the ego's
dissolution in its source (Jung 1971a: 255). In scholarly quarters this mysticism is termed "apophatic" mysticism and culminates in the experience of
a difficult to describe unqualified identity with a power at once devoid of
all form and yet the source of all form. Such dissolution, though a "shat-
tering thought" (Jung 1968o: 135), would go to and perhaps through the
archetypal psyche to rest in a nothingness divested of all urgency to activity
or expression and yet be itself the source of the archetypes and their
insatiable drive to create human consciousness and to become self-
conscious in it.

The experience of dissolution in the nothing would be among the greatest, if not the greatest, experience of the numinous possible to the psyche. It
would be so because it would engage a psychic profundity preceding even
the archetypal dimension of the psyche. Its very profundity would
guarantee the intensity of its residual impact. For Jung ego loss in the depth
of the psyche "is of the utmost importance because it identifies the Deity
with the numinosity of the unconscious" (Jung 1968h: 194). The depths of
the psyche beyond the archetypal would be free of all forms of constrictive
definition and even the latency thereto. Yet they would generate a truly
universal sentiment because as the source of all form they would embrace
all form. It is understandable then why dissolution in this matrix left those

who underwent it convinced that they had experienced a moment of dissolution in the divine itself as source of all that could be or is definable.
Psychologically this experience would always be of the depths of the individual psyche and would unite the individual to the totality because it
would engage the point where individuality and universality, the one and
the many, identify in the originary nothing from which the many proceed.
It is from this domain of the formless in the subsequent process of the
discovery of its own potential through its expression in consciousness that
symbols and myth reach consciousness and become the basis of living the
symbolic life.

Earlier sections of the work make it clear that Jung considered the
numinous as powerfully therapeutic, and identified the practice of religion
with the "careful and scrupulous observation . . . of the *numinosum*" (Jung
1969b: 7, 8). Because the numinous holds so prominent a place in Jungian
theory and therapy and in the contribution his psychology makes to a now
emerging social consciousness, its nature in all its faces, and especially in
the creation of religious and political symbols and faith in them, is worthy
of further examination. Since the experience of the numinous is inescapably
human, so are religious and political faiths. At a time when such faiths
threaten the future of humanity, Jung's psychology forces the mind to
identify the conditions under which the numinous will enhance or destroy
the human project.

Occasionally the inner dream or external hallucination will be so powerful
as to leave an indelible imprint on the psyche of the individual addressed.
St. Paul's experience on the road to Damascus is a prime example (Jung
1969b: 8). More frequently the more sustained scrupulous observation of
the numinous works over time a less dramatic but nonetheless progressive transformation of the total psyche toward a more "compendious"
or "supraordinate" personality (Jung 1969c: 258). Jung understands the
expressions of the unconscious in dream or in external psychic event to be
scripted by the self. When the self depicts itself in its own dream drama it
carries with it an immense numinous impact and becomes the source of the
individual's experience of imaging God. "The God-image is not something
invented, it is an *experience* that comes upon man spontaneously – as
anyone can see for himself unless he is blinded to the truth by theories and
prejudices" (Jung 1968h: 194). Apophatic experience would attribute this
impact to the self's leading the ego into total dissolution in its source and in
the end leading the ego back from such identity in a cyclical movement not
once but many times. Once more, the personality, thus informed by the
progressive incarnation of the self, is characterized by two distinctive traits;
the personal integration of the many energies that make up the unique
individual combined with an ever more extensive embrace of all that is. It is
expressly this second trait of individuation which implies that dissolution in
the universal source of consciousness carries a greatly enhanced universal

sympathy in consciousness returning from the source of consciousness for whatever lies in its purview.

Jung's equation of therapy with the experience of the numinous and with religious conversion, instantaneous or prolonged, has little or nothing to do with religion as commonly understood. Where he speaks of therapy as religious transformation, he is explicit. "This of course has nothing whatever to do with a particular creed or membership of a church" (Jung 1969p: 334). As related to wider society much of Jung's therapeutic effort was to reconnect a culture severed from the experience of the numinous, often by religious agencies themselves, with the numinous and its healing power. Effectively much of Jungian theory and therapy developed from the failure of institutionalized religions to make available a responsible experience of the numinous to their constituencies. The failure of collective religion to fill this role was and is somewhat ironic since the religious institution is a creation of the numinous and has as its only legitimate function the measured mediation of the numinous which created the institution for that purpose. In the societal wake of religion's current failure Jung's psychology had to turn to the natural roots and origin of the numinous in the psyche to restore to his culture the sense of the sacred which had created the religious institutions and their Gods now peculiarly unable to access through their founding revelations the energies that gave them birth. A bumper sticker displayed at a recent meeting of religionists in America could serve as a humorous reflection on the direction of Jung's research. It read, "Christianity has pagan DNA." Recovering such DNA would mean the experienced recovery of the archetypal powers which birthed the various religions and now has fled them through their removal from their natural and pagan roots. As suggested earlier they have done this to themselves through not taking themselves seriously but rather literally and historically to the great detriment of the power of their symbols which will always work as poetry but no longer as fact.

His efforts to identify the psychological nature and dynamics of the numinous in the interests of its personal and social restoration led Jung to the archetypal level of the psyche as the ultimate generator of the numinous. When the powers of these depths impacted on human consciousness the impact left the victim convinced that he or she had been addressed by a divinity beyond the psyche. Only in our time as the result of a "millennial process" did Jung think that the evolution of human consciousness and religious consciousness was becoming fully aware that all divinities are projections of the archetypal ground of the human psyche whose internalization would now serve the divinization of what is (Jung 1969d: 402). As argued in Chapter 8, he concluded that humanity was currently entrusted with the recall of the Gods to their origin in the psyche if humanity was to survive their escape from their origin and the devastating history such escape has written (Jung 1969b: 85). Contained within the psyche, the numinous powers that create the Gods would be experienced as transcending the ego but on a purely intrapsychic basis. Their relation to the ego would then be revisioned as the mutual redemption of both the ego and the archetypal powers now no longer creating divinities beyond the human but working rather to lead the human more fully into its natural divinity. The thrust of Jung's late great work, *Answer to Job*, followed his mystic predecessor Jacob Boehme in describing a psychological cosmology in which God and the human, the archetypal and consciousness, were involved in mutual redemption as the base meaning of personal and collective human history (Dourley 2004: 60–64).

The religious and secular perversion of the numinous

The perilous situation of unrecalled divinity is most obvious in the relationship between monotheistic communities bonded by three different One and Only Gods, a situation that would be humorous if it were not so tragic. Chapter 7 presented Huntington's *The Clash of Civilizations*, which documents the heightened body count along the "fault lines" or borders where these religiously bonded communities intersect (Huntington 1996/ 2003: 246–265). Unfortunately in the end his deepest concern proved to be the maintenance of Western geopolitical power in the clash of religiously based communities of which the West is one. Nevertheless his analysis of the role of collective religion stands as a helpful and accurate alert to the universal danger of faiths breeding unconsciousness in bonding these mutually inimical communities in their national and political embodiments. As argued earlier, Huntington lacks Jung's depth in identifying the archetypal basis of these faiths and the numinous hold they exert over their collective victims. The most significant contribution Jung makes to the lessening of the universal danger of particular communities with universal aspirations resting on the numinous possession informing their collective unconsciousness is to show the human source of this power and in so doing to diminish its destructive capacity. If all three One and Only Gods were traced to their psychic provenance and seen to be variants of one stage of the religious or psychological evolution of humanity, the ability to hate and take life in the name of any one of them would be greatly diminished (Dourley 2003). However, as long as their revelations are taken literally, and historically as from a source extrinsic to the human, the loss of life attendant on such revelations is likely to continue and a myth surpassing what the monotheisms have to offer to remain unborn.

Jung clearly identified the petrifaction of numinous processes of transformation into biblically based dogma. "Belief in dogma is an equally unavoidable stop-gap which must sooner or later be replaced by adequate understanding if our civilization is to continue" (Jung 1966a: 435). In the face of the threat to the species by religious literalism, Jung appealed to the religious and theological communities themselves to produce an apology, not for this or that religion and its allegedly privileged position and unique God(s), but an apology for religious and symbolic discourse itself as a prior step to the recovery of the credibility of any specific religion.

> Even intelligent people no longer understand the value and purpose of symbolical truth, and the spokesmen of religion have failed to deliver an apologetic suited to the spirit of the age . . . Exclusive appeals to faith are a hopeless *petitio principii*, for it is the manifest improbability of symbolical truth that prevents people from believing in it.
>
> (Jung 1966a: 227)

Jung is here criticizing a literal faith as assent to the unbelievable revealed in biblical event and dogmatic amplification, misapprehensions he elsewhere describes as reducing dogmatic propositions to "sacrosanct unintelligibility" and "preposterous nonsense" (Jung 1969e: 109, 110).

What lies deeper in this criticism is the need to recover an extensive societal sense of the archetypal from which numinous religious experience emerges. Jung concedes that in an earlier epoch the numinous still empowered the biblical and even the dogmatic before their degeneration into literal, historical accounts of divinities external to the human interacting with the human. The recovery of the archetypal psyche would coincide with the experiential discovery of the numinous as the source of religious experience whose power can initially be expressed only symbolically before it takes on the more intellectual form of dogma. Any other approach to the numinous basis of religious experience and expression would be akin to asking poets to write prose for the sake of greater clarity. Something would surely be lost in translation. The real question is "Why religion and its symbolic expression at all?" Such a question would demand "reflecting how it came about in the first place that humanity needed the improbability of religious statements and what it signifies when a totally different spiritual reality is superimposed on the sensuous and tangible actuality of this world" (Jung 1966a: 227). Jung was confident that an appreciation of the genesis of the symbol would lead to a recovery of the numinous power of the archetypal unconscious as the source of symbol and so as the source of the sacred itself. Religion thus understood would no longer be a divine imposition on the human mind but a reconnection of the human mind with its own native depth. Thus a conscious reflection on the archetypal unconscious as the mother of the sense of the numinous, always expressed initially in symbol, would remove from religion its appeal to "people for whom thinking and understanding are too much bother" (Jung 1966a: 229). Rather the experience of the symbolic power of religion would restore to it its true nature and this restoration would be greatly enhanced should individuals connect with their own symbolism and myth especially through the dream whether or not they affirmed a particular set of religious symbols and myth.

Religion removed from its psychic roots is not the only major contributor to the current loss of the sense of the numinous and so to the loss of an authentic religious life. In Jung's mind aspects of the so called "secular" world are equally involved in humanity's severance from such a supportive profundity. The Enlightenment contributed mightily to freeing the human spirit from supernatural imposition in the areas of religion, philosophy and political power. It demanded that the religious and theological communities make themselves responsible to reason and that they disengage from the political manipulation of the wider community they allegedly served. In this the Enlightenment freed the mind from heteronomous invasion by extraneous religious authority, divine or human acting in the name of the divine, and, in so doing, separated Church from state. The victory, though to be cherished and maintained, was not without its own defect. In freeing the human spirit from ecclesial imposition on the mind and the body politic it also undermined whatever legitimate value religion might have in accessing the numinous, diminished as this capacity was in the religious situation the Enlightenment faced in the various forms of religious faith that opposed it. The resultant societal and personal religious situation in our epoch is that of a prevailing consciousness unhinged from its depths both within and beyond religious circles.

This current social malaise in Western society rests on two strangely related phenomena. Official religion stands bereft of access to the powers that created it and whose mediation it was meant to serve. Indeed, its current spiritual bankruptcy is due in no small part to its taking on the Enlightenment on rational grounds and losing battle after battle because it could not distinguish the symbolic nature of its own resources and discourse from philosophical and scientific statement (Jung 1969g: 477, 478). On the other hand scientific discourse came increasingly to reject religion on the grounds of its interference with the legitimate working of the autonomous mind, a level of mind which consistently defeated heteronomous or authoritarian religious attacks on it. In a strange sense religion and science, though very different and for different reasons, conspired to defeat authentic religion in our time by jointly denying humanity's natural experience of divinity as the basis of all valid religion, institutional and personal. Religion denied humanity this experience by locating its source in supernatural spheres beyond the human as the basis of divine intervention in the human. Science denied it by rightly rejecting any influence of these divine spheres in its intellectual endeavor within its legitimate sphere. Eventually reason and science came to prevail within their own domains by simply ignoring such supernatural agencies and their earthly proponents and pretensions. In defending its licit autonomy from religious manipulation the question surfaced whether the rational and scientific was the only valid domain of the mind or whether reason itself was connected to depths which transcended it and whose admission into consciousness would enhance and revitalize it. This option would demand a robust sense of an immanental origin of the religious sentiment itself. Traditional religious thought has largely lost this inner sense and consequently could not identify a wholly other with any compelling force because of its loss of contact with the sense of such an other within the human. Science and eventually philosophy itself rightly felt that the identification of a religious other was beyond their power and in their withdrawal muted even the quest for and question about such transcendence. As philosophy degenerated into logic and grammar, and science into a sophisticated and helpful technology, both contributed to a societal consciousness that lost interest in the question of religious transcendence because the basis of its affirmation in human experience had been muted or destroyed.

Yet in a number of ways secular society has itself become a surpassing religion informed by values that institutional religion has historically struggled with only now to be granted a grudging and partial acceptance. Thus various forms of the assertion of human rights evident in the feminist movement, the acceptance of the gay community including gay marriage, the anti-war movement and a preference for democracy over religion's preferred theocracy are foundational to what might well be called a secular religiosity. Admitting that these movements and values are strongly to be fostered and remain somewhat peripheral to mainstream religion, still the shadow side of secularity as religion remains. Its shadow is evident in the reduction of the human cognitive capacity and sensibility to a sense based, meaningless facticity evidenced in a science and scientific society increasingly regressing to a facile fascination with a shallow intellectualism and technological gadgetry. Paradoxically, though sworn enemies throughout much of the Enlightenment epoch, science and institutional religion join hands as common suppressors of the numinous experience. The former functions well within its own jurisdiction of the empirical and rational. In theory it ignores rather than attacks the source and value of the numinous.

Nevertheless the relegation of the numinous to an area of experience from which legitimate science must abstract does tend to discredit the numinous and its expressions and to render the collective mind insensitive to those valuable dimensions of humanity from which the numinous derives. Religion severs itself from these same dimensions by externalizing its Gods and turning their revelations into revealed facts or a higher level body of information. A dead and implausible religious facticity becomes the object of a dehumanizing religious faith. In both the scientific secular and the religious institution the numinous perishes and with it the sense of the mind's connectedness with "its primordial oneness with the universe" as the sole legitimate basis of religion itself (Jung 1969g: 476). A further consequence of this situation is a widespread schizoid split among those who wish to combine a scientific dedication with a formal religious devotion at the personal level. In such minds the weekly day set aside for religious observance, whether it be Friday, Saturday or Sunday, stands unconnected to the scientific or secular engagement throughout the remainder of the week. Such fragmentation is unavoidable when the point of identity of the divine and human in the human is denied or allowed to lapse into a studied forgetfulness at the cost of the individual's connection with the Universal Mind (Jung 1969g: 476).

Though Jung was convinced that the restoration of a lively sense of the numinous was the key to the revitalization of an authentic religious spirit he was far from unaware of its pathogenic power on individual and society. While he appreciated the numinous as the basis of religion universally, he also feared its shadow as the power that could reduce entire communities to unconsciousness. Consequently his endorsement of the recovery of the numinous experience is two sided. He worked for both its responsible restoration to society and to warn society of its possessive power. Religious and political faith were such major concerns for Jung throughout his pages, no doubt, because of their devastating effects and geographical proximity in his lifetime before and during the Second World War. As an anecdote to group possession by the numinous, Jung worked to locate the individual's experience of divinity in some primary manner in the experience of the self. This was the power which sought incarnation in consciousness as the individual's ultimate resource and support. The experience of the self carried with it a numinosity of such intensity that Jung would liken it to the experience of being "anchored in God" (Jung 1957a: 371). Politically such anchoring served as the ultimate source of freedom from the mass movements of ecclesial and political collective mindlessness. But even here Jung would warn that the ego should never identify with the power of the self. Such identity, if residual, would be psychotic and entail the loss of the ego to the self. Of this loss Jung writes, "It must be reckoned a psychic catastrophe when the *ego is assimilated by the self*" (Jung 1968p: 24, italics Jung's). For Jung it becomes crucially important that Jesus would say, "I and the Father are one". If Jesus were to say I am the father he would have been but another religious psychotic whose ego was permanently absorbed by and lost to the divinity of the self.

Functional religion would thus counter religious and political possession through consciously rooting the individual in the supportive numinosity of the self. But no one and no organization can do this when they are themselves uprooted from this human resource. In fact both secular and religious communities encourage such loss of consciousness on their behalf under the banners of faith, patriotism or commitment. "Both [Church and state] demand unqualified submission of faith and thus curtail man's freedom, the one his freedom before God and the other his freedom before the State, thereby digging the grave for the individual" (Jung 1964c: 266).

The questioner of ecclesial systems is typically told that the articles of faith he or she might question are concrete historical facts and so not to be doubted. Jung's words here are again prophetic, this time of the contemporary situation of many church-goers laboring under a theological authority which removes rather than fosters contact with the numinosity of their native divinity. In such an environment to grow up is to grow out and to leave the ecclesial communities to the surging numbers of fundamentalists fearful that their shallow but comforting and collectively reinforced certitudes would be corroded in the face of a human maturation which locates the divine at the basis of each individual life to be directly engaged there. Jung diagnosed this demeaning lust for certitude when he wrote that such faith "is notoriously apt to disappear as soon as anyone starts thinking about it. Belief is no adequate substitute for inner experience, and even a strong faith which came miraculously as a gift of grace may depart equally miraculously" (Jung 1964c: 265). It is no wonder then that the temptation to forego the protracted pain of becoming conscious through membership in communities of collective unconsciousness defeats the demands of engagement with the numinous in the depth of every life.

An equally important cultural correlate of the removal of individual and society from the numinosity of their roots lies in Jung's early indictment of that social blight currently called "patriarchy". In the form of worship of reason and its verbal superficiality, Jung calls Christian patriarchy "the congenital vice of our age" and traces it to "*the supremacy of the word*, of the Logos which stands for the central figure of the Christian faith" (Jung 1964c: 286, italics Jung's). In Jung's view the Word is currently a pathologizing deity because religious literalism and historicism have severed the Word from the abyss which precedes and empowers it and so reduced it to an empty rationalism. The Joannine prologue no doubt contributed to this situation. For Jung in the beginning was not the Word but the silence or the formless (Lammers et al. 2007: 122). Thus denuded through its severance from its source and power, the Logos becomes Blake's Urizen, a consciousness divested of its depths reduced to the relative sterility of reason and made the object of competing religious claims (who has the one true Logos?). A symbol originally pointing to the divine ground of reason in which humanity universally participates and which itself participates in a preceding and vitalizing abyss has "become a source of suspicion and distrust of all against all" (Jung 1964c: 287).

As suggested the radical removal of the pathology of logocentrism in current religion and society would entail the rewriting of the Joannine prologue. In the beginning would no longer be the Word. In the beginning would be the silence of the nothing from which the Word and world proceed and in whom they continue to dwell. Getting behind or deeper than the patriarchal Logos would restore the sense of the Goddess or Great Mother, personal terms Jung uses as synonyms for the collective unconscious as the womb of both the mind and the numinous. Healthy regression beyond the Logos would mean the experiential restoration of the Goddess as the mother of all definable forms including those of particular divinities. In the case of the monotheisms and their male divinities it would mean recovering the Goddess who has birthed all three and could give them a peace they cannot find in relation with each other or in themselves away from their common maternal source even though such a return would gravely threaten their own self-understanding.

The precedence of the Goddess

As Jung developed his psychology the precedence of the Mother Goddess came ever more to the fore. Much of his psychology is devoted to the description of the base dynamic of individuation as repeated immersion in her restorative nothingness as the prelude to a life of enhanced compassionate activity in the world she also authors. This is the numinous maternal in the most extended sense. Jung used referents from a wide spectrum of human experiences to give some content to his conception of the unconscious as the mother of consciousness seeking ever greater incarnation in her child. Thus he relates the collective unconscious, the Goddess, to Plotinus' conception of the "One", "the world soul" and the "unending All of life" whose nature it was to express herself in all that is real and so become real in her expression (Jung 1966a: 138). Jung also understands the Great Mother as water, river and sea (Jung 1966a: 218) as the prime matter (Jung 1970: 18) and gnostic Pleroma or fullness from whom all form derives (Jung 1965b: 379) and as the "Nothing out of which All may grow" (Jung 1964d: 75). These many designations collectively serve to point to her power and precedence as the ultimate source of the archetypal itself and so of the numinous. Renewed vitality through immersion in and return from her numinosity is the goal of the quest of hero and mystic alike (Jung 1966b: 169, 170).

In so extending the conception of numinous energy or libido to every aspect of the "creative force", Jung included in it much more than the sexual and denied its reduction to any specific instinct (Jung 1966a: 137). This extension was at the heart of Jung's break with Freud (Jung 1966a: 135–137). In challenging and transcending Freud's conception of libido as solely sexual, Jung redefined the numinous. Without denying the numinosity of physical sexuality, he increasingly understood the numinous as experienced in a variety of unities of psychologically significant opposites. The greatest was that of the ego with its maternal origin, the Goddess. For Jung intercourse with the Goddess becomes the deepest meaning of incest whose purpose is the renewal of conscious life. As this incest is sustained the great archetypal opposites in the womb of the Mother come into unity in consciousness, the male with the female, the bodily with the spiritual, the evil with the good. In this specific context, and with an extended sense of the spiritual as working the unity of these opposites, Jung would argue that the deepest movement of "the whole nature of man" was to "a spiritual goal" (Jung 1969f: 212). This spiritual goal Jung understood as the unity in consciousness of all the archetypal opposites in life's matrix, among which instinct and spirit are but two of the greatest. Jung colored the "spiritual goal" toward which the psyche moves in shades of violet to get at the idea that successful incest with the Goddess worked toward a unity of all opposites and, in particular in this imagery, the red of passion with the blue of pure spirit (Jung 1969f: 211–213).

Incest is best

When Jung equates the source of all energy with the Great Mother, he describes a process of incest which breaks the incest taboo, not in some physical and literal sense, but in a psychic and profoundly spiritual sense. "It is not incestuous cohabitation that is desired but rebirth" (Jung 1966a: 224). Violation of the incest taboo comes, then, to mean a variety of things all related to the suffering attached to the transformation of consciousness through incest with the Goddess. Such incest invariably means the sacrifice of an immature, though possibly comfortable consciousness, to the demands of self-loss in the interest of growth. Such incest could come to serious confrontation with the reigning patriarchal consciousness interested in maintaining the psychic status quo out of its terror of the new and, in current culture, of the depths of the psyche itself. Full incest means a psychic death of the ego into the womb of the Great Mother with no guarantee of emergence or resurrection. Baptism and resurrection in the Jungian sense carry no sacramental guarantee of a happy return from the waters of dissolution or the grave. Nor are either once upon a time realities. They describe cyclical processes which repeat in the psyche's effort to grow throughout a lifetime.

Though this incest has many faces, failure to enter it has as many dire consequences. One is the severance of consciousness from the energy of the matrix. Primordial wisdom describes the resultant indolence as loss of soul. Such loss carries with it images not only of loss of personal energy but also of a desiccation of all life even the surrounding life of nature. And yet in reestablishing a life-giving connection with the maternal root the hero runs the risk of no return (Jung 1966a: 249–256). Thus intercourse with the Great Mother describes for Jung a volatile process with a variety of outcomes. It is in the ego's birth from her that the original sin, the gift of self-consciousness, is committed and conferred. When the sin of self-consciousness is committed, it brings with it for the first time a sense not only of the individual but also of the individual's inevitable death (Jung

1966a: 271). For Jung, then, fear of conscious individuality and death lies at the heart of the neurotic fear of life away from the Great Mother and leads to the devouring solace of that perennial and unbroken unconsciousness she so readily provides in her negative face to the physically living but spiritually unborn.

And yet those who have committed the original sin of attaining an initial conscious life can never escape the longing for and fear of reimmersion in the numinous eternity of her womb, "the inner longing for the stillness and profound peace of all-knowing non-existence, for all seeing sleep in the ocean of coming to be and passing away" (Jung 1966a: 356, 357). In this sense the initial birth from the Great Mother leads to an inescapable drive for a return to her which can become both "the supreme goal" of life's adventure and life's most "frightful danger" (Jung 1966a: 236). The danger is that of being consumed by the maternal source of renewal herself. "It happens all too easily that there is no return from the realm of the mothers" (Jung 1966a: 310). It is here in the intimate commerce with the Mother that the wholly intrapsychic and numinous drama at the heart of Jung's psychology is most evident. An initial and ongoing othering from the mother, fearful in itself, is the price of the birth of an autonomous consciousness. But the othering itself, to the extent it is achieved, becomes the prelude to the equally imperious drive to reunion, indeed momentary identification, with her. Only when both moments in this cyclical and recurring dialectic are honored and effected as integral to the total process of maturation is the full sweep of Jung's understanding of individuation comprehended.

Incestuous reentrance into the mother, the ultimate form of numinous experience, is a necessary risk in all great tasks of life, or better, in the task of life itself. Without incest the individual is trapped in impotent but often raging reason. But in offsetting incest the individual risks annihilation. Jung describes the moment in these stirring lines,

> that is the dangerous moment when the issue hangs between annihilation and new life. For if the libido gets stuck in the wonderland of this inner world, then for the upper world man is nothing but a shadow, he is already moribund or at least seriously ill. But if the libido manages to tear itself loose and force its way up again something like a miracle happens: the journey to the underworld was a plunge into the fountain of youth, and the libido, apparently dead, wakes to renewed fruitfulness.
>
> (Jung 1966a: 293)

In describing the joy and danger of incest with the Mother, Jung would seem to make this dialectic a fact of life universal. In the end his understanding of the psyche would challenge one to choose between the numinous though dangerous experience of reentering the Great Mother, on the one hand, and the psychic or even physical death of a consciousness paralyzed by its reluctance to do so and so eventually drained of the will to live.

In these passages even Jung is not fully depicting all the forces at play in incest with the Great Mother. In the end not the ego but the self is the only agency that can work the initial birth from the mother, the return to dissolution in her, and the return with the renewal of conscious life the moment of dissolution affords. The completion of the cycle, birth, death and resurrection, is the basis of the hero myth and so of the Messiah or Saviour complex. As a case in point, Christianity identifies its hero in the figure of Christ. However, Jung would strongly suggest that in turning the Christ myth into a personal, historical and literal event, the myth has lost its power and now cloaks rather than reveals the fact that it is a story of everyman (Jung 1966a: 177–178). Restored to its mythical status, the story of Christ would be one among many religious stories serving to make explicit the processes of the renewal of the life of the spirit through the specifically Christian variant focusing on birth, death and resurrection as the ground movements in psychic maturation. At the heart of these stories is the universal "longing to attain rebirth through the return to the womb and to become immortal like the sun" (Jung 1966a: 212). The ultimate prohibition of the incest taboo is the prohibition to live out of one's own self-renewal by becoming "the child or *oneself* in renewed and rejuvenated form" (Jung 1966a: 258, italics Jung's). Put simply, the goal of "magical incest" is "immortality" and the incest taboo forbids it (Jung 1966a: 259). This is the taboo the hero must break to enjoy the numinosity of identity with the mother and rebirth from her into an eternity experienced in time.

Because this process is endemic to the psyche as its deepest movement, it requires no intervention of a divine agency external to the psyche. This is what Jung means when he says that "the reborn is his own begetter" (Jung 1966a: 323). In doing this he identifies processes of spiritual self-renewal as native to and wholly contained within the psyche itself. It is this wholly natural and intrapsychic dynamic of renewal which religious imagery projects above onto relationships with wholly other Gods or onto the past and unique historical events like the life of Jesus. Jung removes the need for divine intervention from above or a relation to past definitive incursions of the divine into human history. He recasts all such sacred texts and events as documenting processes which are meaningful only if they occur in the experienced numinosity of the now of individual psychological life and its renewal.

Against the background of this extended sense of the Great Mother or Goddess, Jung shifts the imagery of his psychology from Freud's Oedipus complex to the "Jonah and the whale complex" (Jung 1966a: 419). In this imagery he hoped to depict the movement of the ego-Jonah into the transformative belly of the unconscious-whale where Jonah would see the "mysteries" of the transpersonal world and then be luckily spewed forth, "with new possibilities of life" (Jung 1966a: 420). And it is here that Jung makes explicit the connection between regression to the whale's belly and the reality of numinous and so religious experience in all its forms. He writes, "the libido which builds up religious structures regresses in the last analysis to the mother and thus represents the real bond through which we are connected with our origins" (Jung 1966a: 429). Jung could hardly be clearer that the whale's belly, the Great Mother or Goddess, the source of all life, gives birth not only to consciousness but also to all the religions. This lust for her life in the return to "origins" takes on a peculiar form in the monotheisms each with its own projection of an individual male divinity dwelling in a supernatural realm. To return these deities to their origin in the psyche and deal with them there would be to cap the volcano of the projection which creates them and now endangers the species. Ironically the search for life in the mother has turned into diverse forms of subjection to foreign, male and transcendent father Gods who hold the fate of humanity in their divine hands. Surviving them and their political incarnations is now humanity's greatest challenge. The key to such survival is the recovery of the capacity to lead a truly interior life in the recovery of the energies of the mother of the all.

Jung's deepest indictment of modern cultural consciousness is that it is uprooted from the source of the numinous which the symbolic sense carried and could restore. For Jung the loss of the symbolic sense threatens the very continuance of humanity for a number of reasons. Such a loss deprives the culture of its will to go on through depriving it of the numinous libido which the symbol mediates to consciousness as the basis of its will to live and thrive in the face of the challenge of the future. Writes Jung on this threat, "Nevertheless, when a living organism is cut off from its roots, it loses the connections with the foundations of its existence and must necessarily perish." The ultimate counter to such death is the "anamnesis of the origins" as "a matter of life and death" (Jung 1968e: 180). In these passages Jung is contending that an individual or culture forgetful of its roots in the unconscious will eventually lose the will to live. Jung frames these remarks in relation to the question of evolution and is asking Teilhard de Chardin's repeated question and quest, "from what source will humanity derive its will to survive and flourish in its task of completing God as the completion of human endeavor?" And Jung would remain open to Teilhard's conclusion: "Sooner or later souls will end up giving themselves to that religion which will most activate them as humans" (translation mine, Teilhard de Chardin 1969: 272). Both are positing the question of accessing that numinous energy that makes life not only possible but also passionate in addressing the problems of human survival and, more than survival, a greatly enhanced well being. Jung and Teilhard would thus eliminate all candidacy to religions or cultures themselves uprooted from their origins in the psyche and infecting their environment with their own pathology. In this sense Jung saw his psychology as in and of itself a religious endeavor in so much as it could restore to those sickened by the uprooting powers of their literalistic, historicist religions the very "foundations of religious experience" in the individual's depths as the source of the numinous made conscious in the religious event. "The medical psychotherapist today must make clear to his more educated patients the foundations of religious experience and set them on the road to where such experience becomes possible" (Jung 1966a: 229).

Jung considered the Christ figure still to be the "culture hero" of his society (Jung 1968c: 36). Using Christianity to exemplify the religious dimension of his psychology, Jung would contend that the recovery of the numinous in full consciousness of its intrapsychic provenance is a necessary prelude to the modern's ability "to participate spiritually in the substance of the Christian message", and, by extension, in any religious or archetypal message (Jung 1966a: 230). Whether this ability to again participate immediately in the archetypal basis of the Christian or of any religion is compatible with their current collective self-understanding is by no means clear at the moment. In not a few passages Jung strongly suggests that the Christian's appropriation of the sense of humanity's natural participation in the divine currently outstrips the Christian's imaginal capacity. He writes, "The latter [the Christian] has far too little introspection to be able to realize what modifications in his present conception of God the homoousia of the self (Atman) would involve" (Jung 1966a: 393). In this passage, as he does elsewhere, Jung extends to every human being the status of two natures, consciousness and the unconscious, in one person, a unity official Christianity reserved in its Christological councils and presently to the unique figure of Christ. In contrast, for Jung, each individual is potentially, and is destined by the psyche itself to become, a Christ figure or equivalent in whatever religious or compelling symbolism this truth might be clothed. In all of these remarks Jung is far from engaging in any Christian imperialism. The psychological reality of Christ is the numinous experience of the self becoming incarnate in consciousness. Other religions and archetypal communities experience the same numinosity through the self figure in whatever variation it takes in them. The question this citation poses is this, "Could Christianity and, indeed, any of the monotheisms, proclaim the natural divinity of the human as the basis of humanity's potential universal experience of the divine and remain faithful to their current self-understanding?" In the wake of the exclusion of gnosticism, and alchemy and the suspicion surrounding mysticism on the part of the great Western religions, it would appear that the recovery of their health would demand the integration of what they have made peripheral or excluded as heresy in the historical processes of their self-debilitation resulting in their current studied distance from the healing numinosity that created them. In this context recovered heresy would serve as their greatest healing resource.

In the end the counter to currently lethal religious consciousness is not a matter of reasoning but the recovery of "spontaneous religious experience which brings the individual's faith into immediate relation with God" (Jung 1964c: 292). Jung, in his more far-reaching statements, was convinced that the psyche taken in its totality participated in eternity. He will write of the self as having "an 'incorruptible' or 'eternal' character on account of its being pre-existent to consciousness" (Jung 1969c: 265). Though he used many images to get at the concept of rerooting, in the final analysis, rerooting is a process of the intrapsychic reunion of the individual with eternity as the source of the finite in the here and now of time. Failure to connect with these roots is a personal disaster. "It means the same thing as the conscious denial of the instincts – uprootedness, disorientation, mean-inglessness, and whatever else these symptoms of inferiority may be called" (Jung 1969q: 415). Nor is this reunion of the individual with eternity a bloodless reunion with some unearthly immortality in a distant or post-temporal state. The consciousness it produces always "retains its con-nection with the heart, with the depths of the psyche, with the tap-root" (Jung 1969q: 410). Out of such rootedness in the eternal, the individual echoing the gnostic, alchemist and mystic of all ages, can say in the face of death itself:

> I am a vessel more precious than the feminine being who made you. Whereas your mother knew not her own roots, I know of myself, and I know whence I have come, and I call upon the imperishable wisdom which is in the Father and is the Mother of your mother, which has no mother, but also has no male companion.
>
> (Jung 1957c: 87, 88)

Such is the confidence that the self induced experience of living out of the mother generates.

In the end it all comes to nothing

Chapter 10 will deal in greater depth with Jung's appropriation of certain streams in Western Christian mysticism. What follows here is a brief recapitulation of the rudiments in the psychological processes of the renewal of life through entry in its reciprocity with the Great Mother as the creative nothing from which all consciousness is born. If the West is to recover its sense of the numinous and so of the humanizing divine, Jung's turn to the individual's inner life through the gnostics, alchemists and mystics is of crucial importance. Mystical scholarship has highlighted the apophatic experience, that moment of nothingness in which mystic and divinity become one without difference as the prelude to a more vital engagement of the mystic with the world (Sells 1994). The thirteenth century Beguines,

Mechthild of Magdeburg, Hadewijch and Marguerite Porete belonged to this tradition (McGinn 1998a: 199–265). Current scholarship reveals that this tradition was a significant influence on Meister Eckhart (*c.*1260–*c.*1328) (McGinn 2001: 9, 144, 148, 181). Mechthild of Magdeburg is present in Jung's work (Jung 1966a: 90; 1968q: 176) and Meister Eckhart is a substantial figure throughout his pages (Jung 1971a: 241–258).

Eckhart is explicit in identifying the Godhead as the fourth in God beyond the Trinity. His experience extended to a moment of identity with the nothingness of the Godhead, an experience of his native divinity which followed him back into the world (Eckhart 1978: 214–220). The only mystic Jung cites more frequently than Eckhart is Jacob Boehme. He too went to the point of identity with God beyond the Trinity but returned from it with the conviction that the unification of the divine opposites did not take place in eternity, as Trinitarian orthodoxy would have it (Boehme 1911: v). Rather the unity of the divine opposites is to take place in human consciousness which alone can perceive the divine conflict and undergo its resolution in processes at once redemptive of the divine and the human (Dourley 2004: 60–64). Boehme was a significant influence on Hegel. Jung's late *Answer to Job* completes Hegel's philosophy by elevating it to the level of psychology. There, in the footsteps of Boehme and Hegel, Jung describes the process in which an unconscious divine life torn between its unresolved absolutes is perceived as such by a discriminating human ego. But this insight carries with it the intimation that only in the human can the reconciliation of the divine antinomy take place. Job is a forerunner of the Christ figure who dies between archetypal opposites despairing of divine intervention (Jung 1969d: 408). Jung contends that this despair becomes the prelude to a death into a risen life in which the opposites come together as the thrust of both the psychological maturation of the individual and the eschatological direction of history (Jung 1969d: 408). Such was Jung's final word on the numinosity of the cycle of death into the mother and resurrection from her as the ground movement of maturation in the individual soul and the base meaning of history.

When the experience of Eckhart and Boehme are united as foundational movements of the psyche, the image of a double quaternity emerges whose key is humanity's dialectical engagement with the creative nothingness of its ground. Eckhart identifies with divinity as the nothing, the fourth, that precedes even Trinity, that is, Eckhart identifies with the mother, herself formless, from whom all form and the drive to form derive (Dourley 1990: 41–68). A moment of dissolution in the nothing frees Eckhart from the compulsion of form, of mind and the imposition of form on matter or others. It is at the heart of his doctrine of resignation or letting be. His dissolution in the mother is the height of the numinosity of the night.

Boehme also went into this night which he calls the *ungrund* or the One. But he realized that the nothing needs the ego to become self-conscious of its own latencies and their union. In effect the return to the nothing demands and enables the reconciliation of its conflictual opposites in consequent consciousness. This reconciliation takes place simultaneously in both the divine and the human as their mutual harmony is achieved in humanity. In Jung's parlance both the divine and the human are mutually redeemed and enhanced when the antinomies in the archetypal ground of the unconscious embrace in consciousness. If Jung's myth could be reduced to a formula it would read: the deeper the ego's penetration into the unconscious, even into that nothingness beyond the archetypal, the greater the ability of the traveler to resolve divinely grounded conflict in oneself as the precondition to its resolution in society.

The gnostics, alchemists and the mystics anticipated the experience of the numinous central to Jung's psychology and Jung's psychology proffers their numinous experience to the contemporary in psychologically theoretical and therapeutic form. The now dawning spirituality in the West is built upon the recovery of the numinosity of one's natural divinity and upon intercourse with the nothing as the mother of the empirical all, to be embraced in its totality as the many and varied faces she shows to the world. To the revisioning of the numinous in the service of a functional spirituality Jung's psychology makes a substantial contribution.

At this point it should be obvious that the mystical values of the myth of the double quaternity move beyond idle psychological, sociological or religious speculation. The myth takes on survival value. If humanity cannot die into that fleeting point of rest in the nothing beyond the inner archetypal wars and their externalizations, then such wars will continue to threaten the species physically. Jung warned of the consequences. "We are threatened with universal genocide if we cannot work out the way of salvation by a symbolic death" (Jung 1976a: 735). Unless humanity does so Jungians will have to continue writing their common paper in its many variants over the decades, "*Why the slaughter must continue.*" This point was belabored in Chapter 6. Let us hope that a time approaches when this paper and chapter will no longer have to be written. Jung died in the Cold War when, then as now, archetypal absolutes pitted communities against each other in potentially lethal interface. The divisions and carnage continue. Lives are daily sacrificed to the archetypal Gods in ever greater abundance. The powers of meaningless death could greatly be lessened, even eliminated, if the all could come again to its origin in the nothing. And so this stream of mysticism is well worth exploring in itself and for what it has to offer to humanity's survival of its own religious propensities toward a more and eventually all inclusive religious compassion.

Chapter 10

Jung, some mystics and the void

Personal and political implications

Recapitulation and foreword

To this point the work has argued that Jung's psychology is a major contributor to an emerging religious consciousness resting on a radical interiority not to be found in the mainstreams of the major monotheistic Western traditions. This consciousness and attendant spirituality would effectively understand the experience of and dialogue with the divine to describe the reciprocity between the wholly intrapsychic agencies of the archetypal unconscious and the ego. Within the total containment of this reciprocity, the unconscious serves to create consciousness in order to become progressively conscious in it in processes of incarnation or penetration that can never be completed nor abandoned individually or collectively. This paradox is due to the fact that the fecundity of the unconscious seeking incarnation in consciousness will always transcend its specific concretions. At the conclusion of Chapter 9, it was suggested that Jung's attraction to certain particular mystics was based on an experience in which the ego was wholly absorbed by the unconscious in a state of rest which for the moment demanded no activity. These mystics took the experience of such total absorption as an experience of their identity with God in which all distinction between creature and creator was negated. This chapter examines such experience and its possible social consequences.

The apophatic

Scholars both within and beyond the Jungian community have failed to give to Jung's thought on mysticism the attention it deserves. Bernard McGinn, a leader in current scholarship on Western mysticism, provides an excellent survey of recent theological, philosophical and psychological commentary on mysticism. Because of its breadth this effort should not be slighted for its occasional dearth of depth. In his section on psychology McGinn writes that Jung "wrote little directly on mysticism though his thought has had great influence on many contemporary students of religion" (McGinn 1998b: 332). McGinn was apparently unaware of Jung's understanding of the nature of mysticism itself as archetypal experience and of his appropriation of certain major Western mystics and their tradition. His archetypal hermeneutic guided Jung's treatment of individual mystics whose experience he construed as dramatic instances of the process of individuation itself. McGinn was obviously unaware of Jung's appreciation of Mechthild of Magdeburg and her fellow Beguines as well as Eckhart himself. Nor was he aware of the affinities Jung established between his psychology and foundational themes in Jacob Boehme. Nevertheless McGinn should be credited with an excellent summation of Neumann's thought on *homo mysticus* (Neumann 1968) leading to the quite accurate conclusion that, for Neumann, mysticism, in the sense given it by Jung, is not only at the heart of the individuation process itself but is nothing less than "the definition and goal of all of human life" (McGinn 1998b: 333). Since this conclusion remains foreign to most Jungian scholars and practitioners and more than somewhat heretical to theologians and historians of theology, concerned more with historical detail than with what the mystics could offer to the modern, it is not surprising that it has failed to receive more widespread interest and acclaim.

The mystics in the Western Christian tradition who drew Jung's more sustained attention were members of the apophatic tradition who had undergone variations of the experience at the heart of this tradition. The experience of apophasis, in this context, refers to their experience of a moment of identity with divinity in a nothingness devoid of all form and, for some, of all urgency to form. The attainment of nothing and some kind of residual rest in it, even after the height of its intensities subsided, was the distinguishing feature of their experience and spirituality. Put simply their journey included a momentary void state which was somehow sustained in their consequent consciousness and activity leaving a permanent impress on it. A residual anomaly in their description of their experience of the nothing lies in the fact that, while in it, they were stripped of all their cognitive resources from sensation through intellection and volition even to a loss of the sense of personal identity. Yet in its wake they were able to remember and convey to others what it meant to them. Fearsome as it was, they cherished the experience and describe it as having transformed their consequent lives and endeavor in a manner that could never be lost. In fact the experience, once undergone, was for them something they would dearly recapture.

Their description of the moment of the void raises the question of how this experience would relate to, illuminate and be illuminated by the model of the psyche Jung draws throughout his life's work. It might be suggested that these mystics simply regressed to an experience of the unconscious as the source of consciousness and so were able to identify for a moment with archetypal energies preceding the creation of consciousness, the sole theatre in which archetypal energies realize themselves in their ascent to conscious apprehension. But in classical Jungian archetypal theory the archetypes themselves, even as potential, constitute a *"facultas praeformandi"* (a faculty of pre-forming), whose nature drives to conscious manifestation in likely limitless variation (Jung 1968r: 79). This compulsive side of archetypal activity is absent from the experience the mystics have of a deeper entry into void states. Rather they seem to depict a state where self-loss into the nothing carries with it no urge to express itself beyond itself or to engage in any activity whatsoever. Though this may have been a crucial moment in their experience, it was not the last, given the intense life these mystics were to live in their relation to their surrounding society in the wake of their void experience. But the void and its absence of urgency was an unmistakable moment commonly cherished in the recording of their experience, one empowering their activity upon their return from it.

Relating their experience to a Jungian perspective supports the conjecture that these women and men seek to describe a dimension of the psyche which precedes archetypally based compulsion of any kind. This immersion in a pre-archetypal world would demand the total extinction of the senses and the ego with its so called "executive faculties" of intellect and will. All distinction between ego and unconscious, the human and God, would surrender to their identity in the nothing from which both derive in consequent differentiation. A well founded suspicion emerges that these mystics have somehow gotten behind or beyond the archetypal world which Jung, in the burden of his work, assumed to be the ultimate foundation of the psyche. And yet at the same time he was obviously drawn to their experience and, on occasion, used their description of it dramatically to describe the major movements in the process of individuation itself. Jung's fascination with these mystics prompts the further suggestion that in his appreciation of them Jung betrays the possibility of a psychic stratum he must have seen in their accounts of their experience but did not develop to any great extent in the paradigm(s) of the psyche he bequeathed to his readers.

What follows is an examination of central motifs in the mystics' accounts of the nothing that drew Jung to them, and a reflection on the possibility that they have surfaced a psychic depth left largely undefined but highly appreciated by Jung himself. The elaboration of the nothing at the depth of the psyche might prove to be of current social value in humanity's individual and collective task of ushering the archetypes into historical consciousness without destroying individual life and collective human history in the process. This sense of a nothingness underlying all archetypal concretions would generate a greater social and political responsibility in humanity's inescapable vocational involvement in the birthing of archetypal forces and so of God into consciousness. Such a sense would foster a safer consciousness because it would cultivate a deeper humanity, sensitivity and compassion, based on the assurance that current highly defined archetypal divides proceed from a nothingness prior to all of them, and look for a higher synthesis beyond each of them in their current divisive and potentially lethal historical manifestations.

Jung on mysticism

Jung describes mystics simply as individuals who have had immediate personal experience of the archetypal unconscious: "Mystical experience is experience of the archetypes" (Jung 1976c: 98). Because he himself underwent many such experiences, Jung would have to admit his own description of mysticism makes him a mystic and imbues his psychology with a certain mystical hue. When understood in his own precise terms there is, therefore, some justification for understanding his psychology as mystical but not in the usual dismissive sense of deliberate obfuscation or needless ambiguity. Indeed, Jung himself wearily confessed that his efforts to link the psyche to unmediated religious experience led to charges of reductionism or a wooly minded mysticism. "Anyone who dares to establish a connection between the psyche and the idea of God is immediately accused of 'psychologism' or suspected of morbid 'mysticism'" (Jung 1969g: 482). A mystical dimension inherent to Jung's psychology may be many things. But it is not morbid.

The first of the above indictments stems from those who would be unable to accept the psychic origin of all religious experience and so of the religions on the ground that this would identify all the religions as "only psychological". This contingent would dismiss Jung's location of the origin of all religions in the impact of the archetypal on consciousness as psychological reductionism. This position is usually taken in the defense of a particular religion, however well disguised beneath the scholarship, as the singular and true religion in relation to all other religions thus reduced to secondary status or entirely discounted in the affirmation of the one true religion whose origins owe nothing to the psyche. Such anti-reductionism usually entails even as it conceals an understanding of religion as supernatural in origin privileging its holder in its provenance from the one true God. The limitations of this position were clearly exposed in Jung's critique of the supernaturalism of Buber and White and the incompatibility of their monotheistic mind with Jung's understanding of the psychic origin of all religion.

The second indictment, that of morbid mysticism, rises from an inability to appreciate the powerful religious role of archetypal impact on consciousness. The accusation of morbidity belongs frequently to those whose natural or induced disposition is toward the reduction of the total human cognitive capacity to the sterile interplay of reason with a reality knowledge of which is confined to the senses. This bleak perspective is frequently buttressed by an equally shallow methodology in matters theological or religious, rendering the victims of such positions immune to or fearful of the role of the unconscious or pre-rational in all things and especially in the creations of religious experience. To them the experiential nature of mysticism remains personally foreign because their truncating rationalism, often metaphysically self imposed by individual or cultural narrowness, makes mystical experience simply incomprehensible to them. To such a caste of mind mystical experience is not only foreign but also threatening because of its origin beyond a constricted conception of reason or mind whose primacy and power is greatly curtailed if not destroyed by the pre-rational powers of the archetypal. In its often voluntarily imposed isolation this mind can be arrogant, smug, and yet aggressive when its defensive certitudes are challenged in their superficiality. In its non-religious form this mind simply dismisses religion as irrational. In its religious form it dismisses the irrational as hostile to the complacency of a mind assured of its abilities in relation to a God further revealed in revelation which goes beyond but never against the God whom reason charts. This is the mind happy alone on top of the iceberg not concerned with or frightened by what may lay beneath the ocean's surface. In short all mysticism is morbid to those who would prefer to lead a life reduced to the rational even in matters of a personal religion and in the more academic study of religion itself. In the latter case the question arises as to their competence as religionists when divested of the sense that gives birth to religion universally. The problem is akin to that of the color blind artist.

In this matter Jung has reversed the meaning of reductionism and psychologism. He argues quite convincingly that the reduction of humanity to the rational and the consequent fear of the power and ambiguities of the unconscious manifest in mystical experience are the most insidious and constrictive form of contemporary reductionism. They are so because they empty humanity of its native experience of divinity by either placing such divinity beyond humanity in supernatural realms and so making all relation to it arbitrary and a matter of alienation or by neglecting religious experience and so emptying life of its depths often in the name of the alleged clarities religion itself provides. To such a mind poets would have much greater impact if only they wrote with the clarity of prose. Jung felt strongly that much would be lost in the translation. Such religious reduction of the totality of the human usually favors two positions which can be combined. Some reduce religion to reason or rational morality, one that can allegedly prove the existence of God and many of his attributes to be supplemented by subsequent additional information conveyed through specific revelations. Outside of religious positions confined to the museums of the history of religion and philosophy by Kant's demonstration that such proofs for God's existence are beyond reason's legitimate capacities, this position enjoys little credibility today at least in responsible academe outside of

Thomistic circles. The second position embraces a salvation more directly through a supernatural revelation or infusion of grace, often itself beyond experience, imported into the soul from a transcendent elsewhere whose alleged purely objective existence is either validated in circular manner by the divine source of the revelation itself or by reason as the grateful recipient of such extraneous revelation. These positions in their many variations substitute for the more intense and immediate religious experience proffered by the direct impact of the archetypal on consciousness itself in the interests of the incarnation of a more total humanity. The global rise of contemporary fundamentalism witnesses the tragedy that these positions are still held by the believing masses today.

In his identification of mystical experience with intense archetypal experience, Jung actually identifies the dynamic of mystical experience with the ground movement of the psyche itself. For instance he will write of the individual's wedding with the abyss and the blotting out of "all memory in its embrace". He continues, "This piece of mysticism is innate in all better men as the 'longing for the mother,' the nostalgia for the source from which we come" (Jung 1966b: 169). For Jung this psychic incest describes the journey of both mystic and hero not once but many times into the maternal womb from which consciousness is born, always with the fear that it may not return from this deepest ingression into a power which is both its originating matrix and a potentially devouring monster (Jung 1966b: 169, 170). Yet Jung is explicit in affirming that, from the perspective of mystic and hero alike, the descent into and hoped for return from the maternal nothingness describe, in perhaps an overly dramatic manner, the dynamic cycle of the process of individuation itself, to some extent operative in every life.

In related passages Jung will describe this mystical regression as a return to the "psychic conditions of prehistory" common to all still functioning religions (Jung 1971a: 255). Here he will go to Indian literature and to the *purusha* as symbolic of an ever present energy running through all of humanity and its epochs with the power to relate the individual to the totality through the experienced recovery of the individual's ever present divine origin (Jung 1966a: 122, 123, 416, 417). In this sense mystical experience is primitive in so much as it returns to the omnipresent origin of humanity in the psyche and, in so doing, relates the human both to current collective humanity and to its cultural historical experience. The loss of this unifying sense of a universal inherence in a source shared by humanity itself was a deep concern for Jung philosophically and psychologically. As an historian of philosophy he traces the fragmentation of current social consciousness in large part to the loss of the philosophical sense of an underlying unity supporting and uniting individual centers of consciousness currently and across time. For instance he will cite Leibniz as the last significant philosopher to uphold such a universal substrate and deplore the social fragmentation that results from the current reality of the atomistic individual as an isolated centre of consciousness severed from his or her personal depth and, through such severance, from a sense of relatedness to nature and to both contemporary and historical humanity (Jung 1969n: 501). Jung sums up the fragmentation of reality by the isolated intellect and by a science unrelated to a significant principle of inclusion as follows. "The development of Western philosophy during the last two centuries has succeeded in isolating the mind in its own sphere and in severing it from its primordial oneness with the universe" (Jung 1969g: 476–477).

Yet there remains in Jung's own texts the question of whether he would embrace the mystics' regression to and identity with the origins of consciousness in a moment of such radical self-divestiture as the Christian mystics of the nothing affirm. In his treatment of Eastern religiosity he greatly appreciates the One Mind (Jung 1969g: 504) and does attribute to it a creative nothingness, a matrix quality, formless itself and yet the mother of all form (Jung 1969g: 490; 1969i: 552). However, his great concern for the maintenance of ego consciousness – even as it is transformed through its interplay with the unconscious under the orchestration of the self – leads him, at times, to draw back from the possibility that the ego and its faculties might undergo a moment of total oblivion in the unconscious portrayed by the very mystics he presents so vividly (Jung 1969g: 484, 485, 504, 505). Part of Jung's concern here may be his reading or misreading of Eastern texts to suggest that such nothingness would induce a permanent loss of ego and not its temporary abeyance as a moment in a process then residual to consequent consciousness. Yet contrary to his tendency to draw back from images of a real and total dissolution of the ego in its origin, his appropriation of Eckhart's work would strongly suggest an openness to so radical a loss of ego-consciousness, and, indeed, an endorsement of it. Such openness rests on textual evidence in Jung's treatment of Eckhart's total experience as one telling paradigm of the foundational movements of the psyche itself. In this account Jung leaves no doubt that the moment of immersion in the unconscious constitutes the loss of ego in an identity with the divine (Jung 1971a: 255). The following account of the mystics and the basis of Jung's appropriation of them raises the real possibility that their experience of the void could take a more central place in Jung's understanding of the full inventory of the psyche than has to date been the case. This would mean that, while Jung recruits certain classical accounts of mystical experience to describe the flow of energies endemic to processes of individuation, the mystics, in their turn may have undergone experiences of the depths of the psyche appreciated by Jung but left largely uncharted in his formal work. These possibilities emerge from a closer examination of the mystics whom Jung appreciated in his works amplified by some in their school whose statements are even more powerful than those of the mystics cited by Jung.

The mystics themselves

Mechthild of Magdeburg (1210–c.1285)

Mechthild was a thirteenth century Beguine, a member of what today would be called a lay movement of women, sometimes living as individuals, sometimes wandering, but most often living in community and dedicated to good works (McDonnell 1954; Babinsky 1993; Hollywood 2004). They shared a mysticism that centered on imagery culminating in total identity with God sometimes depicted as consequent to a sexual encounter with a young Christ figure. Mechthild, whom Jung cites a number of times throughout his work (Dourley 2006d), describes a tryst with an 18-year-old Christ figure in language reminiscent of the courtly love tradition (Mechthild 1953: 20–25, 237–238). The Christ figure approaches her initially as a suitor. At first the senses encourage Mechthild to take up the invitation to intimacy. Soon, however, they realize that they cannot follow her to the consummation of the tryst and so offer a series of virtuous alternatives. Mechthild rejects them all, will only be satisfied with her divine lover with whom she is one by nature, and goes naked to meet him in an intimacy the senses cannot share. In the meantime the senses are to await her return when they will again be useful. This remark would imply that the innermost union with her divine lover is in a psychic state beyond that which the senses can enter or mediate to consciousness but that the senses will again be useful in the wake of such experience. With Mechthild the union of the lovers, herself and Christ figure, goes to climax in an image of mutual loss in the nothingness of sexual satiation (Mechthild 1953: 20–25).

In this vivid account of her intimacy with the divine Mechthild makes some telling psychological and theological points. She speaks of her natural divinity which she shares with the Christ figure with whom her sexually depicted relationship opens out into the total dissolution of their difference culminating in a state of identity. As previously discussed Jung too endorses the extension of a natural experience of divinity to humanity and refers to a state of the identity of the divine and the human, the unconscious and ego, as a certain culmination of the maturational process itself (Jung 1971a: 255). Further Mechthild writes that God can never satisfy the divine lust for intercourse with the soul "of that He can never have enough" (Mechthild 1953: 105). Her words here are easily related to the unremitting drive the archetypal has to be embodied or become incarnate and so aware of itself in human consciousness. Yet a key moment, a prelude to the satisfaction of the lust of the archetypal to become incarnate in human consciousness, occurs in a psychic sphere beyond the competence and reach of the senses and by extension beyond the competence of any image adequately to depict. Her position here is consistent with Jung's dismissal of the truncating contention that there is nothing in the intellect or knowable except through the senses

(Jung 1969g: 492; 1969h: 559). On the contrary Mechthild would support his position that the senses are inadequate to experience the furthest reaches of the natural psyche and so of the divine. Nor can this depth of the psyche be attained by willful striving or virtuous attainment. The virtuous life is no doubt necessary at some preliminary level. Indeed Mechthild will clothe herself with an impressive variety of virtues (Mechthild 1953: 21). But she is stripped naked of them in the final consummation of her love with a youthful Jesus beyond all imagery other than the empty silence of love satisfied (Mechthild 1953: 25). The religious use of the image of nudity needs to be amplified in this context. In the end it points to the paradoxical fact that clothing oneself in a virtuous life, though perhaps necessary at some preliminary stage in maturation, is futile and obstructive to its culmination in an intimacy beyond the distinction of divine and human. This does not indicate a libertine abandonment of the virtuous life. It does indicate that the virtuous life in a spiritual situation in which there is nothing more can be an obstacle to a mature spirituality. As will be seen the same point is made even more explicitly by Marguerite Porete.

The ambiguous relation of virtue to the attainment of identity with God is a common motif in all the mystics of the nothing. In the end only the nothing suffices and it is always given freely, never forced, nor won as the prize of willful virtuous achievement. The experience of the nothing the mystics seek to describe is not antinomian but neither is it ascetic nor moralistic in its achievement. If anything, it happens as a grace when conscious effort can go no further though there still is so much further to go. In line with the fairy tales' demand that the hero's exhaustion precedes his triumph then given as gift, Jung makes much the same point when he writes, "The method [analysis] cannot, however, produce the actual process of unconscious compensation; for that we depend upon the unconscious psyche or the 'grace of God' – names make no difference" (Jung 1969g: 488, 506). From a Jungian perspective the impact of the self, in Mechthild's discourse the Christ figure, is *"always a defeat for the ego"* and beyond the ego's ability to compel or, in the end, to resist (Jung 1970: 546, italics Jung's).

The intimacy between the divine and the human such imagery suggests strongly implies a mutual need and completion foreshadowing modern process philosophy, evolutionary religious thought, and Jung's *Answer to Job*. In these contemporary streams of thought, God and humanity are mutually and inescapably involved in historical and psychological processes of redemptive reciprocity. Mechthild anticipates these modern themes rather dramatically when she portrays the Trinity, in transcendent isolated self-sufficiency, discussing their eternal sterility and the means to overcome it. They decide on the creation of Mechthild and a love relationship with her as the most obvious form of relief (Mechthild 1953: 74, 75). This imagery radically revisions the dialectic between creator and creature. It makes of the creation of the human a divine necessity. It imbues humanity with an essential role in the redemption of the divine. Through her images of sexual love the redemption of the divine is to be achieved through a moment of unqualified unity with it in a moment of return to identity in the nothing beyond all difference, imaged in the mutual loss of lovers into each other at the height of their ecstasy. In this imagery, Mechthild anticipates Jung's all inclusive dialectic of individuation in the flow between the archetypal necessity to create consciousness in order to become conscious in it through the cyclical return of consciousness to an immersion and rebirth in its source. What both are describing is divinity and humanity engaged from the outset in processes of mutual redemption as the deepest dynamic of the psyche and history.

Hadewijch and Marguerite Porete

Though not mentioned in Jung's work, two other Beguine mystics amplify Mechthild and the experience of nothing to make its radical nature even clearer. Hadewijch was a thirteenth century religious poet and visionary. Little is known of her life. One of her visions can hardly be surpassed in its description of apophatic experience. In it the Christ figure first appears as a 3-year-old child and offers her communion in bread and wine. Perhaps a sardonic comment on the infantilism of a literal belief in transubstantiation. Then he appears as a mature adult at the age of his death and again gives her bread and wine in sacramental form. But then they embrace as lovers.

> After that he came himself to me, took me entirely in his arms, and pressed me to him; and all my members felt his in full felicity, in accordance with the desire of my heart and my humanity.
>
> (Hadewijch 1980: 281)

Nor does it end there. Such intimacy goes on to the lovers' mutual dissolution into a state beyond any difference between them. She could find her lover neither "outside me" nor "within me". They become one in a nothingness beyond all differentiation. "Then it was to me as if we were one without difference" (Hadewijch 1980: 281). She concludes, "I wholly melted away in him and nothing any longer remained to me of myself" (Hadewijch 1980: 282). A moment of identity beyond difference could hardly be more vividly described.

The third Beguine in this sequence, Marguerite Porete, centered her entire spirituality on the attainment of the nothing. She was burnt in public in Paris on 1 June 1310 by the secular arm to whom a Church court committed her after convicting her of heresy. Throughout her trial she had remained totally silent, witness to her well founded conviction that the men who condemned her had little capacity to understand or sympathize with her experience (Babinsky 1993: 20, 21). Though her single work, *The Mirror of Simple Souls*, somehow escaped the flames and became a classic through the centuries following her execution, scholarship established her authorship only in 1946 (McGinn 1998a: 244, fn. 237). Her importance both in the history of mystical experience and Jung's appropriation of it lies in the fact that current scholarship has established thematic and possibly literary continuities between her formulations and those of Meister Eckhart, a major figure in Western mysticism and in Jung's work (McGinn 1998a: 246, 263, 297). During his second teaching period at the University of Paris (1311–1312) Eckhart lived with Marguerite's inquisitor, William of Paris, an English fellow Dominican. In this period Eckhart probably read a copy of her condemned work (McGinn 2001: 9). There is some speculation that a major sermon of Eckhart's, "Blessed are the poor", containing most of the foundational elements of his mysticism, reflected and affirmed Marguerite's experience. Eckhart may have written the sermon in later life when he was defending himself at his own heresy trial or had been already condemned and so given up efforts to defend his orthodoxy (Sells 1994: 183).

Marguerite is also indebted to the courtly love tradition but is less explicit sexually than Mechthild or Hadewijch in her occasional references to the divine "Spouse of her youth, who is only One" (Porete 1993: 193). Rather she is much more explicit about the culmination of her psychological and spiritual development in that state she calls the "annihilated soul" (Porete 1993: 102, 120, 135, 153). The annihilated soul achieves an identity with the divine in a nothingness that is at the same time the all. In this radical apophatic state the achievement of the nothing and through it the relation to the totality are but two aspects of the same psychic event. She writes, "Now this soul has fallen from love into nothingness, and without such nothingness she cannot be All" (Porete 1993: 193; 129). Nor does Marguerite attain annihilation as a passing moment. Rather she is "established" in it. Her establishment in the nothing means such experience cannot be lost once undergone. Her consequent life as "unencumbered" by all forms of will and desire describes a residual consciousness (Porete 1993: 127, 129, 159, 171). In Jungian parlance this could well mean that when the self dissolves the ego in the nothing that is also the all it is an unforgettable experience, one which benignly possesses its happy victim for a lifetime as a residual memory and an always present conscious resource. Mechthild may get closest to the absence and presence of this experience when she describes leaving her tryst with the Christ figure. "Where two lovers come secretly together They must often part without parting" (Mechthild 1953: 25). Parting without parting holds true even more when parting from the intimacy of identity in the nothing for the return to the sensate and conscious world. Somehow something remains and these mystics were aware of its continued presence and influence.

As with Mechthild, so for Marguerite the annihilated soul is naked of whatever clothing the virtues can provide. Yet the annihilating identity with the divine nothing does not preclude the virtues. Indeed it presupposes them, even as it lies beyond them and defies attainment through them (Porete 1993: 169). Her position here resonates with Jung's. No doubt individuation requires the virtuous effort of the ego in, for instance, recording and amplifying dreams, but the ego never creates its dreams or works their initial impress. Rather the ego remains throughout in dialogue with the self whose impact is, for Jung, experientially indistinguishable from the agency of "God" (Jung 1970: 546). For Marguerite, souls whose spiritual journey terminates in the virtuous life, are "sad" souls (Porete 1993: 130, 134, 153, 166). For the hopelessly "lost", the depression of leading a virtuous life goes unnoticed because they can imagine nothing beyond the vacuity of virtue perfected and the relatively empty satisfaction it brings (Porete 1993: 132). Though intensely active in good works they are dead to anything beyond such need for activity. In effect their activity masks their religiously induced depression. Marguerite was no doubt familiar with the psychology of the many then and now whose depression is directly proportionate to the degree of virtue and virtuous activity attained. With others, however, the disappointment of virtue attained is the strongest suggestion and prompt that the life of the spirit holds out more. For Marguerite the more becomes the residual living out of a fixed experiential identity with the nothing, the mother of the totality (Porete 1993: 134). In this experience the depth of her humanity would be her connection with all that is and so all that surrounded her. Such spiritual vitality would be its own reward, one that could not be surpassed and one to whose maintenance her life was dedicated.

Especially in her understanding of the will and its role in creation, fall, and return to God, Marguerite reflects the psychology that attracted Jung to Eckhart. Her thrust on these foundational religious themes is this. In the use of the will she has severed herself from the divine with whom she enjoyed an identity, "where she was before she was" (Porete 1993: 218). As will be seen, this quaint but loaded phrase was to recur almost exactly in Eckhart's work. Marguerite's logic is foreign to our modern mindset yet is consistent with its own presuppositions and logic. It argues that, if the alienation between the divine and the human presupposes the willing and the knowing of two distinct subjects, the human and the divine, the ego and the unconscious, this knowing and willing makes them opposites in a creation now fallen from a prior identity. If this alienation is to be defeated it demands the recovery of identity with the divine in that state Marguerite enjoyed prior to her willful removal from this identity and the subsequent false consciousness, namely, that the relation to the divine is a relation to another, or worse, to a wholly other. In contemporary terms which address the same problem only the obliteration of the subject/object distinction can eliminate the alienation between the knower and the known and this is truest in the relation of the divine to the human.

Porete's cosmology and psychology would then endorse the annihilation of the faculties of willing and knowing so that between the human will and the divine will and between the human knower and the divine known and knower, there could be no distinction. It could be assumed that the unqualified attainment of this state would be episodic, though, as stated, endowed with an unforgettable impact. Marguerite and other mystics of the apophatic could hardly be charged with a permanent loss of consciousness given what is known of their active life instanced in Marguerite's writing, her tireless promotion of her work and her stamina through trial and execution. Abstracting from the question of Eckhart's literary dependence on Marguerite and approaching the two through thematic affinity, it cannot be denied that the dynamic of the annihilation of will as well as intellect is at the heart of Eckhart's experience of the return to the nothing or abyss. Nor can it be denied that Jung's attraction to Eckhart rests on the dynamic of the ego as a psychic child of the Nothing, or of the Pleroma or Great Mother, name it as you will, recurrently reentering the womb, the creative nothing, as a precondition to a return to a greatly enhanced consciousness. The process, taken in all its moments, effects an ever deeper bonding and mutually redemptive marriage of ego with its eternal and maternal ground and describes the foundational dialectic of the individuation process itself.

In a striking passage, in which he describes what he thought to be the only authentic though stark spirituality for the contemporary, Jung, citing Goethe, echoes almost literally Marguerite's experience that only in the nothing does one relate to the all. Jung writes,

> Indeed, he is completely modern only when he has come to the very edge of the world, leaving behind him all that has been discarded and outgrown, and acknowledging that he stands before the Nothing out of which All may grow.
>
> (Jung 1964a: 75)

In these passages Jung is referring to Goethe's equivalent statement from *Faust, Part Two*, "In this your Nothing, I may find my All" (Jung 1964a: 75, fn. 2). These statements could be deemed occasional in the context of Jung's total work but they do illustrate a foundational point in his psychology, namely, that he fully appreciated the sense of the deepest unconscious as the nothing from which all definition and form are born. Such appreciation makes access to the nothing a most valuable psychological resource, admitting its dangers, in every age. The recovery of this depth of a common humanity is all the more needed for a living contemporary spirituality and psychology in a culture removed by its mind from its depths.

Meister Eckhart (c. 1260–c. 1328)

Meister Eckhart died in 1328 some time during his trial for heresy at Avignon, then the residence of the papacy. He was a member of the Dominican Order, a leading theologian of his day twice teaching at the University of Paris, who also held at various times in his life a series of high level administrative positions with the Dominicans. After a second period of teaching at the University of Paris (1311–1312) he began to teach and preach along the Rhine in his native Germany. It may have been during this time in his life that he was further acquainted with the female mysticism of the previous century through his work as a spiritual mentor to communities of women. It was also in this period that his preaching first drew the attention of the Inquisition and led to an initial trial in Cologne. At Eckhart's request, appealing to canon law that the court in Cologne had no jurisdiction over him as a member of the Dominican order, he had the venue of the trial moved to Avignon, then the seat of the papacy. After his death the Inquisition declared seventeen articles extracted from his work to be heretical and eleven others to be highly suspicious though capable of an orthodox interpretation (Denzinger 1965c: 290–295).

In the late twentieth century Mathew Fox, then a Dominican himself, was censured for his efforts to revive Eckhart's theology in the interests of a more vital contemporary spirituality friendlier to such current concerns as the ecological movement. That so little has changed in nearly seven hundred years points to the fact that institutional Catholicism, and probably the wider Christian collective, still fear the individual's leading of an intensive interior life that might even go to dissolution in the nothingness underlying the all. This fear could be justly founded on the psychological dread and spiritual dangers of so deep an ingression into human subjectivity. Jung writes: "Human nature has an invincible dread of becoming conscious of itself" (Jung 1969c: 263). This fear could be allayed if more pastoral directors and therapists were aware of the experience itself and the spirituality that is built upon it. But the fear of a deep ingression into human interiority could also be an institutional fear of the individual who would come to live immediately and directly out of such depths and from them relate to all collectivities, ecclesial and secular, from a responsibility resting on loyalty to the self becoming conscious in the individual. The theory has been advanced that the apophatic mysticism characteristic of the earlier and late Middle Ages continued to live in the seventeenth and eighteenth centuries' sense of living directly out of a divine inner resource characteristic of "quietism" grounding the individual's religious life in total dependence on the cultivation of the depths of human subjectivity (Bruneau 1998: 139–141). It is to a spirituality such as this that Jung refers in his justification of a gnostic spirituality for the Christian, "It would not seem to me illogical if a psychological condition, previously suppressed, should reassert itself when the main ideas of the suppressive condition begin to lose their efficacy" (Jung 1969b: 97). The main idea of the suppression referred to here is that of a God wholly other than the psyche as the only licit conception of humanity's relation to the divine.

Many of the foundational elements in Eckhart's experience can be found in his sermon, "Blessed are the Poor" (Eckhart 1978). The rudiments of this sermon serve as a prelude to an examination of Jung's most significant appropriation of Eckhart under the rubric of "The Relativity of the God-concept in Meister Eckhart" (Jung 1971a: 241–258). Eckhart begins the sermon by distinguishing external from inner poverty. He commends the former but concentrates on the latter. Inner poverty is deep seated indeed. It lies in the loss of intellect, will, and of whatever one possesses, even, as it turns out, of one's own distinct personal being and identity (Eckhart 1978: 214). In resonance with his mystic predecessors of the thirteenth century, Eckhart discounts the cultivation of poverty as a virtuous activity here identified as an ego driven asceticism in the form of the divestiture of personal material belongings. Eckhart describes such practitioners who would reduce poverty to literal material diminishment as "asses" (Eckhart 1978: 215).

Rather, true poverty means the loss of the created will and intellect so that the individual returns to that state "when he was not yet". Eckhart repeats this phrase three times throughout the sermon (Eckhart 1978: 215, 216–217, 218). Note the striking similarity to Marguerite's "where she was before she was" (Porete 1993: 218). True poverty implies even the loss of one's personal but lesser being to an identity with the being of God. "Henceforth, in this poverty, man recovers the eternal being that he was, now is, and will eternally remain" (Eckhart 1978: 218). In other words true poverty means a regression to a total identity with God, that is, to a state that existed prior to any distinction between the divine and the human.

To make this point as dramatically as possible, Eckhart twice repeats in this sermon his paradoxical prayer, "I pray to God to rid me of God" (Eckhart 1978: 216, 219). The unpacking of this statement demands a more extensive knowledge of some fine points in Eckhart's theology. Eckhart clearly distinguishes between the Godhead and God as Trinity. The former rests in itself without any urgency to express itself beyond itself. The latter is caught up in a boiling tumult (*bullitio*) which compulsively boils over into creation (*ebullitio*) (McGinn 1981: 31, 39–45). When Eckhart prays to God to rid him of God, he prays that he be taken beyond the God of creation, the Trinity, as a source of the dualism between God and creature, to a state prior to all such dualism in which no distinction exists. This is the reality of the Godhead which is at once nothing and divested of any urgency to enter into the dualism of expressing itself beyond itself, either within or beyond divine life. Eckhart's theology here clearly distinguishes between a dimension of divinity which rests totally in itself, the Godhead, and another dimension, the Trinity, which cannot escape a compulsive creativity in going out beyond itself into a creation othered and so alienated from its source by the very act of creation as the basis of the distinction between creator and creature. On this point Eckhart is explicit. "God and Godhead are as different as active and inactive" (Eckhart 1857a: 143). Eckhart's distinction between Godhead and Trinity as Creator bears affinity with Jung's contention that the archetypes are driven to create consciousness to realize themselves in it. Eckhart equates the Trinity with God as Creator and conceives of the Trinity as incapable of resisting the drive to create. But in experiencing the Godhead as prior to the Trinity and divested of such compulsiveness Eckhart may point to a dimension of the psyche deeper than the archetypal itself and devoid of archetypal compulsion. The recovery of such a state, as a moment in the maturational process, is a valuable spiritual and political resource in the contemporary human situation since it would moderate the intensity and pretensions of all archetypally driven ideologies, religious or secular, by identifying a common source beyond their peculiar particularities and urgencies.

The perception that the Trinity acts necessarily and compulsively in creating and so establishing the state of alienating distance between creature and creator lies behind Eckhart's statement that on coming forth from God every creature speaks of God but none are happy. This universal state is due to the fact that the word that every creature speaks of God is a word of its alienation from God worked by the very act of creation itself (Eckhart 1978: 219). Anticipating Marx by five centuries Eckhart calls for a negation of the negation, i.e., the overcoming of the divide between creatures as wholly other than each other and wholly other than the creator. "I am not what you are and you are not what I am. Suppress the *not* and we are just the same; take naught from creatures and creatures are all the same. The remainder is one" (Eckhart 1857c: 435). This negation entails the recovery of that state when Eckhart and every creature was identical with the Godhead. "There I stood clear of God and of all things" (Eckhart 1978: 216). Eckhart terms the attainment of this state the "breakthrough" and understands it to somehow go beyond and complete a prior experience which he describes as the birth of God in the soul. This birth, remarkable in itself, is somehow preliminary and rather than lead back to an immediate engagement with the external world leads even deeper into the divine toward the breakthrough and unqualified identity with the Godhead. The ongoing birth of God in the soul anticipates the moment of identity in the breakthrough.

Eckhart's paradigm here suggests that the creator God is an energy like the archetypal which lusts for its expression in consciousness, its creature. In this sense the self and the archetypes, as creators of consciousness and seeking expression in it, describe a compulsive side of the psyche driven to become increasingly conscious in humanity. But Eckhart points to a dimension of divinity prior to such compulsion and so to a dimension of psyche which precedes the archetypal and archetypally based urgency to manifest in conscious form. The cultivation of this pre-archetypal stratum of psyche could be a significant restraint in the drive of the archetypal to incarnate currently too often in configurations of archetypal conflict in human individuals and communities to the serious detriment of both. The influence of the nothing would exercise its moderating and humanizing effect by breeding a sense of the relativity of such archetypal concretions as religions, ethnic bonding and political faiths and work to offset the threat their lethal particularity now poses to a more universal embrace of all archetypal differentiation in human consciousness.

Contemporary scholarship of the apophatic makes clear the radical nature of Eckhart's total self loss to identity with divinity. The culmination of the apophatic experience in the nothing describes a union of the divine and the human as a *"unitas indistinctionis"* (a unity without distinction) in sharply drawn contrast to a *"unitas distinctionis"* (a unity of distinction) in which the difference of the divine and the human is retained if not exacerbated in their very relationship (McGinn 1998a: 216, 217, 232–243; 2001: 47, 148). The former is a union in which all differences between the united are obliterated in the identity of a formless nothingness. The latter describes a union in which the difference between the divine and the human is retained and intensified through religious practice throughout their religious commerce. For Eckhart this second type of religious union with the divine would simply maintain and reinforce their differences and so the alienation which creation itself inevitably brings with it. Only dissolution in the nothing that precedes the bifurcation into creature and creator is radical enough to heal the split the act of creation occasions and sustains.

Jung's appropriation of Eckhart is equally radical. He adopts Eckhart's understanding of the divine–human relation in developing his singular and personal conception of "the relativity of God" (Jung 1971a: 241f.). At the heart of this understanding lies Jung's contention that the divine and the human are "functions" of each other (Jung 1971a: 243). Here Jung is clearly arguing that the relation of the divine to the human is the relation of the unconscious to consciousness as wholly intrapsychic functions of each other. For Jung the psychic containment attached to the equation of the relation of the unconscious to the ego with that of the divine to the human effectively terminates the end of all conceptions of God as "absolute" or "cut off from man" (Jung 1971a: 243). Rather the action of God on the human is confined to the psychological fact "that God's action springs from one's own inner being" (Jung 1971a: 243). As he was to make explicit in his *Answer to Job* such an understanding of the psyche corrodes the monotheistic understanding of humanity's relation to any One of the One and Only Gods. "The naive assumption that the creator of the world is a conscious being must be regarded as a disastrous prejudice which later gave rise to the most incredible dislocations of logic" (Jung 1969d: 383, fn. 13). Rather humanity is given a new responsibility of bringing a universally present inner divinity and its total potentiality to birth in human finite consciousness.

And, following Eckhart, Jung goes on to detail precisely the psycho-dynamics of how this birthing of God into consciousness takes place. First, all projections onto any external reality must be withdrawn. External reality here could range from the projection of mana onto things or people to the projective creation of the Gods themselves understood as wholly trans-psychic (Jung 1971a: 246, 248). Such externalism would be the object of Eckhart's and Jung's joint condemnation of fetching "him [God] from without" (Jung 1971a: 245). This latter phrase is Eckhart's though not foot-noted in Jung's use of it. Effectively Jung is here attacking all forms of idolatry on psychological grounds. The Gods and their archetypal equi-valents that escape psychic containment must first be returned to their origin. This retrieval serves as the prelude to the turn within, there to experience immediately the power from which all divinity emanates.

At this point, however, the turn inward is itself replete with danger. For the power or *dynamis* of the unconscious can consume the conscious power, the ego. In Eckhart's terms "the soul is not blissful because she is in God", i.e., when submerged in the unconscious, but "she is blissful when God is in her", i.e., mediating the unconscious to consciousness (Jung 1971a: 251). Yet this moment must be risked, and is, for Jung, the psychological equi-valent to Eckhart's breakthrough into the nothing. Jung is explicit:

> But when the "breakthrough" abolishes this separation [of creature from God] by cutting the ego off from the world, and the ego again becomes identical with the unconscious *dynamis*, God disappears as an object and dwindles into a subject which is no longer distinguishable from the ego.
>
> (Jung 1971a: 255)

This is the union of identity scholars of mysticism now speak of healing the separation of the ego from the unconscious and so wholly undermining any basis for the distinction between the divine and the human. Again Jung could hardly be more precise on the moment of unqualified identity with the nothing. "As a result of this retrograde process the original state of identity with God is re-established and a new potential is produced" (Jung 1971a: 255).

The new potential is what flows into consciousness through the soul in the wake of its moment of identity with its divine and unconscious origin. Obviously for neither Eckhart nor Jung can the moment of pure identity with the nothing be sustained permanently. Its sustenance would approach a catatonic state. Yet neither can it be wholly forsaken if consciousness is to be charged with the vitality and creativity such a moment alone can afford. What Jung and Eckhart are describing is a cyclical psychic rhythm, for Jung citing Goethe, analogous to the systolic and diastolic flow of blood to and from the heart (Jung 1971c: 253). In this ongoing circularity the ego, created by the unconscious, reverts to a moment of total identity with her and returns to consciousness renewed by the graces of the Great Mother to be found in their fullness in the abyss of her dark and fearsome recesses. In the return from the Mother the soul carries her energies to consciousness in the form of the symbol. Here Jung introduces another radical side of his psychology. He denies the substantiality of the soul and contends that the energies of the symbol born from the unconscious as it moves to consciousness becomes the soul herself ever in processes of revivifying consciousness through her regression to and return from the deeper unconscious. This cycle is the legitimate basis of what certain Jungian schools term "soul-making". It means that God, the energies of the deeper unconscious, is constantly being born in the soul in her return from the preceding depths. In this perspective the soul is removed from substantialist categories and simply becomes the power of the symbols and the energy they bear to consciousness (Jung 1971a: 251). "Loss of soul" is the severance or diminution of conscious access to these energies. On this the primordial mind was correct. The recovery and growth of soul lies in her role as mediating the energies or graces of the abyss to a more vital consciousness out of her moment of dissolution in the abyss.

Jacob Boehme (1575–1624)

In an intriguing statement in *Memories, Dreams, Reflections* Jung allows that humanity has long held the "premonition" of "the creature that surpasses its creator by a small but decisive factor" (Jung 1965a: 220). The premonition probably refers most directly to the dawning consciousness that divinity can become conscious only in humanity depicted in Jung's appropriation of the Book of Job but his remark would equally apply to Jacob Boehme, the only mystic cited more frequently in the *Collected Works* than Eckhart. Boehme's mystic genius lay in his experience that divinity had not resolved its self-contradiction in eternal life. Rather it was forced to create historical human consciousness as the sole power able to discern and so discriminate the opposites in the divine as the precondition of suffering their unification in processes of personal and collective history. Again such an organic understanding of the divine–human relationship would lodge a certain necessity in both the divine and the human. The divine would have to create consciousness in order to become conscious in it, where alone its antinomies could be perceived and united. Humanity's divinely imposed vocation would then become the working of these unities both demanded and enabled by the divine in the redemption of both the divine and the human in their hopefully ever more comprehensive synthesis in humanity (Dourley 1995a: 239; 1999).

Boehme's unmediated personal religious experience forced him to these positions. His experience also involved a moment of identity with the nothing. Sometimes he calls the nothing the *"ungrund"*, at other times the "One" or the "unity" (Boehme 1911: iv, sec. 6, v, sec. 8; Weeks 1991: 193). Making explicit what Eckhart left ambiguous and in so doing completing him, Boehme will clearly identify the preceding nothing as the source of the Trinity, now framed as the first manifestation of the nothing (Boehme 1911: 4, sec. 24). In doing this he removes a difficulty left by Eckhart's depiction of the nothing as totally at rest beyond all impulse toward self-definition or action. In Boehme's experience the Trinity is the first emanation of the nothing or stillness within divine life itself. However, Boehme departs from orthodox understandings of Trinity by denying to it the resolution of conflict within Trinitarian life itself. Rather the antinomies within the divine can only be perceived and resolved by and in the created mind. In the dialectic reciprocity between the nothing and its expression through Trinity and into humanity, the nothing seeks the I of human consciousness and the I seeks its healing in return to its source cast as "the cure of nothingness" (Weeks 1991: 192, 193). Again the cycle of regression to dissolution in the nothing and the return to a fuller life becomes evident as the underlying dynamic in Boehme's experience and Jung's appreciation of it as describing the foundational dynamic in psychological maturation. With Boehme and Jung, however, there is the implication that this movement to the nothing and return therefrom has as its major effect the unification of the divinely grounded opposites in human life and consciousness.

With both Boehme and Jung good and evil are two of the primary powers grounded in conflict within divine life and operative in humanity. Boehme's Trinity is made up of a dark, masculine, fiery figure in unison with a light bearing and gentle opposite. The first is a power of unrelated self-affirmation. The second is a power of light and gentle disclosure. They seek in humanity a unity they could not find in divinity. In this imagery Boehme locates the source of evil and good in the first and second moments of the Trinity, Father and Son, and details the agony of their embrace in humanity (Dourley 1995b: 434–439). It should be noted in passing that Boehme is also engaging the opposites of masculine and feminine in this imagery. The Father is an overwhelming male figure. The Son is more feminine and at times blends into the female characterization of Sophia and the Spirit as unifying powers whose unification is worked beyond Trinity in humanity. Thus Boehme's experience is that of an androgynous God whose androgyny is manifest in creation as male and female and demands the unity of these opposites in each individual.

In this imagery Boehme anticipates a number of elements foundational to Jung's understanding of the psyche. The most obvious is the dynamic of a conflicted power as the source of consciousness seeking the resolution of its conflicted life in consciousness. Boehme foreshadows Jung's understanding of the archetypal unconscious as generative of apparently irreconcilable opposites whose nature is to seek their unlikely union in a humanity driven to it by, in effect, the power of a divinity beyond reason and the limited hope to unite opposites that reason can afford. Boehme's vesting of the origin with good and evil, then expressed in its creational consequences, predates and anticipates Jung's position that Christ and Satan are the light and dark sons of the same creative power and, once differentiated as absolute opposites, are destined to embrace in history (Jung 1969e: 174–175).

Boehme also anticipates the profound teleology that informs Jung's psychology and philosophy of history as the site where the transcendent function by its nature works toward more inclusive forms of consciousness through suffering the clash of opposites out of which a compassion of wider embrace arises. In this regard Jung will make important statements about eschatology, a theological term usually referring to the ultimate resolution of the movement of history in a final or end state. In describing the suffering of the Christ figure as a crucifixion between archetypal opposites Jung refers to its imagery as being "as 'eschatological' as it is 'psychological'" (Jung 1969d: 408). By this he means that by suffering between intractable opposites, the thieves on right and left, the symbol of the crucified Christ points to their union in a consciousness beyond all three. Rather than seeing this imagery as a definitive and past historical event Jung understands it as an imaginal depiction of the deepest movement of the psyche and so of history to the more inclusive and so empathic consciousness pointed to in the symbol of resurrection. In the focus of this work it is important to note that the transcendent function works in the imagery of the crucifixion, to a higher consciousness through an immersion in the prior nothingness symbolized as physical death and three days in the tomb. The mystics who undergo this experience psychologically and spiritually would confirm the adequacy of the image of death to depict the suffering entailed in the return to the nothing and its ultimate reward in a resurrected consciousness of much greater embrace.

With his emphasis on the movement toward the unity of opposites in historical humanity Boehme in some sense completes Eckhart through his extending Eckhart to the insight that the moment of identity with the nothing or the One beyond the Trinity leads back to, urges, and enables the resolution of divine opposites in humanity. In both minds the One or Nothing is maternal and the source of all. Thus Boehme's emphasis on the historical resolution of the divine opposites involves both the experience of that dimension of divinity that precedes these opposites and the attendant drive to their unification in finite human history. In Boehme's paradigm as in Jung's, the undifferentiated unity of the primordial nothing is one devoid of consciousness in which the opposites lay latent. The eschatological unity toward which the historical psyche moves is one in which all opposites latent in the original nothingness are differentiated in consciousness and resolved through suffering toward their unity. This forward state could also be termed a "nothing" in that it is made up of a unity beyond opposites but with the crucial difference that all opposites are contained beyond their difference as the substance of its wealth. Indeed in one of his sketches of an all inclusive quaternity, the familiar inverted square or ogdoad, Jung depicts a process that begins in a pre-differentiated "formlessness" and culminates in a wholly differentiated "formlessness". It is interesting that he would describe this final state as also "formless", implying that the full eschatological unity of opposites is itself beyond form as a state in which formal conflict has been consciously unified in a wealth itself beyond form (Jung in Lammers et al 2007: 122). The movement to the final formlessness presupposes the circular movement of repeated immersion in the form-lessness of the maternal origin.

Summary and conclusions

What follows serves as a conclusion to the foregoing remarks on mysticism but also as an implicit summary of what has preceded this concluding chapter.

Mysticism and the psychodynamics of compassion

If the persons and mysticism of the Beguines, Eckhart and Boehme could by some imaginary process become one, they would contribute greatly to the cultivation of a truly universal sentiment and a greatly extended compassion. Eckhart's breakthrough to a total identity with the Godhead describes a psychological process in which ego and unconscious achieve an ephemeral state in a nothingness negating all difference between them. Psychologically Eckhart's return to the fourth, the Godhead, beyond the Trinity and in some sense its origin as Boehme makes clear, would describe a state of identity of ego and unconscious with, paradoxically, no urgency toward form, manifestation or activity. Such a state is the basis of Eckhart's understanding of resignation. Its attainment could be helpful in the unavoidable task of ushering the archetypal powers into consciousness because it would equip the individual who attained it with a position beyond the unmitigated compulsion of archetypal energies to take on form in human history and consciousness which, once assumed, function as intransigent absolutes. Such consciousness would be prior to and so tran-scend any form of archetypal concretion and so stand always in relation to them as the source of their iconoclastic dissolution. This perspective would be particularly helpful in the relief or softening of the collectively possessed consciousness currently evident in paroxysms of individual and collective faith and fanaticism and in the loss of life they induce. Eckhart's experience and Jung's attraction to it thus point to a dimension of psyche which in fact may precede the archetypal and be of immense value in a more humane mediation of the archetypal in its inevitable finite incarnations. Could Jung have been referring to this domain of the unconscious when he wrote of "archetypal statements", "There is nothing to stop their ultimate ramifications from penetrating to the very ground of the universe. We alone are the dumb ones if we fail to notice it" (Jung 1969e: 200). Neither Eckhart nor Jung were "dumb" in this sense. Both knew that the "ground of the universe" was the nothing that mothers the all. Resonance with her would graciously moderate the claims of each of her religious and political children to a privileged or even exhaustive possession of her graces.

But the regression to the fourth, beyond all form and inclination to it, has to include Boehme's experience for its completion. Boehme also traveled to such nothingness but upon his return, through the conflict of Trinitarian life to finite consciousness, realized that the eternal antinomies of divine life could only be resolved in the human. In this sense humanity becomes the fourth in which the divine itself seeks incarnation and redemption. This is the psychology that Jung develops most fully in his late work on Job. Only human consciousness can perceive and provide the locus for the unity of the opposites which divinity itself could not work. The task of cooperating in the redemption of the divine through the unification of its opposites becomes then the task of individual and collective humanity. "Everything now depends on man" (Jung 1969d: 459). Jung's understanding of the unconscious as the seat of contradiction seeking its resolution in consciousness through the latter's return to its source is at the heart of his attraction to Boehme. When the insights of both mystics are united the full sweep of the maturational process would entail a total self loss in the maternal nothingness as the source of a wisdom bearing a wider and ultimately a universal compassion in subsequent human consciousness. In this compassion no other or opposite could be excluded from the conscious embrace of the totality the Goddess strives to birth into reality in its completion and hers.

An all-inclusive psychic containment

Jung's appropriation of the mystics suggests an extension of the psyche to include the totality of the cognitive possibility. It becomes clear, especially in his treatment of Eckhart, that the potentiality of the unconscious infinitely transcends ego-consciousness but that nothing transcends the psyche. The divine nothingness into which the mystics merge is not a power extrinsic to the psyche. It is the primordial level of the psyche itself from which all consciousness, form and culture derive. Commerce with divinity becomes commerce with the depths of a common psyche to which each individual centre of consciousness has unmediated access. This all-inclusive nature of the psyche eliminates in principle that religious imagination which would visualize a relationship to the divine as to an entity or entities wholly beyond the psyche. Transcendence becomes a wholly intrapsychic reality, that of the inexhaustible energies of the Great Mother in relation to the layer of human historical consciousness to which she gives birth and in which she seeks to become self-conscious and incarnate in the full expression of her potential.

Jung's work on the mystics identifies the moments of intercourse with the Goddess in the process of her coming to an ever fuller consciousness in humanity. Once born beyond its origin, the ego is called upon to reenter her to be born again. The depth this reentry reaches with the mystics is that point of their unqualified self-loss in identity with the maternal nothingness from which all consciousness proceeds. Though few individuals may experience the harrowing nature of such total annihilation, Jung makes it clear that it is a moment in the process of individuation itself and to be undergone, at least to some degree, in the maturational process of everyone. "This is as much as to say that anyone who is destined to descend into a deep pit had better set about it with all the necessary precautions rather than risk falling into the hole backwards" (Jung 1968c: 70). The descent is not only for the few nor is it a single isolated event. It is recurrent and operative in all processes of becoming fully human.

In this sense the cyclical or repeated entrance into and return from the void describes a dynamic in the maturational process that can be neither avoided nor completed. It cannot be wholly avoided because only in its return to the energies of its origins is the ego renewed for its tasks in life. Were it not to welcome these depths in whatever form they take in each individual life, the ego would sever its link with the source of its life and eventually lose the will to continue, often after periods of alternating rage and despair occasioned by an ego seeking its renewal out of its relatively puny resources. But the movement to identity with its matrix and the return to consciousness can never be completed because the return, though it always carries with it an increase in consciousness, can never exhaust the fecundity of the infinite maternal. The wealth of her possibility will always outstrip the level of consciousness she has achieved in her manifestations or concretions in time. The human task of bringing her to birth will remain the basic drive of humanity but will never allow humanity to say, "Now her wholeness is fully incarnate in our consciousness and culture. We may rest from our labors." To such arrogance she would reply, "My fecund nothingness offers ever more to be made conscious in our never ending intercourse and so you are never free from its demands and from the agony and ecstasy of serving it."

Social/religious/political relativity

When Jung appropriates Eckhart under the rubric of "the relativity of God", the relativity he envisages would extend to and undermine any form of a particular and exhaustive claim to be in possession of the absolute in any of its forms, cultural, political or religious. The relativity of God for Jung means that the divine and human, the archetypal and ego-consciousness, are functions of each other and in an active dialectic which brings divinity to consciousness in humanity through humanity's reimmersion in the creative nothingness of its divine origin and return therefrom. Because one of the poles in the dialectic, the nothing, is infinite, the process can never end. This paradigm illustrates how smoothly the sacramental and iconoclastic blend in Jung's understanding of the psyche. Because they are functions of each other engaged in mutual redemption, human consciousness cannot remain totally unaware of a divine impress on it directing each human life toward the contribution it is to make to divinity becoming self-conscious in the circumstances of that unique life. Nor can it remain wholly unaware of this same power addressing it from without through natural forces. Because the psyche is continuous with nature, a point at the heart of Jung's understanding of synchronicity and the *unus mundus*, one world of alchemy, the numinous power that manifests within the psyche of the individual can manifest through nature beyond the individual with whom the individual is continuous through the universal ground of the psyche. Jung's understanding of the numinous as a psychic force bearing the power of the sacred is the basis of his compelling sense of the sacred and its sacramentalism addressing humanity always from within and on occasions such as the synchronistic event, from without. The psyche itself takes precedence as the source of the sacramental in bearing the sense of the sacred to the individual most dramatically in the containment and numinosity of the dream. But the same power that appears unmediated to the individual in the dream can manifest in any power in nature since nature too is grounded in the same psyche as is the individual. Indeed without such a universal sense of the sacred particular enactments of the sacred in sacrament or rite degenerate quickly to magic.

Paul Tillich is quite correct in pointing out that the sacred can appear through any level of nature from the vegetative through the animal to the human because all of nature is grounded in the divine, with Jung, the archetypal psyche. It is not surprising then that these powers of nature are used liturgically or ritually by religions great and small to induce the sense of the sacred in the individual and collective. Some of the more common forms of the natural as bearer of the divine are water, food, wine, fire, sound and smell. Yet this sacramental sense is betrayed when it identifies the holy with that through which the holy appears in the form of objects, persons, institutions or, most importantly in the objectification of the Gods themselves. In treating of Eckhart, Jung is explicit in affirming that the deity-creating externalization of humanity's native sense of the divine is a form of debilitating idolatry. Before humanity can turn inward and regress to its native identity with the divine, it must free itself from the creation of the Gods beyond itself, in whatever form they may take, ranging from the projection of the sacred onto holy individuals to lodging the holy in Gods understood to be wholly other or beyond the psyche. In this idolatrous conversion the creature becomes the creator of the divine and robs the creature of its native divinity by giving it to Gods beyond itself.

The iconoclasm of this dynamic would forbid anything beyond the soul as sole mediator of the archetypal to be identified with the divine. The soul carries the experience and images of the divine to consciousness but none of them exhausts the wealth of the unconscious whose images and energies the soul mediates to mind. This psychology is at the heart of Eckhart's thought on the birth of God in the soul. It leads to the breakthrough and to an immersion in the boundless whose expressions in historical consciousness are never more than relative. Obviously this dynamic denies to any con-cretion of the unconscious the status of an unqualified claim to be an expression of the totality. On the contrary it makes relative all such claims, while appreciating their limited contribution to the progress of historical consciousness through whatever aspect of archetypal truth they mediate to humanity in past and present.

Jung's union of the sacramental and the iconoclastic would thus under-mine all political and religious claims to unlimited ultimacy, claims which continue to be made with dire consequences for the human future. In relativizing God Jung relativizes all religious and political claims and proffers some hope to the resolution of the religious or cultural wars currently threatening an ever widening segment of humanity if not the species itself (Dourley 2006a). If it could be realized that the Gods, both religious and political, create themselves through the psyche, consciousness could then ask if any of them is worth the life of a human through whom they are created? Usually such death is enabled by devotion to one or other God, religious or political, in a variety of endless combinations. The pan-theism endemic to Jung's understanding of the psyche's role in the creation of such Gods would undermine them all. Jung claims that the awareness, "that God is reality itself" is only now coming to the fore, and that as a result of a "millennial process" of religious development (Jung 1969e: 402). A consciousness dwelling in the experience that God is reality itself would be much less likely to offend human dignity, let alone kill, for a limited truth and no consciousness is more aware that God is reality itself than those who have experienced divinity as the nothing from which the surrounding all proceeds. Again such consciousness would point to the specifically political benefits it would yield in pointing to the commonly possessed human ground generative of the archetypal differentiation that pits individual and collective faiths against each other.

Consequences for religion and Jungian psychology

Jung's linking of the mystics of the nothing with his psychology has repercussions both for the study of mysticism and for his own psychology. It raises the study of mysticism to the psychological level where its value can be revealed both to those in a religious tradition and to those beyond any. For the believer, Jung's equation of mystical experience with psychological experience opens up depths of the soul and of human interiority which orthodoxy can close over, remain insensitive to, or consciously reject. The believer may find a certain refreshing depth in going beyond biblical stories, their dogmatic formulation, and cultic enactment, to the personal depth from which they all proceed and into which they are intended to lead. This movement inward led to Eckhart's occasional radical formulations about dispensing with all imagery and even ecclesial devotion as preliminary, shallow and exterior to the inner life of immersion in the nothing. Boehme also distinguished between "stone churches", i.e., formal religion, and the immediate experience of the sacred, which he extended to "wise heathens" and to members of other religions as well as to the inhabitants of the newly discovered Americas (Weeks 1991: 50, 133, 202, 203). On the other hand the experience of the depths of human interiority prior to their symbolic expression can enable the individual who appreciates the nothing to appreciate the symbolic forms such depth takes on when expressed. Such appreciation of the pre-symbolic leads to a deeper symbolic life even within specific religious institutional allegiances since these institutions, their symbols and rites, are, in the final analysis, themselves expressions of the nothing created to mediate her power through return to her.

For those who never were in a tradition or have for many reasons – some excellent – left their tradition, Jung's elevation of the mystical experience to the psychological level makes of it a universal human propensity, one that can enrich the life of any one. Consciousness itself lives over the abyss, and the attainment of a fullness of life means, at some point, a return to that abyss. The only real human option is to deal with the abyss consciously or unconsciously. The mystics went in consciously and through a spiritual death came into a consciousness so enhanced that their dissolution in the nothing would never leave them. Such experience intensifies the vitality of those who undergo it. It equips them with a surer sense of an always evolving personal myth or truth and so with a sense of a unique vocation in relation to their society and its embedded myths upon their return from the nothing to engagement with their immediate environment. Though the experience is intensely private it is just as intensely, and always, political.

As suggested earlier, Jung's appreciation of the mystics he admired points to depths of the psyche he did not formally incorporate into the model of the psyche in his written work. These mystics and especially Eckhart endorse a state of resignation, of "Why ask why", beyond the archetypal urgency to transform consciousness and the world beyond it. Obviously none of the mystics dealt with here remained in a nothingness prohibitive of interaction with their surroundings. One died during his heresy trial. Another was executed for making public her views. Boehme was harassed by the institutions in reformed Christianity. They certainly caught the attention of the collective. But what they gloried in was the peace, tranquility and true resignation they experienced in their removal from all personal identity and effort in their return to the universal womb. Again, such experience would help immensely in the incessant incarnation that archetypal powers seek religiously and politically by moderating their compulsive attractiveness through an experience deeper than and prior to the source of their frequently irresistible but swamping allure. Jung was fearful of the archetypally induced societal unconsciousness of the "isms" and of the archetypal energies informing the "psychic epidemics" they so fluently sponsored (Dourley 2003). Yet he never made the link to a consciousness aware of the nothing as a power that could counteract the influence of the "isms" by getting behind them and so undermining them, at least, in their more barbaric affirmation. Bringing the nothing to bear on them in processes of their humanization and moderation is an option that the pre-archetypal dimension of the psyche could provide. Indeed there are indications, sporadic at the moment that Jungian reflection is turning to the experience of the nothing. Works by Paul Ashton (2007), Stanton Marlan (2005) and Kathryn Wood Madden (2008) turn directly to images of the imageless and to the experience of the nothing from a specifically Jungian perspective. It may now be time to further such inquiry on the psychological and political benefits of a consciousness aware of the presence of the nothing in the depth of the psyche as an ultimate human resource in mining a wealthier and more tolerant humanity and so humanizing the redemptive impulse now revisioned on God and humanity as functions of each other engaged in an endless creativity.

Afterword: clinical relevance

Jung devoted three volumes of his *Collected Works* to alchemy and tended to relate alchemy to gnosis and to mysticism on the basis of their shared intense sense of the divine emanating to consciousness from the depths of the natural psyche itself. With the energy Jung put into his mature research into these neglected areas of the Western spirit it is difficult to escape the conclusion that mystical/gnostic/alchemical consciousness constitutes a specifically clinical resource in the doing of Jungian analysis. This chapter has shown the energy he invested in reading so acutely the mystics who gained his attention and who, at least with Eckhart and Boehme, influenced the subsequent development of the Western mind and spirit. Jung was to write that only the experience of the numinous was really capable of effecting a healing transformation.

You are quite right, the main interest of my work is not concerned with the treatment of neuroses but rather with the approach to the numinous. But the fact is that the approach to the numinous is the real therapy and inasmuch as you attain to the numinous experiences you are released from the curse of pathology. Even the very disease takes on a numinous character.

(Jung 1945c: 377)

The experience of the numinous is at the heart of mystical experience and Jung rightly extended the sense of the numinous to the experience of the gnostics, alchemists and the seekers of the grail. He argues throughout his work that the sensitivity for the numinous shared by these neglected traditions of the Western spirit is really the major if not the only resource in a specifically Jungian approach to therapeutic transformation. These resources would then take on a specifically "clinical" value in Jungian therapy and refuse to be excised in the interest of a less esoteric and confining understanding of what the clinical is. The extension of the boundaries of the "clinical" as Jung extended them in the doing of Jungian therapy adds a mystical sensitivity, an appreciation of the numinous, to the specifically "clinical" resources his psychology has to offer. As cited above, Jung might wonder if anything else is "real therapy" and if the absence of a mystical sense in therapy is really Jungian therapy in a clinical sense. The danger is that so much of current commentary could miss the total Jungian clinical resource by excising the mystery of the numinous on which it rests. This would reduce his psychology theoretically and therapeutically to a purely conscious gambit or to a mechanistic and psychometric technology of the psyche. This trend may be evident especially in the neglect of the numinosity endemic to some extent in all dreams and the mystery of the individual they seek to unveil. A so called "clinical" approach based on a conscious distancing from the healing mystery of the psyche's depth Jung would understand as a total defeat for his psychology, one that could be offset only by the recovery of the deeper sensitivities of mystic, alchemist and gnostic in their common yet differing respect for the divine ground of nature and of human nature. There may be a great need to rethink what is clinical and what not in a Jungian world view and what the removal of the experienced arcane from the clinical does in divesting the clinical of a specifically Jungian tone and efficacy. The issue of Jung and the recovery of a modern viable religion based on human interiority has been addressed at some length (Dourley 2008). This is but one side of a needed recovery. What is equally important is the recovery of the fullness of Jung's understanding of the psyche and its societal dissemination. Its recovery may now be a survival issue if humanity is not to be consumed by the very source that has imbued it with the gift of self-consciousness.

References

Ashton, P. (2007) *From the Brink: Experiences of the Void from a Depth Psychological Perspective*, London: Karnac.

Babinsky, E. (1993) "Introduction", in *Marguerite Porete, The Mirror of Simple Souls*, New York: Paulist, 6–20.

Barth, K. (1968) *Epistle to the Romans*, London: Oxford University Press.

Berdyaev, N. (1958) "Unground and Freedom", in J. Boehme *Six Theosophic Points*, J. Earle (trans.), Ann Arbor, MI: University of Michigan Press, v–xxxvii.

Boehme, J. (1911) *The Forty Questions of the Soul and the Clavis*, J. Sparrow (trans.), London: John M. Watkins.

—— (1958) *Six Theosophic Points*, J. Earle (trans.), Ann Arbor, MI: University of Michigan Press.

—— (1978) *The Way to Christ*, P. Erb (trans.), New York: Paulist.

Bruneau, M. (1998) *Women Mystics Confront the Modern World*, Albany, NY: State University of New York Press.

Buber, M. (1988a) "Religion and Modern Thinking", in *Eclipse of God*, Atlantic Highlands, NJ: Humanities Press International, 65–92

—— (1988b) "Supplement: Reply to C.G. Jung", in *Eclipse of God*, Atlantic Highlands, NJ: Humanities Press International, 133–137.

Corbett, L. (1996) *The Religious Function of the Psyche*, London: Routledge.

—— (2007) *Psyche and the Sacred: Spirituality Beyond Religion*, New Orleans, LA: Spring Journal.

Cunningham, A. (2007) "Appendix 2, Victor White, a Memoir", in A, Lammers, A. Cunningham and M. Stein (eds) *The Jung-White Letters*, Hove, UK: Routledge, 307–336.

Cupitt, D. (1998) *Mysticism after Modernity*, Oxford: Blackwell.

Dawkins, R. (2006) *The God Delusion*, New York: Bantam.

Dennett, D.C. (2006) *Breaking the Spell: Religion as a Natural Phenomenon*, New York: Viking.

Denzinger, H. (ed.) (1965a) "Pascendi Dominici Gregis", 8 September 1907, in *Enchiridion Symbolorum*, Rome: Herder, 675–682.

—— (1965b) "Humani Generis", 12 August 1950, in *Enchiridion Symbolorum*, Rome: Herder, 772–780.

—— (1965c) "In agro dominico", 27 March 1329, in *Enchiridion Symbolorum*, Rome: Herder, 290–295.

Dourley, J. (1987) "Of Human Faiths and Kidney Stones", in *Love, Celibacy, and the Inner Marriage*, Toronto: Inner City Books, 91–105.

—— (1990) *The Goddess Mother of the Trinity*, Lewiston, NY: Edwin Mellen Press.

—— (1993) "Jung and Metaphysics: A Dubious Disclaimer", *Pastoral Sciences*, 12(1): 15–24.

—— (1994) "In the Shadow of the Monotheisms: Jung's Conversations with Buber and White", in J. Ryce-Menuhin (ed.) *Jung and the Monotheisms*, London: Routledge, 125–145.

—— (1995a) *Jung and the Religious Alternative: The Rerooting*, Lewiston, NY: Edwin Mellen Press.

—— (1995b) "Jacob Boehme and Paul Tillich on Trinity and God: Similarities and Differences", *Religious Studies*, 31(4): 429–445.

—— (1998) "Recalling the Gods: A Millennial Process", in J.M. Spiegelman (ed.) *Psychology and Religion at the Millennium and Beyond*, Tempe, AZ: New Falcon, 23–35.

—— (1999) "Bringing Up Father: C.G. Jung on History as the Education of God", *The European Legacy: Toward New Paradigms*, 4(2): 54–68.

—— (2003) "Archetypal Hatred as Social Bond: Strategies for its Dissolution", in J. Beebe (ed.) *Terror, Violence and the Impulse to Destroy, Perspectives from Analytical Psychology, Papers from the 2002 North American Conference of Jungian Analysts*, Einsiedeln, Switzerland: Daimon Verlag, 135–160.

—— (2004) "Jung, Mysticism and the Double Quaternity: Jung and the Psychic Origin of Religious and Mystical Experience", *Harvest*, 50(1): 47–74.

—— (2006a) "C.G. Jung, S.P. Huntington and the Search for Civilization", *Studies in Religion*, 35(1): 65–84.

—— (2006b) "Jung and the Recall of the Gods", *Journal of Jungian Theory and Practice*, 8(1): 43–53.

—— (2006c) "Rerooting in the Mother: The Numinosity of the Night", in A. Casement and D. Tacy (eds) *The Idea of the Numinous, Contemporary Jungian and Psychoanalytic Perspectives*, Hove, UK: Routledge, 171–185.

—— (2006d) "Love, Celibacy and the Inner Marriage: Jung and Mechthild of Magdeburg", in *The Intellectual Autobiography of a Jungian Theologian*, Lewiston, NY: Edwin Mellen Press, Part Three, 25–43.

—— (2007) "The Jung-White Dialogue and Why it Couldn't Work and Won't Go Away", *Journal of Analytical Psychology*, 52(3): 275–295.

—— (2008) *Paul Tillich, Carl Jung and the Recovery of Religion*, Hove, UK: Routledge.

Eckhart, Meister (1857a) Sermon LVI, "The Emanation and Return", in *Meister Eckhart*, F. Pfeiffer (ed.) C. de B. Evans (trans.), Volume 1, London: John M. Watkins, 1947, 142–143.

—— (1857b) Sermon LXXVII, "The Poor in Spirit", in *Meister Eckhart*, F. Pfeiffer (ed.) C. de B. Evans (trans.), Volume 1, London: John M. Watkins, 1947, 217–221.

—— (1857c), "Sayings", in *Meister Eckhart*, F. Pfeiffer (ed.) C. de B. Evans (trans.), Volume 1, London: John M. Watkins, 1947, 417–441.

—— (1978) Sermon, "Blessed are the Poor", in *Meister Eckhart, Mystic and Philosopher*, R. Schurmann (trans.), Bloomington, IN: Indiana University Press.

Hadewijch (1980) *Hadewijch: The Complete Works*, Mother Columba Hart, O.S.B. (trans.), New York: Paulist.

Harris, S. (2006) *Letter to a Christian Nation*, New York: Knopf.

Hegel, G.W.F. (1970) "The Spirit of Christianity and its Fate", in *On Christianity: Early Theological Writings*, T.M. Knox and R. Kroner (trans.), Gloucester, MA: Peter Smith, 182–301.

—— (1990) *Lectures on the History of Philosophy, Volume III, Medieval and Modern Philosophy*, R.F. Brown (ed.), Berkeley, CA: University of California Press.

Hollywood, A. (2004) "Begin the Beguines: A Review of Walter Simons' *Cities of Ladies: Beguine Communities in the Medieval Low Countries*", *Spiritus: A Journal of Christian Spirituality*, 4(1): 91–97.

Huntington, S.P. (1993) "The Clash of Civilizations?" *Foreign Affairs*, 72(3): 22–49.

—— (1996/2003) *The Clash of Civilizations and the Remaking of World Order*, New York: Simon & Schuster.

—— (2004) *Who Are We? The Challenges to America's National Identity*, New York: Simon & Schuster.

James, W. (1979) *The Varieties of Religious Experience*, Glasgow: Collins.

Jung, C.G. (1933) "Brother Klaus", *Psychology and Religion: West and East, Collected Works, Volume 11*, Princeton, NJ: Princeton University Press.

—— (1935) Letter to Freidrich Seifert, 31 July 1935, in G. Adler and A. Jaffe (eds) *C.G. Jung Letters, Volume I, 1906–1950*, Princeton, NJ: Princeton University Press, 1973.

—— (1940) Letter to Anonymous, 20 May 1940, in G. Adler and A. Jaffe (eds) *C.G. Jung Letters, Volume I, 1906–1950*, Princeton, NJ: Princeton University Press, 1973.

—— (1942) Letter to B. Milt, 8 June 1942, in G. Adler and A. Jaffe (eds) *C.G. Jung Letters, Volume I, 1906–1950*, Princeton, NJ: Princeton University Press, 1973.

—— (1945a) Letter to Father Victor White, 26 September 1945, in G. Adler and A. Jaffe (eds) *C.G. Jung Letters, Volume I, 1906–1950*, Princeton, NJ: Princeton University Press, 1973.

—— (1945b) Letter to Father Victor White, 5 October 1945, in G. Adler and A. Jaffe (eds) *C.G. Jung Letters, Volume I, 1906–1950*, Princeton, NJ: Princeton University Press, 1973.

—— (1945c) Letter to P.W. Martin, 20 August 1945, in G. Adler and A. Jaffe (eds) *C.G. Jung Letters, Volume I, 1906–1950*, Princeton, NJ: Princeton University Press, 1973.

—— (1946a) Letter to Father Victor White, 6 November 1946, in G. Adler and A. Jaffe (eds) *C.G. Jung Letters, Volume I, 1906–1950*, Princeton, NJ: Princeton University Press, 1973.

—— (1946b) Letter to Father Victor White, 18 December 1946, in G. Adler and A. Jaffe (eds) *C.G. Jung Letters, Volume I, 1906–1950*, Princeton, NJ: Princeton University Press, 1973.

—— (1947a) Letter to Father Victor White, 27 March 1947, in G. Adler and A. Jaffe (eds) *C.G. Jung Letters, Volume I, 1906–1950*, Princeton, NJ: Princeton University Press, 1973.

—— (1947b) Letter to Father Victor White, 23 April 1947, in G. Adler and A. Jaffe (eds) *C.G. Jung Letters, Volume I, 1906–1950*, Princeton, NJ: Princeton University Press, 1973.

—— (1947c) Letter to Father Victor White, 6 July 1947, in A, Lammers, A. Cunningham and M. Stein (eds) *The Jung-White Letters*, Hove, UK: Routledge, 2007.

—— (1947d) Letter to Father Victor White, 19 December 1947, in G. Adler and A. Jaffe (eds) *C.G. Jung Letters, Volume I, 1906–1950*, Princeton, NJ: Princeton University Press, 1973.

—— (1947e) Letter to Father Victor White, 27 December 1947, in G. Adler and A. Jaffe (eds) *C.G. Jung Letters, Volume I, 1906–1950*, Princeton, NJ: Princeton University Press, 1973.

—— (1948a) Letter to Father Victor White, 30 January 1948, in G. Adler and A. Jaffe (eds) *C.G. Jung Letters, Volume I, 1906–1950*, Princeton, NJ: Princeton University Press, 1973.

—— (1948b) Letter to Father Victor White, 21 May 1948, in G. Adler and A. Jaffe (eds) *C.G. Jung Letters, Volume I, 1906–1950*, Princeton, NJ: Princeton University Press, 1973.

—— (1948c) Letter to Father Victor White, 24 September 1948, in G. Adler and A. Jaffe (eds) *C.G. Jung Letters, Volume I, 1906–1950*, Princeton, NJ: Princeton University Press, 1973.

—— (1948d) Letter to Father Victor White, 16 December 1948, in G. Adler and A. Jaffe (eds) *C.G. Jung Letters, Volume I, 1906–1950*, Princeton, NJ: Princeton University Press, 1973.

—— (1949a) Letter to Father Victor White, 8 January 1949, in G. Adler and A. Jaffe (eds) *C.G. Jung Letters, Volume I, 1906–1950*, Princeton, NJ: Princeton University Press, 1973.

—— (1949b) Letter to Father Victor White, 31 December 1949, in G. Adler and A. Jaffe (eds) *C.G. Jung Letters, Volume I, 1906–1950*, Princeton, NJ: Princeton University Press, 1973.

—— (1950a) Letter to Father Victor White, 12 May 1950, in A, Lammers, A. Cunningham and M. Stein (eds) *The Jung-White Letters*, Hove, UK: Routledge, 2007.

—— (1950b) Letter to Father Victor White, 25 November 1950, in G. Adler and A. Jaffe (eds) *C.G. Jung Letters, Volume I, 1906–1950*, Princeton, NJ: Princeton University Press, 1973.

—— (1952a) Letter to Dorothee Hoch, 28 May 1952, in G. Adler and A. Jaffe (eds) *C.G. Jung Letters, Volume II, 1951–1961*, Princeton, NJ: Princeton University Press, 1975.

—— (1952b) Letter to Father Victor White, 30 June 1952, in G. Adler and A. Jaffe (eds) *C.G. Jung Letters, Volume II, 1951–1961*, Princeton, NJ: Princeton University Press, 1975.

—— (1952c) Letter to Father Victor White, Spring 1952, in G. Adler and A. Jaffe (eds) *C.G. Jung Letters, Volume II, 1951–1961*, Princeton, NJ: Princeton University Press, 1975.

—— (1952d) Letter to Pastor Walter Uhsadel, 6 February 1952, in G. Adler and A. Jaffe (eds) *C.G. Jung Letters, Volume II, 1951–1961*, Princeton, NJ: Princeton University Press, 1975.

—— (1952e) Letter to Dr. Hoch, 23 September 1952, in G. Adler and A. Jaffe (eds) *C.G. Jung Letters, Volume II, 1951–1961*, Princeton, NJ: Princeton University Press, 1975.

—— (1953a) Letter to Father Victor White, 24 November 1953, in G. Adler and A. Jaffe (eds) *C.G. Jung Letters, Volume II, 1951–1961*, Princeton, NJ: Princeton University Press, 1975.

—— (1953b) Letter to Rudolph Jung, 11 May 1956, in G. Adler and A. Jaffe (eds) *C.G. Jung Letters, Volume II, 1951–1961*, Princeton, NJ: Princeton University Press, 1975.

—— (1953c) Letter to Carleton Smith, 9 September 1953, in G. Adler and A. Jaffe (eds) *C.G. Jung Letters, Volume II, 1951–1961*, Princeton, NJ: Princeton University Press 1975.

—— (1953d) Letter to Pastor Willi Bremi, 11 December 1953, in G. Adler and A. Jaffe (eds) *C.G. Jung Letters, Volume II, 1951–1961*, Princeton, NJ: Princeton University Press, 1975.

—— (1953e) Letter to Pastor Willi Bremi, 26 December 1953, in G. Adler and A. Jaffe (eds) *C.G. Jung Letters, Volume II, 1951–1961*, Princeton, NJ: Princeton University Press, 1975.

—— (1954a) Letter to Erich Neumann, 30 January 1954, in G. Adler and A. Jaffe (eds) *C.G. Jung Letters, Volume II, 1951–1961*, Princeton, NJ: Princeton University Press, 1975.

—— (1954b) Letter to Father Victor White, 10 April 1954, in G. Adler and A. Jaffe (eds) *C.G. Jung Letters, Volume II, 1951–1961*, Princeton, NJ: Princeton University Press, 1975.

—— (1954c) "Analytical Psychology and Education", *The Development of Personality, Collected Works, Volume 17*, Princeton, NJ: Princeton University Press.

—— (1955a) Letter to Father Victor White, 19 January 1955, in G. Adler and A. Jaffe (eds) *C.G. Jung Letters, Volume II, 1951–1961*, Princeton, NJ: Princeton University Press, 1975.

—— (1955b) Letter to Father Victor White, 2 April 1955, in G. Adler and A. Jaffe (eds) *C.G. Jung Letters, Volume II, 1951–1961*, Princeton, NJ: Princeton University Press, 1975.

—— (1955c) Letter to Father Victor White, 6 May 1955, in G. Adler and A. Jaffe (eds) *C.G. Jung Letters, Volume II, 1951–1961*, Princeton, NJ: Princeton University Press, 1975.

—— (1957a) Letter to Bernard Lang, 8 June 1957, in G. Adler and A. Jaffe (eds) *C.G. Jung Letters, Volume II, 1951–1961*, Princeton, NJ: Princeton University Press, 1975.

—— (1957b) Letter to Bernard Lang, 14 June 1957, in G. Adler and A. Jaffe (eds) *C.G. Jung Letters, Volume II, 1951–1961*, Princeton, NJ: Princeton University Press, 1975.

—— (1957c) Letter to Bernard Lang, June 14, 1957, in G. Adler and A. Jaffe (eds) *C.G. Jung Letters, Volume II, 1951–1961*, Princeton, NJ: Princeton University Press, 1975.

—— (1959a) Letter to Mother Prioress of a Contemplative Order, September 1959, in G. Adler and A. Jaffe (eds) *C.G. Jung Letters, Volume II, 1951–1961*, Princeton, NJ: Princeton University Press, 1975.

—— (1959b) Letter to Joseph F. Rychlak, 27 April 1959, in G. Adler and A. Jaffe (eds) *C.G. Jung Letters, Volume II, 1951–1961*, Princeton, NJ: Princeton University Press, 1975.

—— (1959c) Letter to Father Victor White, 22 October 1959, in G. Adler and A. Jaffe (eds) *C.G. Jung Letters, Volume II, 1951–1961*, Princeton, NJ: Princeton University Press, 1975.

—— (1960a) Letter to Father Victor White, 25 March 1960, in G. Adler and A. Jaffe (eds) *C.G. Jung Letters, Volume II, 1951–1961*, Princeton, NJ: Princeton University Press, 1975.

—— (1960b) Letter to Mother Prioress of a Contemplative Order, 19 October 1960, in G. Adler and A. Jaffe (eds) *C.G. Jung Letters, Volume II, 1951–1961*, Princeton, NJ: Princeton University Press, 1975.

—— (1960c) Letter to Mother Prioress of a Contemplative Order, 29 April 1960, in G. Adler and A. Jaffe (eds) *C.G. Jung Letters, Volume II, 1951–1961*, Princeton, NJ: Princeton University Press, 1975.

—— (1960d) Letter to C.K. Ginsberg, 3 June 1960, in G. Adler and A. Jaffe (eds) *C.G. Jung Letters, Volume II, 1951–1961*, Princeton, NJ: Princeton University Press, 1975.

—— (1960e) Letter to Father Victor White, 30 April 1960, in G. Adler and A. Jaffe (eds) *C.G. Jung Letters, Volume II, 1951–1961*, Princeton, NJ: Princeton University Press, 1975.

—— (1960f) Letter to Mother Prioress of a Contemplative Order, 6 February 1960, in G. Adler and A. Jaffe (eds) *C.G. Jung Letters, Volume II, 1951–1961*, Princeton, NJ: Princeton University Press, 1975.

—— (1960g) Letter to A.D. Cornell, 9 February 1960, in G. Adler and A. Jaffe (eds) *C.G. Jung Letters, Volume II, 1951–1961*, Princeton, NJ: Princeton University Press, 1975.

—— (1964a) "Wotan", in *Civilization in Transition, Collected Works, Volume 10*, Princeton, NJ: Princeton University Press.

—— (1964b) "A Rejoinder to Dr. Bally", in *Civilization in Transition, Collected Works, Volume 10*, Princeton, NJ: Princeton University Press.

—— (1964c) "The Undiscovered Self", in *Civilization in Transition, Collected Works, Volume 10*, Princeton, NJ: Princeton University Press.

—— (1964d) "The Spiritual Problem of Modern Man", in *Civilization in Transition, Collected Works, Volume 10*, Princeton, NJ: Princeton University Press.

—— (1964e) "Women in Europe" in *Civilization in Transition, Collected Works, Volume 10*, Princeton, NJ: Princeton University Press.

—— (1964f) "Archaic Man", in *Civilization in Transition, Collected Works, Volume 10*, Princeton, NJ: Princeton University Press.

—— (1964g) "Mind and Earth", in *Civilization in Transition, Collected Works, Volume 10*, Princeton, NJ: Princeton University Press.

—— (1964h) "Editorial 1935", in *Civilization in Transition, Collected Works, Volume 10*, Princeton, NJ: Princeton University Press.

—— (1964i) "Epilogue to 'Essays on Contemporary Events'", in *Civilization in Transition, Collected Works, Volume 10*, Princeton, NJ: Princeton University Press.

—— (1964j) "After the Catastrophe", in *Civilization in Transition, Collected Works, Volume 10*, Princeton, NJ: Princeton University Press.

—— (1965a) *Memories, Dreams, Reflections*, A. Jaffe (ed.), New York: Vintage, Random House.

—— (1965b) *"Septem Sermones ad Mortuos"*, Appendix V, in *Memories, Dreams, Reflections*, A. Jaffe (ed.), New York: Vintage, Random House.

—— (1966a) *Symbols of Transformation, Collected Works, Volume 5*, Princeton, NJ: Princeton University Press.

—— (1966b) "The Relations Between the Ego and the Unconscious", in *Two Essays on Analytical Psychology, Volume 7*, Princeton, NJ: Princeton University Press.

—— (1966c) "The Psychology of the Transference", *The Practice of Psychotherapy, Volume 16*, Princeton, NJ: Princeton University Press.

—— (1966d) "Anima and Animus", in *Two Essays on Analytical Psychology, Volume 7*, Princeton, NJ: Princeton University Press.

—— (1966e) "On the Relation of Analytical Psychology to Poetry", in *The Spirit in Man, Art and Literature, Volume 15*, Princeton, NJ: Princeton University Press.

—— (1966f) "Fundamental Questions of Psychotherapy", in *The Practice of Psychotherapy, Volume 16*, Princeton, NJ: Princeton University Press.

—— (1966g) "The Assimilation of the Unconscious", in *Two Essays on Analytical Psychology, Volume 7*, Princeton, NJ: Princeton University Press.

—— (1967a) "Commentary on 'The Secret of the Golden Flower'", in *Alchemical Studies, Collected Works, Volume 13*, Princeton, NJ: Princeton University Press.

—— (1967b) "The Philosophical Tree", in *Alchemical Studies, Collected Works, Volume 13*, Princeton, NJ: Princeton University Press.

—— (1968a) "Introduction to the Religious and Psychological Problems of Alchemy", in *Psychology and Alchemy, Collected Works, Volume 12*, Princeton, NJ: Princeton University Press.

—— (1968b) "Individual Dream Symbolism in Relation to Alchemy", in *Psychology and Alchemy, Collected Works, Volume 12*, Princeton, NJ: Princeton University Press.

—— (1968c) "Christ, A Symbol of the Self", in *Aion, Collected Works, Volume 9ii*, Princeton, NJ: Princeton University Press.

—— (1968d) "Concerning Rebirth", in *The Archetypes and the Collective Unconscious, Collected Works, Volume 9i*, Princeton, NJ: Princeton University Press.

—— (1968e) "Background to the Psychology of Christian Alchemical Symbolism", in *Aion, Collected Works, Volume 9ii*, Princeton, NJ: Princeton University Press.

—— (1968f) "Melchior Cibinensis and the Alchemical Paraphrase of the Mass", *Psychology and Alchemy, Collected Works, Volume 12*, Princeton, NJ: Princeton University Press.

—— (1968g) "The Structure and Dynamics of the Self", in *Aion, Collected Works, Volume 9ii*, Princeton, NJ: Princeton University Press.

—— (1968h) "Gnostic Symbols of the Self", in *Aion, Collected Works, Volume 9ii*, Princeton, NJ: Princeton University Press.

—— (1968i) "A Study in the Process of Individuation", in *The Archetypes and the Collective Unconscious, Collected Works, Volume 9i*, Princeton, NJ: Princeton University Press.

—— (1968j) "Archetypes of the Collective Unconscious", in *The Archetypes and the Collective Unconscious, Collected Works, Volume 9i*, Princeton, NJ: Princeton University Press.

—— (1968k) "Conscious, Unconscious and Individuation", in *The Archetypes and the Collective Unconscious, Collected Works, Volume 9i*, Princeton, NJ: Princeton University Press.

—— (1968l) "The Concept of the Collective Unconscious", in *The Archetypes and the Collective Unconscious, Collected Works, Volume 9i*, Princeton, NJ: Princeton University Press.

—— (1968m) "Concerning the Archetypes and the Anima Concept", in *The Archetypes and the Collective Unconscious, Collected Works, Volume 9i*, Princeton, NJ: Princeton University Press.

—— (1968n) "The Shadow", in *Aion, Collected Works, Volume 9ii*, Princeton, NJ: Princeton University Press.

—— (1968o) "The Fish in Alchemy", in *Aion, Collected Works, Volume 9ii*, Princeton, NJ: Princeton University Press.

—— (1968p) "The Self", in *Aion, Collected Works, Volume 9ii*, Princeton, NJ: Princeton University Press.

—— (1968q) "The Psychology of the Child Archetype", in *The Archetypes and the Collective Unconscious, Collected Works, Volume 9i*, Princeton, NJ: Princeton University Press.

—— (1968r) "Psychological Aspects of the Mother Archetype", in *The Archetypes and the Collective Unconscious, Collected Works, Volume 9i*, Princeton, NJ: Princeton University Press.

—— (1969a) "Psychological Commentary on 'The Tibetan Book of the Dead'", in *Psychology and Religion: West and East, Collected Works, Volume 11*, Princeton, NJ: Princeton University Press.

—— (1969b) "Psychology and Religion", in *Psychology and Religion: West and East, Collected Works, Volume 11*, Princeton, NJ: Princeton University Press.

—— (1969c) "Transformation Symbolism in the Mass", in *Psychology and Religion: West and East, Collected Works, Volume 11*, Princeton, NJ: Princeton University Press.

—— (1969d) *Answer to Job*, in *Psychology and Religion: West and East, Collected Works, Volume 11*, Princeton, NJ: Princeton University Press.

—— (1969e) "A Psychological Approach to the Dogma of the Trinity", in *Psychology and Religion: West and East, Collected Works, Volume 11*, Princeton, NJ: Princeton University Press.

—— (1969f) "On the Nature of the Psyche", in *Collected Works, Volume 8*, Princeton, NJ: Princeton University Press.

—— (1969g) "Psychological Commentary on 'The Tibetan Book of the Great Liberation'", in *Psychology and Religion: West and East, Collected Works, Volume 11*, Princeton, NJ: Princeton University Press.

—— (1969h) "The Psychology of Eastern Meditation", in *Psychology and Religion: West and East, Collected Works, Volume 11*, Princeton, NJ: Princeton University Press.

—— (1969i) "Foreword to 'Suzuki's Introduction to Zen Buddhism'", in *Psychology and Religion: West and East, Collected Works, Volume 11*, Princeton, NJ: Princeton University Press.

—— (1969j) "The Transcendent Function", in *Collected Works, Volume 8*, Princeton, NJ: Princeton University Press.

—— (1969k) "Foreword to White's 'God and the Unconscious'", in *Psychology and Religion: West and East, Collected Works, Volume 11*, Princeton, NJ: Princeton University Press.

—— (1969l) "General Aspects of Dream Psychology", in *Collected Works, Volume 8*, Princeton, NJ: Princeton University Press.

—— (1969m) "Psychological Factors in Human Behaviour", in *Collected Works, Volume 8*, Princeton, NJ: Princeton University Press.

—— (1969n) "Synchronicity: An Acausal Connecting Principle", in *Collected Works, Volume 8*, Princeton, NJ: Princeton University Press.

—— (1969o) "On Psychic Energy", in *Collected Works, Volume 8*, Princeton, NJ: Princeton University Press.

—— (1969p) "Psychotherapists or the Clergy", in *Psychology and Religion: West and East, Collected Works, Volume 11*, Princeton, NJ: Princeton University Press.

—— (1969q) "The Soul and Death", in *Collected Works, Volume 8*, Princeton, NJ: Princeton University Press.

—— (1970) *Mysterium Coniunctionis, Collected Works, Volume 14*, Princeton, NJ: Princeton University Press.

—— (1971a) "The Relativity of the God-concept in Meister Eckhart", in *Psychological Types, Collected Works, Volume 6*, Princeton, NJ: Princeton University Press.

—— (1971b) "The Problem of Types in the History of Classical and Medieval Thought", in *Psychological Types, Collected Works, Volume 6*, Princeton, NJ: Princeton University Press.

—— (1971c) "Schiller's Ideas on the Type Problem", in *Psychological Types, Collected Works, Volume 6*, Princeton, NJ: Princeton University Press.

—— (1971d) "Definitions", in *Psychological Types, Collected Works, Volume 6*, Princeton, NJ: Princeton University Press.

—— (1976a) "Techniques of Attitude Change Conducive to World Peace", in *The Symbolic Life: Miscellaneous Writings, Collected Works, Volume 18*, Princeton, NJ: Princeton University Press.

—— (1976b) "The Symbolic Life", in *The Symbolic Life: Miscellaneous Writings, Collected Works, Volume 18*, Princeton, NJ: Princeton University Press.

—— (1976c) "The Tavistock Lectures", in *The Symbolic Life: Miscellaneous Writings, Collected Works, Volume 18*, Princeton, NJ: Princeton University Press.

—— (1976d) "Jung and Religious Belief", in *The Symbolic Life: Miscellaneous Writings, Collected Works, Volume 18*, Princeton, NJ: Princeton University Press.

—— (1976e) "Religion and Psychology: A Reply to Martin Buber", in *The Symbolic Life: Miscellaneous Writings, Collected Works, Volume 18*, Princeton, NJ: Princeton University Press.

—— (1976f) "The Archetype in Dream Symbolism", *The Symbolic Life: Miscellaneous Writings, Collected Works, Volume 18*, Princeton, NJ: Princeton University Press.

—— (1976g) "The Healing Split", *The Symbolic Life: Miscellaneous Writings, Collected Works, Volume 18*, Princeton, NJ: Princeton University Press.

—— (1979) *General Index, Collected Works, Volume 20*, Princeton, NJ: Princeton University Press.

Lammers, A. (1994) *In God's Shadow: The Collaboration of Victor White and C.G. Jung*, Mahwah, NJ: Paulist.

Lammers, A. Cunningham, A. and Stein, M. (eds) (2007) *The Jung-White Letters*, Hove, UK: Routledge.

Livingston, J. (1997) *Modern Christian Thought, Volume 1, The Enlightenment and the Nineteenth Century*, 2nd edn, Upper Saddle River, NJ: Prentice Hall.

McDonnell, E. (1954) *The Beguines and Beghards in Medieval Culture*, New Brunswick, NJ: Rutgers University Press.

McGinn, B. (1981) "Theological Summary", in *Meister Eckhart*, E. Colledge and B. McGinn (trans.), New York: Paulist, 24–61.

—— (1998a) *The Flowering of Mysticism: Men and Women in the New Mysticism – 1200–1250*, New York: Crossroad Herder.

—— (1998b) "Appendix: Theoretical Foundations – The Modern Study of Mysticism", in *The Flowering of Mysticism: Men and Women in the New Mysticism – 1200–1250*, New York: Crossroad Herder, 265–343.

—— (2001) *The Mystical Thought of Meister Eckhart*, New York: Crossroad Herder.

Madden, K.W. (2008) *Dark Light of the Soul*, Great Barrington, MA: Lindesfarne.

Marlan, S. (2005) *The Black Sun, The Alchemy and Art of Darkness*, College Station, TX: Texas A and M University Press.

Mechthild of Magdeburg (1953) *The Revelations of Mechthild of Magdeburg or the Flowing Light of the Godhead*, L. Menzies (trans.), London: Longmans, Green.

Neumann, E. (1968) "Mystical Man", in *The Mystic Vision Papers from the Eranos Yearbooks*, J. Campbell (ed.), Princeton, NJ: Princeton University Press, 1968, 375–415.

Pagels, E. (1981) *The Gnostic Gospels*, New York: Vintage.

—— (1982) "The Gnostic Jesus and Early Christian Politics", The University Lecture in Religion, Arizona State University, 28 January 1982.

Pearson, L.B. (1955) *Democracy in World Politics*, Princeton,7 NJ: Princeton University Press.

Petrement, S. (1990) *A Separate God: The Christian Origins of Gnosticism*, C. Harrison (trans.), New York: Harper & Row.

Pontifical Council for Culture and the Pontifical Council for Interreligious Dialogue (21 February 2003), *Jesus Christ, the Bearer of the Water of Life*, Rome: Vatican Press.

Porete, M. (1993) *Marguerite Porete, The Mirror of Simple Souls*, E.L. Babinsky (trans.), New York: Paulist.

Quispel, G. (1992) "Jung and Gnosis", in R. Segal (ed.) *The Gnostic Jung*, Princeton, NJ: Princeton University Press.

Sells, M. (1994) *Mystical Language of Unsaying*, Chicago, IL: University of Chicago Press.

Stein, M. (2007) "Foreword", in A, Lammers, A. Cunningham and M. Stein (eds) *The Jung-White Letters*, Hove, UK: Routledge, 2007.

—— (2008) "'Divinity Expresses the Self . . .': An Investigation", *Journal of Analytical Psychology*, 53(3): 305–327.

Stoudt, J. (1957) *Sunrise to Eternity*, Philadelphia, PA: University of Pennsylvania Press.

Teilhard de Chardin, P. (1964) *Le Milieu Divin*, London: Fontana.

—— (1969) "Contingence de l'univers et gout humain de survivre", 1953, in *Comment Je Croix*, Paris: Seuil.

Tillich, P. (1951) *Systematic Theology, Volume I*, Chicago, IL: University of Chicago Press.

—— (1952) *The Courage to Be*, New Haven, CT: Yale University Press.

—— (1957) *Dynamics of Faith*, New York: Harper & Row.

—— (1963) *Systematic Theology, Volume III*, Chicago, IL: University of Chicago Press.

—— (1964) "Two Types of Philosophy of Religion", in R.C. Kimball (ed.) *Theology of Culture*, New York: Oxford University Press, 10–29.

—— (1967) *Perspectives on 19th & 20th Century Protestant Theology*, C.L. Braaten (ed.), New York: Harper & Row.

Walsh, D. (1983) *The Mysticism of Innerworldly Fulfillment: A Study of Jacob Boehme*, Gainesville, FL: University Presses of Florida, 1983.

Weldon, C. (2007) *Fr. Victor White, O.P. The Story of Jung's "White Raven"*, Scranton, PA: University of Scranton Press.

Weeks, A. (1991) *Boehme: An Intellectual Biography of the Seventeenth Century Philosopher and Mystic*, Albany, NY: State University of New York Press.

White, V. (1945) Letter to C.G. Jung, 27 December 1945, in A, Lammers, A. Cunningham and M. Stein (eds) *The Jung-White Letters*, Hove, UK: Routledge, 2007.

—— (1950) Letter to C.G. Jung, 4 May 1950, in A, Lammers, A. Cunningham and M. Stein (eds) *The Jung-White Letters*, Hove, UK: Routledge, 2007.

—— (1952) Letter to C.G. Jung, 5 April 1952, in A, Lammers, A. Cunningham and M. Stein (eds) *The Jung-White Letters*, Hove, UK: Routledge, 2007.

—— (1953a) Letter to C.G. Jung, 15 September 1953, in A, Lammers, A. Cunningham and M. Stein (eds) *The Jung-White Letters*, Hove, UK: Routledge, 2007.

—— (1953b) Letter to C.G. Jung, 8 November 1953, in A, Lammers, A. Cunningham and M. Stein (eds) *The Jung-White Letters*, Hove, UK: Routledge, 2007.

—— (1953c) Letter to C.G. Jung, 29 November 1953, in A, Lammers, A. Cunningham and M. Stein (eds) *The Jung-White Letters*, Hove, UK: Routledge, 2007.

—— (1954a) Letter to C.G. Jung, 4 March 1954, in A, Lammers, A. Cunningham and M. Stein (eds) *The Jung-White Letters*, Hove, UK: Routledge, 2007.

—— (1954b) Letter to C.G. Jung, 15 May 1954, in A, Lammers, A. Cunningham and M. Stein (eds) *The Jung-White Letters*, Hove, UK: Routledge, 2007.

—— (1954c) Letter to C.G. Jung, 25 September 1954, in A, Lammers, A. Cunningham and M. Stein (eds) *The Jung-White Letters*, Hove, UK: Routledge, 2007.

—— (1955a) Letter to C.G. Jung, 8 January 1955, in A, Lammers, A. Cunningham and M. Stein (eds) *The Jung-White Letters*, Hove, UK: Routledge, 2007.

—— (1955b) Letter to C.G. Jung, 17 March 1955, in A, Lammers, A. Cunningham and M. Stein (eds) *The Jung-White Letters*, Hove, UK: Routledge, 2007.

—— (1955c) Letter to C.G. Jung, 10 May 1955, in A, Lammers, A. Cunningham and M. Stein (eds) *The Jung-White Letters*, Hove, UK: Routledge, 2007.

—— (1955d) Letter to C.G. Jung, 21 May 1955, in A, Lammers, A. Cunningham and M. Stein (eds) *The Jung-White Letters*, Hove, UK: Routledge, 2007.

—— (1958) Letter to C.G. Jung, 26 July 1958, in A, Lammers, A. Cunningham and M. Stein (eds) *The Jung-White Letters*, Hove, UK: Routledge, 2007.

—— (1959) Letter to C.G. Jung, 18 October 1959, in A, Lammers, A. Cunningham and M. Stein (eds) *The Jung-White Letters*, Hove, UK: Routledge, 2007.

—— (1960a) *God and the Unconscious*, London: Fontana.

—— (1960b) Letter to C.G. Jung, 18 March 1960, in A, Lammers, A. Cunningham and M. Stein (eds) *The Jung-White Letters*, Hove, UK: Routledge, 2007.

—— (1960c) Letter to C.G. Jung, 6 May 1960, in A, Lammers, A. Cunningham and M. Stein (eds) *The Jung-White Letters*, Hove, UK: Routledge, 2007.

—— (1960d) Letter to C.G. Jung, 8 May 1960, in A, Lammers, A. Cunningham and M. Stein (eds) *The Jung-White Letters*, Hove, UK: Routledge, 2007.

Wulff, D. (1997) *Psychology and Religion: Classic and Contemporary*, 2nd edn, New York: John Wiley & Sons.

Index